Modern Critical Views

Chinua Achebe
Henry Adams
Aeschylus
S. Y. Agnon
Edward Albee
Raphael Alberti
Louisa May Alcott
A. R. Ammons
Sherwood Anderson
Aristophanes
Matthew Arnold
Antonin Artaud
John Ashbery
Margaret Atwood
W. H. Auden
Jane Austen
Isaac Babel
Sir Francis Bacon
James Baldwin
Honoré de Balzac
John Barth
Donald Barthelme
Charles Baudelaire
Simone de Beauvoir
Samuel Beckett
Saul Bellow
Thomas Berger
John Berryman
The Bible
Elizabeth Bishop
William Blake
Giovanni Boccaccio
Heinrich Böll
Jorge Luis Borges
Elizabeth Bowen
Bertolt Brecht
The Brontës
Charles Brockden Brown
Sterling Brown
Robert Browning
Martin Buber
John Bunyan
Anthony Burgess
Kenneth Burke
Robert Burns
William Burroughs
George Gordon, Lord
  Byron
Pedro Calderón de la Barca
Italo Calvino
Albert Camus
Canadian Poetry: Modern
  and Contemporary
Canadian Poetry through
  E. J. Pratt
Thomas Carlyle
Alejo Carpentier
Lewis Carroll
Willa Cather
Louis-Ferdinand Céline
Miguel de Cervantes

Geoffrey Chaucer
John Cheever
Anton Chekhov
Kate Chopin
Chrétien de Troyes
Agatha Christie
Samuel Taylor Coleridge
Colette
William Congreve & the
  Restoration Dramatists
Joseph Conrad
Contemporary Poets
James Fenimore Cooper
Pierre Corneille
Julio Cortázar
Hart Crane
Stephen Crane
e. e. cummings
Dante
Robertson Davies
Daniel Defoe
Philip K. Dick
Charles Dickens
James Dickey
Emily Dickinson
Denis Diderot
Isak Dinesen
E. L. Doctorow
John Donne & the
  Seventeenth-Century
  Metaphysical Poets
John Dos Passos
Fyodor Dostoevsky
Frederick Douglass
Theodore Dreiser
John Dryden
W. E. B. Du Bois
Lawrence Durrell
George Eliot
T. S. Eliot
Elizabethan Dramatists
Ralph Ellison
Ralph Waldo Emerson
Euripides
William Faulkner
Henry Fielding
F. Scott Fitzgerald
Gustave Flaubert
E. M. Forster
John Fowles
Sigmund Freud
Robert Frost
Northrop Frye
Carlos Fuentes
William Gaddis
Federico García Lorca
Gabriel García Márquez
André Gide
W. S. Gilbert
Allen Ginsberg
J. W. von Goethe

Nikolai Gogol
William Golding
Oliver Goldsmith
Mary Gordon
Günther Grass
Robert Graves
Graham Greene
Thomas Hardy
Nathaniel Hawthorne
William Hazlitt
H. D.
Seamus Heaney
Lillian Hellman
Ernest Hemingway
Hermann Hesse
Geoffrey Hill
Friedrich Hölderlin
Homer
A. D. Hope
Gerard Manley Hopkins
Horace
A. E. Housman
William Dean Howells
Langston Hughes
Ted Hughes
Victor Hugo
Zora Neale Hurston
Aldous Huxley
Henrik Ibsen
Eugène Ionesco
Washington Irving
Henry James
Dr. Samuel Johnson and
  James Boswell
Ben Jonson
James Joyce
Carl Gustav Jung
Franz Kafka
Yasonari Kawabata
John Keats
Søren Kierkegaard
Rudyard Kipling
Melanie Klein
Heinrich von Kleist
Philip Larkin
D. H. Lawrence
John le Carré
Ursula K. Le Guin
Giacomo Leopardi
Doris Lessing
Sinclair Lewis
Jack London
Robert Lowell
Malcolm Lowry
Carson McCullers
Norman Mailer
Bernard Malamud
Stéphane Mallarmé
Sir Thomas Malory
André Malraux
Thomas Mann

Modern Critical Views

Modern Critical Views

WILLIAM BUTLER YEATS

Edited and with an introduction by
Harold Bloom
Sterling Professor of the Humanities
Yale University

CHELSEA HOUSE PUBLISHERS
New York ⋄ Philadelphia

© 1986 by Chelsea House Publishers, a division of
Main Line Book Co.

Printed and bound in the United States of America

10   9   8   7   6

Library of Congress Cataloging-in-Publication Data
Main entry under title:

William Butler Yeats.

   (Modern critical views)
   Bibliography: p.
   Includes index.
   1. Yeats, W. B. (William Butler), 1865–1939—
Criticism and interpretation—Addresses, essays,
lectures.   I. Bloom, Harold.   II. Series.
PR5907.W484   1986   821'.8   85-29060
ISBN 0-87754-700-9

A129083338

Contents

Editor's Note

This book gathers together what in its editor's judgment is the most useful criticism yet published on the writings of William Butler Yeats. The essays included are reprinted in the order of their original publication. I am grateful to Peter Childers for his labors in helping to locate and choose the commentaries presented here.

The editor's introduction is a revisionary overview of Yeats's achievement as a lyric poet, with an emphasis upon his overt Gnosticism, his authentic religion. Helen Vendler begins the chronological sequence of criticism with an informed analysis of *The Player Queen*, the most problematical of Yeats's dramas, and the most crucial for the entire development of all his diverse writings. An acute analysis of "Leda and the Swan" by Priscilla Washburn Shaw serves as a paradigm for the reading of the poet's strongest and most influential lyrics. With Thomas R. Whitaker's learned and sensitive exegesis of Yeats's deliberately Anglo-Irish poems, we enter the vexed area where modern Irish and modern European cultural politics meet and clash.

Ian Fletcher, our leading scholar of the Nineties and of Edwardian literature, analyzes Yeats's artful *Autobiographies* as the grandly Paterian "Imaginary Portrait" that shrewd and beautiful book constitutes. The early lyric Yeats, who culminated in *The Wind among the Reeds*, is captured memorably in the poet Allen Grossman's portrayal of the Paterian "moods" that dominate those poems. This aspect of the early Yeats is finely caught also by Richard Ellmann, definitive biographer of both Yeats and Oscar Wilde, in his humorous and loving study of the way in which Yeats subsumed Wilde.

Yeats's overt System, his mythology, is outlined in its two separate formulations in two separate chapters from the editor's synoptic book on the poet. The first investigates Yeats's mythological alphabet, *Per Amica Silentia Lunae,* a marmoreal reverie in the mode of Sir Thomas Browne and of Walter Pater. This prelude to *A Vision* is seen here as a secret meditation upon poetic influence, a meditation expanded and rendered into both psychology and cosmology in *A Vision*'s fascinating and exasperating interweavings of Yeats's two great *topoi,* the dead and history. Some of the same thematic obsessions are explored in Denis Donoghue's survey of Yeats's art as a dramatist, and in Herbert J. Levine's tracing of Yeats's relation to daimonic tradition.

The last two essays in this volume are both distinguished instances of the newest rhetorical criticism, Deconstruction, with its concerns for the epistemology of metaphor and the conceptual limits that poetry both suffers and evades. The first of them, by the late Paul de Man, though only recently published, is actually one of the critic's earliest ventures, yet uncannily prophesies his later advanced and subtle probings of conceptual rhetoric. His friend and colleague, J. Hillis Miller, properly closes this book with a strong attempt to reconcile the linguistic skepticism of Deconstruction with Yeats's aggressive faith that words alone are certain good. The world knows nothing because it has invented nothing, Yeats liked to observe, since he believed that the poets have invented everything. Deconstructive criticism can be said to explore some of the darker consequences of that inventiveness, while knowing always what Freud knew, that the poets have been there before us.

Introduction

The Valentinian Speculation chronicles the Fall of the Muse-principle, the Sophia, who in her leap forward found herself alone in the primal abyss, the Sacred Void, suffering a state that is called "ignorance" by the central Valentinian text, *The Gospel of Truth*:

> It was this ignorance concerning the Father which produced Anguish and Terror. Anguish became dense like a fog, so that no one could see. Therefore Error became fortified. It elaborated its own Matter in the Void.

Yeats was slyly fond of the epithet that the Neoplatonist Proclus bestowed upon Christianity; Proclus called it "the barbarian theosophy," and declined to distinguish it from Gnosticism. The classical scholar E. R. Dodds, rather more detachedly than Proclus or Yeats, concludes that the Gnostic tendency was strong in St. Paul, and agrees that it is impossible to divide sharply between Church and Gnosis.

Yeats is the most canonized poet of the twentieth century, more so even than Eliot, and most criticism of Yeats gives the impression of having been written while the critic was posturing upon his knees. Yeats was a supernaturalist (with much skepticism mixed in) and in some sense a religious poet, but the religion was a syncretic Gnosticism. In itself, of course, this is matter neither for praise nor for blame, but we ought to be clear about it. Canonical misreading provokes anticanonical misreading as a corrective, but since I published a 500-page commentary attempting just that, in 1970, I intend to devote this discourse on Yeats to a rather more sympathetic account of the Gnostic tendency in him. Yeats is safely in the canon, and nobody, myself included, wants him out, or could get him out even if that were desired. Himself a great revisionist, and so an unscrupulous distorter of Romantic tradition, Yeats has suffered and will go on suffering the weak misreadings that canon-formation affords. This hardly matters, and is pe-

1

culiarly inevitable anyway, because Yeats was deliberately an *antithetical* poet and interpreter. The dominant influences upon him were the antithetical fourfold: Shelley, Blake, Nietzsche, Pater, to whom as an *antithetical* theorist he added himself as a fifth.

My own personal interest in the problems of formulating an *antithetical* practical criticism, founded on a view of poetic influence as misprision and revisionism, started with the difficulties I encountered in trying to write a book upon Yeats's relationship to his precursors, a book that found itself compelled first to center upon Yeats's systematic treatise, *A Vision,* and ultimately upon the far more beautiful and suggestive tractate by Yeats, *Per Amica Silentia Lunae,* now easily available in the collection of Yeats's prose called *Mythologies.* From 1902 on, Yeats was a steady reader of Nietzsche. I suggest that the crucial influences upon a poet must come early in his development, even as Shelley, Blake, and Pater affected Yeats early on. That Nietzsche, whom he read after he turned thirty-seven, influenced Yeats so strongly is due to Nietzsche's reinforcement of the earlier influences. Yeats himself associated Nietzsche with Blake, saying that "Nietzsche completes Blake and has the same roots." He might have said, more accurately, that Nietzsche was allied to Pater, but then the Yeatsian misprision soon compounded Nietzschean elements with aspects of Shelley, Blake, and Pater into one composite *antithetical* precursor anyway.

The term "antithetical" Yeats took from the Third Essay of the *Genealogy of Morals,* where Nietzsche asked for the antagonist of the ascetic ideal to come forward: "Where do we find an antithetical will expressing itself in an antithetical ideal?" In *The Will to Power,* no. 884, Nietzsche speaks of "the *strong* German type" as "existing blithely among antithesis, full of that supple strength that guards against convictions and doctrines by employing one against the other and reserving freedom for itself." Denis Donoghue is accurate in locating Nietzsche as the origin of Yeats's concept of the hero; as Donoghue says: "The hero is an antithetical fiction; his idiom is power, will; his sense of life dynamic, theatrical." In *Per Amica Silentia Lunae,* Yeats first stated his formula of the *antithetical:* "The other self, the anti-self or the antithetical self, as one may choose to name it, comes but to those who are no longer deceived, whose passion is reality."

From Plutarch and the Gnostics and Neoplatonists, Yeats took the notion of the Daimon as the proper figure for the *antithetical.* The evolution of the Daimon in Yeats is curious. In *Per Amica,* it is clearly a father or precursor-figure, "an illustrious dead man," but Yeats insists that "the Daimon comes not as like to like but seeking its own opposite, for man and Daimon feed the hunger in one another's hearts." "The Daimon is our

destiny," Yeats says, thinking he cites Heraclitus, but Heraclitus actually
said that character or *ethos* was fate or the *daimon,* whereas Yeats's remark
is a powerful tautology. The tautology suits Yeatsian solipsism, with its
drive towards the ultimate suprarealism that Yeats, following Shelley and
Pater, called the Condition of Fire. At the center of *Per Amica* is Yeats's
Gnostic version of what I have called the Scene of Instruction, the state of
heightened demand that carries a new poet from his origins into his first
strong representations. Yeats mediates his Scene of Instruction through the
agency of the Daimon, which we can translate here simply as "precursor":

> The Daimon, by using his mediatorial shades, brings man again
> and again to the place of choice, heightening temptation that
> the choice may be as final as possible, imposing his own lucidity
> upon events, leading his victim to whatever among works not
> impossible is the most difficult.

In *A Vision,* the double cone or vortex or gyre is the dominant image,
with the subjective cone "called that of the *antithetical tincture* because it is
achieved and *defended* by continual conflict with its opposite." This image
in turn is made coherent through a more complex and advanced doctrine of
the Daimon, which I have expounded at some length in my commentary
upon *A Vision,* but briefly the Daimon for Yeats is now both the Muse-
principle and the self-destructive principle that expresses itself in passionate
heterosexual love. Neither of these meanings is wholly traditional, and
Yeats's transformation of the daemonic is therefore worth some explanation.
E. R. Dodds observes that for the second and third centuries A.D. the
daemonic simply meant what the unconscious means now. By using the
daemonic in his special senses, Yeats relates the term to repression, both to
the aesthetic repression that gives poetry, and to the mode of repression we
call or miscall sexual "love." But the traditional meaning of the daemonic,
as Dodds shows, is ultimately the Platonic one: the daemonic interprets the
gods to men, and men to the gods, which means that the daemonic is the
channel between divine will and mortal wish, or simply constitutes the
whole basis of Eros.

Freud's essay in the daemonic is his striking investigation of the *Unheimlich* or "Uncanny" of 1919, which relates the uncanny or daemonic to
repetition-compulsion:

> Our analysis of instances of the uncanny has led us back to the
> old animistic conception of the universe, which was characterized
> by the idea that the world was peopled with the spirits of human

beings, and by the narcissistic overestimation of subjective mental processes (such as the belief in the omnipotence of thoughts, the magical practices based upon this belief, the carefully proportioned distribution of magical powers or "mana" among various outside persons and things), as well as by all those other figments of the imagination with which man, in the unrestricted narcissism of that stage of development, strove to withstand the inexorable laws of reality. It would seem as though each one of us has been through a phase of individual development corresponding to that animistic stage in primitive men, that none of us has traversed it without preserving certain traces of it which can be re-activated, and that everything which now strikes us as "uncanny" fulfills the condition of stirring those vestiges of animistic mental activity within us and bringing them to expression.

On this view, the daemonic is the survival of an archaic narcissism, which is defined as our faith that mind can triumph over matter. Let us, as readers of poetry, be very wary about what Freud is saying, for he is destroying the whole enterprise of literary Romanticism, if we give him our entire allegiance, as surely we do not. He is coming to us here as the greatest of reductionists, wiping away moonlight like mud. It is painful to see Sigmund Freud as Mrs. Alfred Uruguay, but it would be more painful still to abandon the mount of vision. The central formula of Coleridgean Romanticism, of which Yeats, Stevens, Hart Crane may have been the last Sublime representatives, is "the power of mind over the universe of death," in which the mind's power means the Imagination, and the universe of death means all of the object-world. This formula, Freud is telling us, is only a survival, a trace returned from the repression of an archaic narcissism. The daemonic or Sublime is thus merely another evasion of the unacceptable necessity of dying. But Freud is harsher even than this, and his analysis of the uncanny takes us even farther into the problematics of repression:

> In the first place, if psychoanalytic theory is correct in maintaining that every emotional affect, whatever its quality, is transformed by repression into morbid anxiety, then among such cases of anxiety there must be a class in which the anxiety can be shown to come from something repressed which *recurs*. This class of morbid anxiety would then be no other than what is uncanny, irrespective of whether it originally aroused dread or some other affect. In the second place, if this is indeed the secret nature of the uncanny, we can understand why the usage of speech has

extended *das Heimliche* into its opposite *das Unheimliche;* for this uncanny is in reality nothing new or foreign, but something familiar and old-established in the mind that has been estranged only by the process of repression. This reference to the factor of repression enables us, furthermore, to understand Schelling's definition of the uncanny as something which ought to have been kept concealed but which has nevertheless come to light.

On Freud's view, we cannot distinguish the daemonic, or uncanny, or Sublime, from a particular variant of repetition-compulsion, whose affect is morbid anxiety. Translated into Yeatsian terms, early or late, this means that awareness of the precursor, or of the presence of the Muse, or of sexual love, are all compulsive repetitions of an obsessional anxiety. Here I have no quarrel with Freud, though I wish I did. But Yeats had such a quarrel, as would have had the entire tradition of the daemonic in poetry, from Homer through Goethe. Here is Goethe on the daemonic, as recorded by Eckermann:

> I cannot rid myself of the notion that the daemons, who enjoy teasing us and joy at our pain, set up individuals so alluring that everyone aspires towards them, yet so great that no one can reach them. So they set up Raphael . . . Mozart . . . Shakespeare . . .

The daemonic, Goethe added at a later time, was not present in his Mephistopheles, for the daemonic had nothing in it of the spirit that denies, being positive and efficacious, as in Goethe himself. The argument between poetry and Freud, I would judge, reduces to this: can there be, as Goethe thought, a daemonic without morbid anxiety, or is the daemonic only an archaic and narcissistic survival?

I think that this argument, between Freud and the daemonic poets, is an ancient one, and could be traced back through different versions until we reached the quarrel between Plotinus and the Gnostics. Plotinus, unlike his later followers, finally evolved into an Hellenic rationalist, and his great essay against the Gnostics marked the crucial point of this evolution. Let us venture the following formula: the conflict here, whether between Plotinus and the Gnostics, or Descartes and Vico, or Freud and the poets, is between two views of the human condition as flawed or fallen. The more rational dualisms—Plotinian, Cartesian, or Freudian—accept as natural and inevitable the separation between body and consciousness, as well as the continued association of the two entities. So even Plotinus speaks of a descent of the soul into the body as being an instinctual necessity. The less rational dualisms—Gnostic, Vichian, and poetic-daemonic—maintain not only the prestige of monistic origins but assign a particular prestige to the phenomenon of the uncanny, that Freud analyzes as being marked always by evidences of acute anxiety. What Freud sees as archaic narcissism is seen by Gnosticism as the call to salvation, by Vico as Poetic Wisdom, and by Yeats as the *antithetical* imagination.

I do not believe that this argument between Freud and a permanent element in poetic tradition can or should be reconciled or explained away. There is, as I have indicated previously, no fully articulated Freudian view of art, because Freud in his final phase never got round to working one out, but he would have had grave difficulties in persuading himself that the strongest art represented a sublimation of human instinctual drives, whether sexual, or whether aggressively directed towards death. I am not inclined however to blame Freud for what is now called psychoanalytic literary criticism, since none of it that I have read merits being called either psychoanalysis or literary criticism.

Yeats's Gnosticism was in small part a consequence of his reading Gnostic texts, though generally in dubious versions or misleading contexts, but primarily I think that Yeats's Gnosticism was inherent in him, temperamentally and spiritually. Yeats's various occultisms, including his own System, with its often bizarre ventures into philosophy of history, Yeats himself took rather dialectically. He was invariably skeptical of his own credulity but also impatient with his own skepticism. There was also a fair amount of posturing in his stances, particularly in his Nietzscheanism, which was essentially theatrical. But his Gnosticism seems to me his natural religion: sincere, consistent, thoroughgoing, and finally a considerable aid to his poetry, however dubious it may seem in its human or social consequences. I hope to be clear on this; I am *not* saying that Yeats was a Gnostic adept, in the same way that he did become an Hermeticist, a quasi-Kabbalist, a member of the theosophical Order of the Golden Dawn. I *am* saying that the actual religion of Yeats's poetry seems to me closer to the Valentinian Speculation than to any other organized, historical faith of which I have knowledge. Like the Valentinian entity called Error, Yeats elaborated his own matter in the void, and like his masters Pater and Nietzsche he came to regard that void as being in itself partly sacred.

Yeats is hardly unique in his modern Gnosticism. Indeed, it could be argued that a form of Gnosticism is endemic in Romantic tradition without, however, dominating that tradition, or even that Gnosticism is the implicit, inevitable religion that frequently informs aspects of post-Enlightenment poetry, even where that poetry has seemed to be primarily a late phase of Protestantism. I am in no position to condemn Gnosticism anyway, as the kind of criticism I am attempting to develop takes a later Kabbalistic view of textuality and influence as its paradigm, and later Kabbalah relies ultimately upon Gnostic models of catastrophe-creation. Yeats is the representative of more than his own choices, and any reservations I have expressed before or will make now about his Gnostic tendencies have to do with certain consequences he deduced from those tendencies, and not with the tendencies themselves.

Various attempts have been made to account for both ancient and modern Gnosticism, in terms of supposed psychological and social causations, but these have satisfied very few scholars, including those who have formulated them. E. R. Dodds disposes of Erich Fromm on Gnostic and Christian origins by showing that Gnosticism and Gnostic tendencies in early Christianity all came into being in the Antonine period, the last phase of peace and prosperity in the Roman Empire, rather than during the third-century time-of-troubles that Fromm posited as the context in which doctrines of despair arose. Indeed, as Dodds shows, Gnosticism was a prophecy of trouble to come, rather than a reaction to a declining world:

> When Marcus Aurelius came to the throne no bell rang to warn
> the world that the *pax Romana* was about to be succeeded by an
> age of barbarian invasions, bloody civil wars, recurrent epidemics,
> galloping inflation and extreme personal insecurity.

Whatever its historical causations, ancient or modern, Gnosticism is a highly distinctive religion or religious tendency. A brief summary of its salient characteristics may be misleading, but some such summary seems necessary if I am to explore its relevances to Yeats's poetry. Gnosis, as the word itself indicates, means a kind of "knowledge," rather than a mode of thought. This "knowledge" is itself the form that salvation takes, because the "knower" is made Divine in such a "knowing," the "known" being "the alien God." This kind of "knowledge" is anything but what the West has meant by rational "knowledge," from the Greeks until our time, but it is precisely what Yeats means by "knowledge" in his poetry. It is also *not* what normative Judaism and orthodox Christianity have meant by any human "knowledge" of God, for Gnostic "knowledge" transforms man *into* God.

Gnosticism is a doubly radical dualism, a dualism between man and nature, and also between nature and God. Here is a usefully brief summary of the essentials of Gnostic doctrine by Hans Jonas:

In its theological aspect this doctrine states that the Divine is
alien to the world and has neither part nor concern in the physical
universe; that the true god, strictly transmundane, is not revealed
or even indicated by the world, and is therefore the Unknown,
the totally Other, unknowable in terms of any worldly analogies.
Correspondingly, in its cosmological aspect it states that the
world is the creation not of God but of some inferior principle
whose law it executes; and, in its anthropological aspect, that
man's inner self, the *pneuma* ("spirit" in contrast to "soul" =
psyche) is not part of the world, of nature's creation and domain,
but is, within that world, as totally transcendent and as unknown
by all worldly categories as is its transmundane counterpart, the
unknown God without.

It is what Jonas calls the "anthropological aspect" of Gnosticism that
is prominent in Yeats, since Yeats's characteristic poem tends to be a dramatic
lyric, frequently turning upon the distinction between what Yeats calls the
antithetical self and the *primary* soul, which are precisely the *pneuma* and the
psyche, respectively, of Gnostic formulation. The place of the Gnostic alien
or transmundane true God in Yeats is taken, alternately, by death or by the
imagination, which in Yeats is closer to Gnostic transcendence than it is to
the Romantic Sublime. What Jonas says of the Gnostic alien God is true
also of the Yeatsian imagination; it "does not stand in any positive relation
to the sensible world. It is not the essence or the cause of the sensible world,
but rather the negation and cancellation" of nature. I think that these
similarities of Yeats and the Gnosis account for Yeats's obsession with transmigration, since only Yeats and the Gnosis, so far as I know, make a causal
connection between libertinism and reincarnation. The following is the account given of the Cainite Gnostics by Irenaeus (as cited by Jonas), but it
could come out of several contexts in Yeats's systematic treatise, *A Vision:*

> The souls in their transmigrations through bodies must pass
> through every kind of life and every kind of action, unless some-
> body has in one coming acted everything at once . . . their souls
> before departing must have made use of every mode of life and
> must have left no remainder of any sort still to be performed:
> lest they must again be sent into another body because there is
> still something lacking to their freedom.

This Gnostic notion of "freedom" as meaning an absolute *completion* of
every human impulse, however destructive, is strikingly Yeatsian. But the

central Gnostic element in Yeats is the crucial trope of *A Vision* and its "System": the Phases of the Moon, which goes back to the most Yeatsian personage among the Gnostic speculators, the flamboyant Simon Magus, who when he went to Rome took the cognomen of *Faustus,* "the favored one," and so became the ancestor of the Renaissance Faust. Simon, a Samaritan almost uniquely hated by the early Church Fathers, asserted that he was the Messiah. With unrivalled and admirable audacity, Simon picked up a whore in a Tyre brothel, named her Helena, and called her also the fallen Sophia, the "Thought" of God scattered into the broken vessels, whom he now restored and raised up to salvation. Simon also named his Helena *Selēnē,* the Moon, and gathered twenty-eight disciples, who together with himself and his whore made up the Valentinian *pleroma,* the thirty Aeons constituting the manifold of unfallen Divinity. The symbolism of salvation was transferred by Simon to the great image of the waxing and the waning of the moon, which in Yeats becomes the central emblem of the primary and the antithetical cones, or objective and subjective cycles of history. Rather than continue to adduce Gnostic patterns in Yeats, or link up immediately Yeats's Gnosticism to his daemonic intensities and both, whether positively or negatively, to the Freudian defense of repression, I will proceed now to a consideration of two of Yeats's most ambitious works in the Sublime mode: "The Second Coming" and "Byzantium," and to very nearly his last poem, "Cuchulain Comforted," in order to ask and perhaps answer the following question: was Yeats's daemonic Gnosticism his repressive defense against the anxiety of influence, and in particular against the composite Romantic precursor he had formed out of Shelley, Blake, and Pater? Is the Yeatsian Sublime a triumph (however equivocal) of a very belated Romantic questor over and against the enormous pressures of poetic anteriority? Or, to put the question most plainly: was Yeats's poetic variety of Gnosticism his own wilful misprision of Romantic tradition?

"The Second Coming" is a very powerful piece of rhetoric, and one of the most universally admired poems of our century. I attempted a few enlightened reservations about it in my book on Yeats, and provoked a great deal of defensive abuse from reviewers and Yeats-idolators, a reaction that helped instruct me further in the theory of misprision as defensive troping. I am at least as skeptical about "The Second Coming" now as I was earlier, but I think I can elucidate my reservations rather more sharply, by having recourse to my Kabbalistic map of misprision.

Take the poem's celebrated opening. I would say that the first six lines require to be read as reaction-formation or rhetorical irony, while the next two represent a turning against the self that is a despairing or masochistic synecdoche. In the opening figuration, the center is man, unable as falconer to maintain a control over a "turning and turning" movement that he has trained. But a falconer is also every poet, and the falcon is his trope, and we can translate "turning and turning" as "troping and troping," so that the discipline of falconry represents not only a mastery of nature, but a mastery of language. This representation, either way, is breaking down, or rather falling and shattering outwards, and so the "ceremony of innocence" is indeed an élitist ritual, whether it be the aristocratic sport of falconry, or the poet's art in praise of aristocracy. Yeats, reacting with dismay to the excesses of the Russian Revolution, and with counterrevolutionary fervor and gladness to the excesses of the assault of the German *Freikorps* upon Russia, is saying one thing (falconry) while meaning another (poetry). His reaction-formation is the defense against anteriority (specifically against Shelley, as we will see) that masks his emotional exultation by a deceptive, only apparent emotional revulsion, a rhetorical irony that has been canonically misread as a literal statement. But Yeats is unified in his emotional and intellectual reaction to the Gnostic vision that dominates this poem. He welcomes the second birth of the Egyptian Sphinx both emotionally and intellectually, all canonical misreadings to the contrary.

Yet this opening *illusio* or rhetorical irony indeed limits or withdraws more meaning than it represents, which is why the opening images are so bewildered a dialectical interplay of presence and absence. Meaning has fled or wandered or, more likely, been driven out; the trope will not obey its master, anarchy itself is not significant, coherence is withdrawn, and the image of an élite, of a being chosen, without which poetry is not possible, is engulfed. Out of this flood of limitation, Yeats rescues a single trope of representation, a part/whole image wholly turned against the deepest desires of his own *antithetical* self or Gnostic *pneuma*. A self that worships passionate intensity finds intensity manifested only by the rabblement, while the best, the aristocrats of Britain, "lack all conviction." The best gloss on this last phrase can be found in Yeats's letters of that time, where he bitterly accuses the British royal family of lacking the conviction to avenge the murders of their blood-relations, the Czar's family, recently executed by the Bolsheviks. The second movement of the poem is lines 9–17, which itself divides exactly in half with the full colon after "troubles my sight" in line 13. Here is the poem's *kenosis,* its radical humbling of its own meaning, by way of a metonymic displacement, an emptying-out substitution of the Christian Second Coming for the Gnostic Second Birth, not of the Antichrist, but of the mere Demiurge or god of the fallen world:

Surely some revelation is at hand;
Surely the Second Coming is at hand.
The Second Coming! Hardly are those words out
When a vast image out of *Spiritus Mundi*
Troubles my sight:

"Words" is the crucial word here, for Yeats "surely" is showing us
how unsure he is, the repetition of "surely" betraying his yearning uncertainty. Having used the word "revelation" he substitutes for it the Christian
interpretation. Self-startled into repeating the words "the Second Coming,"
he is confronted by a vast image out of a book he himself has written, for
Spiritus Mundi is identical with "Anima Mundi," the second part of *Per
Amica Silentia Lunae,* written just two years before. In "Anima Mundi,"
following the lead of the Cambridge Kabbalist and Neoplatonist, Henry
More, Yeats had spoken of images that came before the mind's eye, images
out of the Great Memory. Here, Yeats attains to one of those images through
a defensive act of *isolation,* which on the cognitive level momentarily burns
away the Gnostic context of Yeats's visionary cosmos. This acute limitation
of meaning is restituted as Yeats achieves his daemonic version of the Sublime, in the truly uncanny passage of his poem:

somewhere in sands of the desert
A shape with lion body and the head of a man,
A gaze blank and pitiless as the sun,
Is moving its slow thighs, while all about it
Reel shadows of the indignant desert birds.

I think that if we could answer the question: *what is being repressed here?,*
we would find ourselves better able to clarify the Yeatsian Sublime. Let us
divide our question, for there are two parts to this repression: literary and
religious-sexual. Yeats is describing a male Sphinx, Egyptian rather than
Greek, and in an earlier draft spoke of "An eye blank and pitiless as the
sun," meaning the one-eyed Egyptian Sphinx associated with the sun-god.
The deepest literary repression here is of Shelley's famous sonnet "Ozymandias," which described the "colossal wreck" of the tomb of Rameses II, a
monument that was in the shape of a male Sphinx. "A gaze blank and
pitiless" goes back to the "shattered visage" of Ozymandias, with its "sneer
of cold command" but particularly to the complex phrase describing the
sculptor's "hand that mocked" Ozymandias, where "mocked" means both
"represented" and "disdained." Yeats does not mock *his* male Sphinx, in

either sense. His exultant welcome to the Sphinx is both the sadistic consequence of his relative repression, even in 1919, of a really violent, over-exuberant sexuality and, more intensely, the return of his repressed Gnosticism, repressed in respect to its real hostility both to nature and to fallen human history. All of these aspects of repression will return us to Yeats's notion of the Daimon, once we have completed our mapping of the poem.

Here is the poem's third and final movement, five climactic lines of which the first three are a revealingly limiting metaphor, and the last two a powerful but confused and confusing attempt at a metaleptic reversal or scheme of transumption:

> The darkness drops again; but now I know
> That twenty centuries of stony sleep
> Were vexed to nightmare by a rocking cradle,
> And what rough beast, its hour come round at last,
> Slouches towards Bethlehem to be born?

The "stony sleep" of the Sphinx associates him with the "stony sleep" of Blake's Urizen in *The Book of Urizen*. Those twenty "Christian" centuries can be taken as the outside term in this metaphor; they represent nature, the fallen object-world. The "rocking cradle" is the inside term, standing for the subjective consciousness that is aware of the Incarnation. Yeats says that his vision is over, but that he has put on knowledge, if not power, because he has seen and *known*. He has acquired a "knowing" which tells him that the *antithetical* influx is at hand, and that the Christian age is over. This "knowing," like other acts of knowledge in Yeats's poetry, is a sublimation, a condensation of a greater desire or dream, which would be the Gnostic "knowing" in which Yeats as "knower" would become one with the vision "known," here the antithetical beast. But every poetic sublimation is an *askesis* or self-curtailment, or another limitation of meaning. From this limitation Yeats recoils to his poem's closing representation, which is a rhetorical rather than an open question. The hour of the rough beast has come round at last, and yet Yeats stands in no time at the poem's close, while projecting the twenty Christian centuries and introjecting the *antithetical* age, where the epiphany at Bethlehem will see the Second Birth of the Sphinx.

We can read "The Second Coming" as a misprision of Shelley, or perhaps an assimilation of Shelley to Nietzsche, and then of both to the Gnosis. Echoing throughout the poem, but particularly in its synecdochal lines 7–8 ("The best lack all conviction, while the worst / Are full of passionate

intensity") is the major Shelleyan synecdoche, the lament of the Last Fury
in *Prometheus Unbound:*

> The good want power, but to weep barren tears.
> The powerful goodness want: worse need for them.
> The wise want love; and those who love want wisdom;
> And all best things are thus confused to ill.

The final form of this central Shelleyan insight is achieved, as Yeats
knew, in *The Triumph of Life:*

> And much I grieved to think how power & will
> In opposition rule our mortal day—
>
> And why God made irreconcilable
> Good & the means of good, and for despair
> I half disdained mine eye's desire to fill
>
> With the spent vision of the times that were
> And scarce have ceased to be

Nietzsche, in *Towards the Genealogy of Morals,* saw art as the *antithetical*
opponent of what he had attacked as "the ascetic ideal" since it was art "in
which precisely the *lie* is sanctified and the *will to deception* has a good
conscience," and so art was much more fundamentally opposed to the ascetic
ideal than was science. Yet Nietzsche saw the Romantic artist (Wagner in
particular) as being corrupted by the ascetic ideal, and I suspect he would
have agreed with Yeats that Shelley was so corrupted, since Shelley *did* try
to give human suffering a meaning. What Nietzsche called the "ascetic
ideal," Yeats called the *primary,* which he called also the "objective" and
the "sentimental," the realm of the soul, and not the Gnostic *pneuma* or
antithetical self.

I would summarize this account of "The Second Coming" by saying
that what the poem reveals is a successful, Sublime repression of the Shelleyan
influence, by way of a making daemonic or uncanny the characteristic pat-
terning of the post-Wordsworthian crisis-lyric. But that returns me to this
discussion's starting point; how can a Gnostic defense be understood from
a more rational perspective, whether it be Freud's or belong to some other
Western rationalism? If the beast of Yeats's vision in "The Second Coming"
is an emanation from his Daimon, as it appears to be, then what is Yeats's
relationship to his own vision? Who is making the poem, poet or Daimon?

On Freud's view, Yeats's vision is a partial or distorted Return of the
Repressed, manifesting a repetition-compulsion, but that is too partial a

view, covering only the poem's *kenosis* or metonymic reduction of itself through isolation, as we have seen. In Yeats the uncanny or repressed spills over into every major trope and into every major psychic defense. And this, I would argue, is the triumph of Yeats's Gnosticism, which is not only beyond Good and Evil (though not quite in the subtler sense that Nietzsche would have desired) but which has broken the bounds also of what Vico meant by Poetic Wisdom or Poetic Divination. Yeats, as a figure or mask *in his own poems,* is much closer to, say, Browning's Childe Roland than he is to Browning, or much closer to Tennyson's Tithonus or Percivale than he is to Tennyson. Following Nietzsche's notion of the Mask as well as Oscar Wilde's, Yeats is the Solitary or *antithetical* quester of his own poetry, and as such he seeks a god who is at once death and the aesthetic state that in *A Vision* is called Phase 15, which is a purely supernatural incarnation. He seeks, like the Error of Valentinus or of Nietzsche, to elaborate his own matter in the Void, but his highly personal swerve away even from Gnosticism allows him to regard the Void itself as being Sacred or daemonic, for does it not contain the splendor of his elaborations?

Let us consider another splendid elaboration in Yeats's Sublime mode, "Byzantium." I will begin with another exercise in misprision and its patterns, no doubt mine own as well as Yeats's, by tracing in "Byzantium" the shadows of revisionism. The poem's first stanza divides equally between *clinamen* and *tessera,* four lines of reaction-formation followed by four lines of reversal-into-the-opposite. The *kenosis* of a defensive undoing occupies the first six lines of the second stanza, and is then followed by a sudden mounting into the repressive Sublime of *daemonization,* with "I hail the superhuman," a movement that continues all through the third stanza. The fourth stanza, with its characteristic Romantic metaphor of fire doing the work of sublimation, is this poem's *askesis,* replaced in the fifth and final stanza by the transumptive *apophrades,* with its peculiar balance of introjection and projection defensively represented by the Yeatsian version of the chariot, which is a being borne by dolphins from life to death.

This is the poem's defensive pattern, and it follows the Romantic crisis-poem paradigm more closely even than "The Second Coming" does. I will not pursue this mapping into imagistic detail here, except to note that again it follows the traditional pattern closely, with the imagery of absence at the opening, and the synecdochal representation of "all that man is" reversed into the opposite of the "human form divine," as "the fury and the mire of human veins." The metonymic undoing follows, with the image of unwinding as a kind of emptying out, and the direct metonymies of mouth and breath replacing even the superhuman. The daemonic imagery of high and low is invoked in the third stanza, while the fourth opposes fire and spirits, as inside terms, to storm and dance, as outside ones, with the purgatorial fire refined or sublimated beyond physicality. In the final stanza, "bitter" becomes the equivalent of "late" while "fresh" equals transumptive "early." Our chart of evasions is demonstrated as proleptically accurate in regard to the image patterns of a poem that represses powerfully its very close indebtedness to Shelley and Blake.

I have not attempted a reading/misreading here, whether against the canonical misreadings or my own earlier account of this poem in my book on Yeats. One more misreading, however strong, of "Byzantium" would be a redundancy; my quarry here is still what Freud called repression or the *Unheimlich*, and Yeats the daemonic or the *antithetical*, and what literary tradition has called the Sublime. I want to approach this oxymoronic notion of poetic repression, or hyperbolical representation, through Freud's theory of "Negation," as set forth in his essay of that title, written in 1925, a decade after his essays on "Repression" and on "The Unconscious." I realize now that I employed the Freudian concept of Negation without being aware I was using it in my two books on misprision, particularly in my discussions of the revisionary ratio of *daemonization* or the belated strong poet's Counter-Sublime. In my struggle to understand Yeats's Gnostic Sublime, my repression of Freudian Negation seems to have been startled into a Negation of my own.

Freud defines *Verneinung* as a process in which the ego expresses a repressed thought or desire, but continues the defense of repression by disowning the thought or desire even as it is made overt. "Disowning" here is a kind of "disavowal" rather than a refutation. Negation then, in the Freudian rather than any philosophical sense, means that the repressed rises into cognition, and yet is still to be spoken of as "the repressed":

> Thus the subject-matter of a repressed image of thought can make its way into consciousness on condition that it is *denied* . . . Negation only assists in undoing *one* of the consequences of repression—namely, the fact that the subject-matter of the image in question is unable to enter consciousness. The result is a kind of intellectual acceptance of what is repressed, though in all essentials the repression persists.

At the end of the essay on "Negation," Freud remarks that since we never discover a "No" in the unconscious, it is fitting that the ego's recognition of the unconscious should be expressed in a negative formula. Certainly we can relate Freud's conceptual insight to the negative element always present in the Romantic Sublime, that self-negation in loss, bewilderment, error, even in an approach to death, that always haunts the *Unheimlich* or daemonic aspect of poetic sublimity. A Gnostic Sublime, we must now add, necessarily emphasizes this process of Negation, since both the Gnostic true God and the Gnostic *pneuma* or true, *antithetical* self are utterly alien to all natural or even cosmic imagery. Hence, the powerfully negative aura of the Gnostic Sublime in Yeats's "Byzantium," where the superhuman is hailed equivocally as "death-in-life" and "life-in-death," respectively Phases 15 and 1 of *A Vision,* both of them phases where human incarnation is negated and so made impossible.

But where then have we taken the interpretation of Yeats's poem? Nowhere much, as yet, for this is still only a clearing of the ground. A poem is a triad, as I have said earlier, following the unlikely combination of Peirce and Proclus. As an idea of thirdness, "Byzantium" involves us in working out the relation of its own text to a composite precursor-text, and of both of these to the reader, who as a reader constitutes a third text. Yet only the overlay effect of our map is preparatory to criticism, for a closer look at the poem's availability to mapping will be a critical act proper. The use of a map is not only to find one's way and to chart the hidden roads that go from poem to poem, but also to train us to see what is truly *there* in the poem, yet might never have been observed if we had not seen it first flatted out upon a necessarily somewhat distorting surface.

The first critical insight that our mapping gives us into "Byzantium" is that this is, intensely, a High Romantic crisis-lyric, a Wordsworthian poem despite all its *antithetical* yearnings; indeed this is a kind of Yeatsian "Intimations" Ode. The biographical facts support such a characterization, since they tell us that Yeats was recovering from a severe illness, at the age of sixty-five, and that by his own account he was attempting to warm himself back into life, through writing this poem. In a clear sense, "Byzantium" is an elegy for the poetic self, and though Yeats was to live for nine more years, he did not know that when he wrote the poem. The poet has a prolepsis of his own death, or rather he achieves a representation of such a prolepsis, by describing a vision of catastrophe-creation, of the Gnostic sort, but confined here to the creation of images, and not of worlds.

The first major representation of the poem is "a starlit or a moonlit dome" that the original publication of the text said "distains / All that man is," not "disdains." In Yeats's Anglo-Irish pronunciation, he would not have distinguished between "distains" and "disdains," but "distains," which means "outshines," appears to have been his original intention, and so "disdains," in his pronunciation, may be taken as meaning both "mocks" and "outshines." "Distains" carrries also the memory of Shelley's comparison of life to a dome of many-colored glass, that *stains* the white radiance of eternity. Whereas Shelley's "stains" is a paradox, meaning both "defiles" and "colors," Yeats's "distains" or "disdains" has only negative meaning.

Yeats said repeatedly of the Daimon that it was both the poet's muse and the poet's enemy, an ambivalence that reflects the original meaning of the Daimon in Yeats's work: an "illustrious dead man," the precursor. In "Byzantium," Yeats-as-Dante, or as the Shelley of *The Triumph of Life,* confronts his Virgil or Rousseau, his guide to the afterlife, as the Daimon: "Shade more than man, more image than a shade." But an image of the precursor, the "numinous shadow" of an ancestor-god, as Nietzsche called it, can be far more powerful than the precursor himself. Three entities are called "images" in the poem. There are natural images or the *primary*; these, being unpurged, recede as the poem opens. There is the image of the daemonic precursor; its status is ambiguous, and Yeats cannot tell us whether it belongs to Phase 15, complete beauty and "death-in-life," or Phase 1, complete plasticity and "life-in-death." That means Yeats cannot say whether the daemonic image is perfect form, or mere formlessness. That leaves the "bitter furies of complexity," which at the poem's close are broken apart, as in the Gnostic and Kabbalistic breaking-of-the-vessels, and so become images that beget fresh images, catastrophes that are also creations. But here, too, Yeats is equivocal, as he was about previously named "images" in the poem. Syntactically, the last three lines stand alone, even though grammatically all three are governed by the verb "break." This gives a curious rhetorical edge to the three final lines, hinting an autonomy both to "those images" and to "that sea" which the dancing floor actually does not surrender to them.

I suggest that this ambiguity about the status of the "image" in the poem "Byzantium" is a product of what Freud calls "negation," that is, of the daemonic repressed which is revealed and disavowed simultaneously. Yeats, as an authentic strong poet, achieves a belated Sublime at a rather heavy cost. "Byzantium" is a poem about Gnostic salvation or transcendence, which is achieved by an act of *knowing,* but such knowing involves a descent and a loss. We can juxtapose to the close of "Byzantium" a passage from the Valentinian *Gospel of Truth,* which Yeats could not have read, though he had read other Valentinian texts in A. E. Waite's compilation, *The Hermetic Museum.* The advent of salvation or transcendence is necessarily catastrophic in a Gnostic vision:

> When the Word appeared, the Word which is in the hearts of those who pronounce It—and It was not only a sound, but It had taken on a body as well—a great confusion reigned among

the vessels, for some had been emptied, others filled; some were provided for, others were overthrown; some were sanctified, still others were broken to pieces. All the spaces were shaken, and confused, for they had no fixity nor stability. "Error" was agitated, not knowing what it should do. It was afflicted, and lamented and worried because it knew nothing. Since the Gnosis, which is the perdition of "Error" and all its Emanations, approached it, "Error" became empty, there being nothing more in it.

In the ancient Gnostic text such as this we frequently miss the Sublime, even when we encounter a doctrine of transcendence. There are strong passages in the Valentinian *Gospel of Truth,* but this is a weak one, since all Gnostic texts, out of the ancient world, become rhetorically weaker or more blurred when they speak of salvation, as opposed to when they speak of disaster, of the Creation-Fall. Yeats was not so much a doctrinal Gnostic, however eclectic, as he was a naturally Gnostic artist whose consciously belated situation adapted itself efficiently to the employment of Gnostic hypostases and images. His immense advantage, in poems like "The Second Coming" or "Byzantium," over ancient Gnostic texts, is not only the advantage of poetry over the spilled poetry that is doctrine, however heterodox, but is also the peculiar strength wrested by him out of his struggle with Romantic tradition. But again, I find myself circling back to the defensive process of poetic repression, and to Yeats's variations upon the Sublime mode.

I would choose, as Yeats's finest achievement in the Sublime, his death-poem, "Cuchulain Comforted," a Dantesque vision of judgment that is Yeats's condensed equivalent of *The Fall of Hyperion* and *The Triumph of Life.* The prose draft of this poem identifies the shades as being of three kinds, all cowards: "Some of us have been put to death as cowards, but others have hidden, and some even died without people knowing they were cowards. . . ." When Yeats versified the poem, he omitted this last group, thus giving us a hint as to a repressed element in this last daemonic Sublime of his life.

The poem's beautiful last line is its *apophrades,* echoing Dante's Brunetto Latini, who is described as being among the victorious, though justly placed among the damned in the Inferno. As I have shown in my book on Yeats, the poem places itself rather precisely, in terms of *A Vision's* systematic mapping-out of the phases of the life-after-death. The shades have passed through what Yeats calls the *Meditation,* and have purged themselves of everything in their past incarnations except their sense of cowardice. They are at the very end of the state Yeats names as the *Shiftings,* until in the poem's last line they pass out of the *Shiftings* and enter into the state of *Beatitude.* Cuchulain, type of the hero, "a man / Violent and famous," is a stage behind them, and so needs to be instructed by them, in an heroic irony on Yeats's part that is much more a figure-of-thought than a figure-of-speech. Cuchulain, at the poem's start, is passing out of the *Phantasmagoria,* the third and last stage of the *Meditation,* and has entered the *Shiftings* as soon as he accepts instruction, takes up a needle, and begins to sew the shroud that marks his acceptance of passing-over into his antithesis, the world in which heroism and cowardice blend together as one communal ecstasy.

I think it palpable that "Cuchulain Comforted" is a much better poem than "The Second Coming" and "Byzantium," for it seems wholly coherent and they do not, but I think also that its majestic, chastened Sublimity is necessarily the consequence of a completer repression than the earlier poems indicate, and moreover a repression in which there is less disavowal or negation. The mystery of "Cuchulain Comforted" is concealed in the implications of its view of the afterlife, where what appears to matter is not at all how you behaved in your last incarnation, but what you *know,* as the leader of the shades says, implying strongly that this knowledge is only attained in the afterlife. Certainly this is Gnosis again, though of a peculiarly original sort, firmly based upon Yeats's own mythology of death as worked out in Book III, "The Soul in Judgment," of *A Vision.*

Gnostic eschatology, particularly of the Valentinian sect, is close to Yeatsian eschatology in its larger outlines, though certainly not in any detail. A good motto to "Cuchulain Comforted" would be the best-known Valentinian formula of salvation, significant for its differences as well as its similarities to the poem:

> What liberates is the knowledge of who we were, what we became; where we were, whereunto we have been thrown; whereto we speed, wherefrom we are redeemed; what birth is, and what rebirth.

"Equipped with this *gnosis,*" Hans Jonas observes, "the soul after death travels upwards, leaving behind at each sphere the psychical 'vestment' contributed by it." As in Yeats's System, this journey of the *pneuma* has no relation whatsoever to moral conduct in the fallen world, for Yeats and the Gnostics share the same antinomianism. Since Yeats's theoretical human values were always of a kind that made him abstractly welcome Fascist violence, whenever it became available for his approval, we need not be surprised that his self-punishment, in his purgatorial death-poem, involves a leveling equation of what he believed to be the highest virtue, heroism, with its antithesis in shameful cowardice. We encounter here a repetition of the closing vision of Browning's "Childe Roland," where Roland, like Cuchulain the hero, is blent with his opposites, the band of brothers who were cowards or traitors, into one Condition of Fire. There is both a repression and a self-recognition that Browning and Yeats share, and to this sharing I will devote the rest of this [introduction].

I will center on two phrases, one spoken by the "Shroud that seemed to have authority" in Yeats's poem, and the other by Roland. "Mainly because of what we only *know* / The rattle of those arms makes us afraid," says the Shroud, while Roland cries out, magnificently, "in a sheet of flame / I saw them and I *knew* them all." Both knowings are Gnostic, in that they transcend natural knowing or rational knowing, and also in that the knower becomes one with the known, and that which becomes known is uncanny, daemonic. The Shrouds, in the terms of Yeats's *A Vision,* know what Cuchulain yet must learn, that all must be born again, and they will not cease to fear the hero until they are in the Beatitude. More deeply, they know what Yeats had learned by reading Nietzsche: that all must *recur* again. After their communal ecstasy, they must be reborn as solitary souls, and be cowards again, just as Cuchulain, after his communal ecstasy, must be a hero again. By hinting at this Nietzschean vision, and by implying his own acceptance of it, Yeats indicates the limits of his Gnosticism, for the Eternal Recurrence, however we take it, is hardly a Gnostic ideal. Roland, seeing *all* his precursors, and *knowing* them all, can be said to transcend his own earlier, pragmatic gnosticism that dominated his poem until its climax. Yeats, obliquely, attains to a similar self-recognition at the end. I want to conclude by noting this self-recognition, and by indicating its relationship to a repressive Sublime.

In his *Mixed Opinions and Maxims* (1879), Nietzsche utilized one of the central tropes of the repressive Sublime, the descent to Hades, as a vision of self-recognition in regard to the precursors:

> —I, too, have been in the underworld, like Odysseus, and shall be there often yet; and not only rams have I sacrificed to be able to speak with a few of the dead, but I have not spared my own blood. Four pairs it was that did not deny themselves to my sacrifice: Epicurus and Montaigne, Goethe and Spinoza, Plato and Rousseau, Pascal and Schopenhauer. With these I must come

to terms when I have long wandered alone; they may call me
right and wrong; to them will I listen when in the process they
call each other right and wrong. Whatsoever I say, resolve, or
think up for myself and others—on these eight I fix my eyes and
see their eyes fixed on me.

This fixation of eyes is akin to the primal fixation that Freud finds at
the origins of all repression. Repression, in Freud, is too rich and varied a
concept to be subsumed by any formula or definition. Indeed, Freudian
"repression" is an astonishing array of possibly incompatible theories,
whereas Freudian "sublimation" is by comparison an underdeveloped and
intellectually unsatisfactory notion. I find useful enough Paul Ricoeur's summary of primal repression, as meaning "that we are always in the mediate,
in the already expressed, the already said," for this is the traumatic predicament that results in what I have termed "the anxiety of influence," the
awareness that what might be called, analogically, the infantile needs of the
beginning imagination had to be met by the primal fixation of a Scene of
Instruction. Nietzsche, hyperbolically descending to the dead, confronts just
such a Scene, as do Cuchulain and Roland in their purgatorial ordeals. . . .

I want to attempt to find the analogical formula that can give criteria
to the degrees of repression in various instances of a poetic Sublime. In
Freud, the criterion for determining the degree of repression depends upon
the extent of estrangement and distortion that the unconscious displays in
its derivative forms, such as dreams and errors, and also upon the malform-
ings of repressed instincts in various defensive maskings. Analogically, we
can say that the degree of repression in one poem, as opposed to another,
can be judged by a comparison of estrangement, distortion, and malforming,
in tropes and images. The formula may well be that catachresis, or abuse
of all figurations, attends really intense poetic repression, so that images,
in consequence, become not only more grotesque where repression is aug-
mented, but also outlandishly hyperbolical as depictions of elevated or quasi-
divine states of mind or of being. This means, in Freudian terms, that
resistance or defense is truly being turned against inward dangers, indeed
against dangers that result from an *exaggerated inwardness*. Precursors, as I
have remarked in many contexts, become absorbed into the poetic equivalent
of the id, and not of the superego. Poems by Shelley are, for Browning and
for Yeats, the equivalent of impulses, rather than of events. When such
poems are repressed, then negation or disavowal can play little part in the
repression, because that would mean mythicizing renunciation or negation,
and so coming to worship Ananke or Necessity as one's poetic Word or

davhar, which would be a terrible worship for a poet who wishes to continue as a poet. Emerson came to such a worship, but ended as a poet, partly in consequence; Whitman repeated this Emersonian pattern, as did Thoreau, and I think Frost. Dickinson and Stevens are very nearly unique in having made such worship the staple of much of their best work, without suffering irreparable poetic loss.

How do Browning and Yeats compare upon our scale of poetic repression, that is, in the catachreses and grotesqueries and hyperbolical visions that we have judged to characterize an even more repressed Sublime? Though Browning is reputed to be primarily a poet of the Grotesque, and Yeats has little such reputation, they will be found to be very nearly equal in the figurations of an acute primal repressiveness. Both turned to dramatizations of the self, Browning in monologues and Yeats in lyrics and lyrical plays, in order to evade the prime precursor's romances of the self, but the death-drive of poems like "Alastor" and *Adonais* was detoured by them only in part. Browning repressed his memories of the kind of cowardice he had shown in his early confrontation with his mother and, through her, with the supernaturalist strictures of Evangelicalism. But the figurations produced by this poetic repression were the catachreses of self-ruining, of all those failed questers of whom Roland is the most Sublime. Yeats's repressed cowardice is more mysterious, biographically speaking, and we will need unauthorized biographies before we know enough about it to understand how it came to undergo the magnificent distortions and haunting estrangements of his greatest poems. We can see, now, that his Gnostic tendencies aided Yeats by giving him a wider context in a traditional ontology, however heterodox, for his own *antithetical* longings, since the Yeatsian *antithetical,* like the Nietzschean, can be defined as the ultimate resistance against the almost irresistible force of a primal repression, or as a fixation upon precursors whose integrity was finally a little too terrifying. Shelley and Schopenhauer were questers, in their very different ways, who could journey through the Void without yielding to the temptation of worshiping the Void as itself being sacred. Yeats, like Nietzsche, implicitly decided that he too would rather have the Void as purpose, than be void of purpose.

HELEN VENDLER

The Player Queen

"I began in, I think, 1907, a verse tragedy, but at that time the thought I have set forth in *Per Amica Silentia Lunae* was coming into my head, and I found examples of it everywhere. I wasted the best working months of several years in an attempt to write a poetical play where every character became an example of the finding or not finding of what I have called the Antithetical Self; and because passion and not thought makes tragedy, what I made had neither simplicity nor life . . . At last it came into my head all of a sudden that I could get rid of the play if I turned it into a farce."

The germinal idea for *The Player Queen* was tragic, if we are to believe Yeats, and there is no reason why we should not. One aspect of its finale—the banishment of a poet from the kingdom—has something in common with *The King's Threshold*, which though conceived as a comedy, was published as a tragedy. In the early scenarios of *The Player Queen*, the heroine, like Socrates, was forced to drink poison, but in spite of this tragic ending, even the early drafts are full of wit and high spirits. As we now have the play, Yeats's irony plays perpetually over the potentially tragic surface, giving the play a charm that not even its confusions can entirely obscure. It is the irony of the poet foreseeing his own overthrow.

In spite of its appeal, *The Player Queen*, like most of Yeats's plays, is not really stageworthy. Private, chaotic, allegorical in the bad sense, it has in spite of its faults a claim on our attention, if only because Yeats devoted so much time to it. As it stands, it is patched together, and shows it: the

From *Yeats's* Vision *and the Later Plays.* © 1963 by the President and Fellows of Harvard College. Harvard University Press, 1963.

23

action is confused, the allegory is only sporadically remembered, and the issues are rarely clear.

However, some things are at once obvious. Like "The Second Coming" and "Leda and the Swan," *The Player Queen* takes place at the moment of revolution, as one dispensation ends, another begins. "Leda and the Swan" had asked whether a new species of power inevitably brings with itself a correlative knowledge, and we saw that the question was understandable primarily in respect to the aesthetic order. "The Second Coming" asked what shape the new dispensation would take; and *The Player Queen,* dealing with the flirtations of the Muse, asks, among other things, what stance the poet should adopt when he becomes obsolete.

The great obstacle in writing about *The Player Queen* is that the characters tend to melt into each other and into their allegorical types. Are both Septimus and the Beggar figures for the poet? Is Decima a Muse or an Oracle? What relation does the Unicorn have to Septimus and Decima? The action of the play is equally slippery, so much so that it is hard not to falsify the story in the retelling. Briefly put, Septimus the poet is deserted by his wife Decima because he has been unfaithful to her. She takes a new husband, the Prime Minister, and by her own arrogant confidence makes herself queen, banishing Septimus, his mistress Nona, and the troupe of players, whose play about Noah's Ark never takes place. The timid former Queen retires to a convent, and Decima and her commoner-husband inaugurate the new dispensation.

Decima, as the only link between old and new, is the center of the play, while Septimus and the Queen, the representatives of the old order, are her satellites. Nona, Septimus's mistress, is only a device; and the countrymen, citizens, and players are on stage simply to fill in bits of information and to make minor points. The Unicorn, on whom the play depends, never appears, and we infer his actions from the remarks of the other personages. Evidently the meaning of the play depends on Decima, and her apotheosis at the end, comic as it is, is constructed so as to resolve, if possible, the action. The resolution is not the banishment of Septimus; if it were, the play would be a tragedy. (As it stands, an undercurrent of possible tragedy can be glimpsed through the ripples of farce.) If the play were focused on Septimus, he would not exit expostulating and incredulous, but rather bereft and doomed. His last words in a tragedy would be in the tone of

> And what rough beast, his hour come round at last,
> Slouches towards Bethlehem to be born?

Instead, he is carried off to prison protesting obdurately that Decima still belongs to him: "She is my wife, she is my bad, flighty wife."

I have said before that there is a certain approval of disaster and change implicit in "The Second Coming," but it is more an intellectual approval than a felt one. In *The Player Queen,* a gayer and more ironic manner of vision is trained on the prospect of cataclysm. Yeats is amused, in the first place, at the untoward nature of the expected destruction. It will not be a grievous second Deluge, but rather a commonplace reversal of fashion; the players may have pleased Kubla Khan in Xanadu, but their images do not suit here and now. Mental experience (once again, I do not believe that Yeats was writing politically) never repeats itself: the new chaos does not resemble the old, and the new Queen in no way imitates her predecessor. Yeats is wryly appreciative (it is a joke on himself) at the way revelation is announced, coming by its own evangelist, a braying beggar. The beggar is a comic parody of Leda, and his speeches give a sardonic answer to the question posed by "Leda and the Swan"—the beggar puts on no knowledge with his power. "When I roll and bray," the beggar tells Decima, "I am asleep. I know nothing about it, and that is a great pity. I remember nothing but the itching in my back." This is the reduction to absurdity of poetic inspiration. Septimus the poet recognizes the affinities between himself and the beggar, giving us leave to do the same. The old beggar says to him, "Don't you know who I am—aren't you afraid? When something comes inside me, my back itches. Then I must lie down and roll, and then I bray and the crown changes." Septimus replies, "Ah! you are inspired. Then we are indeed brothers." And so they are—Septimus drunk, the beggar tranced; oddly enough, the gaiety of the scene springs from their blowsy kinship. In some undefined way, the beggar's bray causes the Revolution by poetical contingency, as a sunrise in poetry is contingent upon cock-crow. Septimus has "caused" the Revolution by his infidelity to Decima; together he and the beggar represent the contributory causes of the shift in power.

What we do not find in *The Player Queen* are images of horror and disintegration like those which pervade *A Vision* as well as "The Second Coming." Both may have been present in the germinal conception of the tragic *Player Queen,* but as it now stands, the play represents a gay shift of positions all down the line, with no tragic consequences at all.

Septimus begins and ends the play by complaining about Decima, and in his complaints the cranky relation between poet and Muse (for Decima is at least one possible incarnation of the Muse) is made immediately explicit. More interesting is the fact that Septimus defines himself in terms of Decima:

THIRD OLD MAN. Who are You? What do you want?

SEPTIMUS. I am Septimus. I have a bad wife. I want to come in
and sleep.

THIRD OLD MAN. You are drunk.

SEPTIMUS. Drunk! So would you be if you had as bad a wife.

Decima has proved too much for him; her flightiness exposes him to too
much discomfort.

SEPTIMUS. Bad wife—others have had bad wives, but others were
not left to lie down in the open street under the stars,
drenched with cold water, a whole jug of cold water, shiv-
ering in the pale light of the dawn, to be run over, to be
trampled upon, to be eated by dogs, and all because their
wives have hidden themselves.

Septimus is not taken in by his own self-pity any more than he is later taken
in by his own drunken oratory. Rhetoric is his natural mode, and he knows
it. He has not the slightest intention of abandoning his romantic poses:
"Robbed, so to speak; naked, so to speak—bleeding, so to speak—and they
pass by on the other side of the street." This is the last romantic, conscious
of his romantic absurdity, a mode which Decima's brisk poetry is to make
obsolete. In fact, the revolution of this play is posed in terms of fashion; it
represents the light view of a serious phenomenon. Change is, after all, one
of the attributes of the Supreme Fiction, and consequently has its cheerful
as well as its terrifying aspects. *The Player Queen* is like a chapter from *A
Vision* read with an eyebrow cocked.

Yeats pictures his revolution in terms of a change of religion. For
Septimus, Christianity has become another cache of similes, useful for the
grandiloquent gesture ("Bring me to a stable—my Saviour was content with
a stable"), but when he declares his allegiance it is to "Venus and Adonis
and the other planets of heaven." The countrymen have recourse to religion
only to sanction their own clamor for violence ("The Bible says, Suffer not
a witch to live. Last Candlemas twelve-month I strangled a witch with my
own hands") and the Queen's Christianity is indistinguishable from her
apprehensiveness and furtive masochism. We have been given, then, enough
examples of the irrelevance of the traditional religion to prepare us for the
promulgations of a new one, and we are hardly surprised that it is Septimus
who enunciates it, praising its symbol, the Unicorn.

It is a most noble beast, a most religious beast. It has a milk-
white skin and milk-white horn, and milk-white hooves, but a

mild blue eye, and it dances in the sun. I will have no one speak
against it, not while I am still upon the earth . . . For I will
not have it said that there is a smirch, or a blot, upon the most
milky whiteness of an heroic brute that bathes by the sound of
tabors at the rising of the sun and the rising of the moon, and
the rising of the Great Bear.

This is the language of evangelism: superlatives, absolutes, cosmic rituals.
It makes no difference that Septimus is drunk; Septimus has a stake in the
Unicorn, insists that he is "no longer drunk, but inspired," and is affronted
that his countrymen can be indifferent to his divine afflatus, "my breast-
feathers thrust out and my white wings buoyed up with divinity."

The only trouble with Septimus's view of the Unicorn is that it is a
mistaken one. Conditioned by the existing tradition, Septimus cannot imagine the Unicorn as anything but chaste, and he insists that its chastity is as
integral as its beauty. Decima, of course, knows better, but the reader has
only Septimus' speeches to go on in the first scene of the play. For Yeats
himself, the Unicorn was clearly a symbol for the daimon and therefore for
artistic inspiration. Sturge Moore had done a bookplate for Yeats with a
unicorn springing out of a broken tower, and Yeats refers to it as "that
admirable faun or stag springing from the broken tower . . . That beast is
the daemon." Though Yeats's terms are vague, the "beast," in the reproduction of the bookplate on page 35 of the Yeats-Moore correspondence, is
clearly a unicorn. One suspects that Yeats or his wife suggested the symbolism to Sturge Moore.

Yeats was courting danger in using religious imagery for his point
about the Unicorn, but ever since Arnold, the aesthetic and the religious
have been interchangeable, for literary purposes. Whenever art begins to
speak of itself, as Northrop Frye has said, it uses religious terminology. In
a sober context, the language no longer shocks at all, but in a comic context,
we are somewhat at a loss to know what reaction to provide. The fact remains,
uncomfortable as it sometimes is, that Yeats chose to use, in *A Vision* and
in *The Player Queen,* religion as the only adequate symbol for art. Religion
is the only symbol which can combine the revelatory and prescriptive elements which art possesses, but the connotations aroused by religious images
tend to be so strong that the images draw all attention to themselves and
cease to be windows to symbolic meaning. Politics possesses a similar type
of prime force, and consequently the temptation to read Yeats as a prophet
of religious or political disaster is still with us.

Warned that we must look beyond the religion of the Unicorn to what it symbolizes, we can proceed with the play. Just as Septimus wants some link between the Unicorn and the religion he knows, so do the townspeople, who like to think that the beggar who brays to announce the new regime is a reincarnation of the donkey that carried Christ to Jerusalem. Both are harking back to a former time, wishing things to be as they have always been, or as they were in the past. Septimus is similarly unwilling to accept a change in his relationship to his wife Decima, preferring to recall earlier days, when she was not the spirited creature she has now become: "All creatures are in need of protection at some time or other. Even my wife was once a frail child in need of milk, of smiles, of love, as if in the midst of a flood, in danger of drowning, so to speak." This is the way Septimus would like Decima, obviously, but the Decima he now has is in no danger from a deluge; she, in fact, is the only person who will survive the coming one. The troupe of actors, with their play of Noah's Ark, are unfitted to deal with the flood they know only symbolically. Decima alone has an open mind, will not demand a unicorn or a cataclysm cut to order. The second scene of the play (to which the first is really only a curtain-raiser) belongs to her, and the rest of the personages are essentially her comic foils: the timid Queen, the sluttish Nona, the impatient Prime Minister, the evangelistic Septimus.

On the surface, Scene II joins a new theme to the cataclysm-revelation of Scene I: we see in the second half of the play the rivalry for Septimus between Nona, his mistress, and Decima, his wife. It is not the only time Yeats treated, with some wryness, the relation between poet, mistress, and lady. Always, in his musings on inspiration, we sense the uneasy relation between spirit and flesh. *The Player Queen* shows one solution: the wrong one. In the late poem "The Three Bushes" Yeats plays equivocally with what might be the right solution: deception into harmony. To the lady (who is the inspiration for all her lover's songs and is therefore a surrogate for the Muse) chastity is the essential virtue, and chastity for Yeats always denotes a certain final aloofness and self-possession, an almost inhuman independence. The lady, to keep her chastity, sends her maid in to her poet-lover; he is deceived and continues to write his love songs, all unsuspecting. Between them, lady and chambermaid stage the whole deception with a wryly compassionate indulgence for the poet's need and his innocence. Both women are vastly more sophisticated than the lover, and it is through the lady's three songs that the burden of the poem is made clear, as she passes from resentment of her maid to a metaphysical reconciliation of spirit and flesh. Her subjunctive wish has in fact the force of a decree.

When you and my true lover meet
And he plays tunes between your feet,
Speak no evil of the soul,
Nor think that body is the whole,
For I that am his daylight lady
Know worse evil of the body;
But in honour split his love
Till either neither have enough,
That I may hear if we should kiss
A contrapuntal serpent hiss,
You, should hand explore a thigh,
All the labouring heavens sigh.

While the poem clearly has a purely human meaning as an expression of the soul's traffic with both ideal and real, it seems to me no accident that Yeats made the lover a singer and his sexual relation with the lady a necessary condition of his singing. The sexual act is the most accurate symbol for the "fine delight that fathers thought," that "strong spur, live and lancing like the blowpipe flame" which, according to Hopkins, engenders poetry, and most of Yeats's poems about sexual love can be read symbolically. With some, it is hardly necessary to press the point, but when Yeats writes specifically about a poet or singer (as in *The Player Queen, A Full Moon in March, The King of the Great Clock Tower*, and "The Three Bushes") it is logical to place in the foreground the application to the poetic act. In "The Three Bushes" it is up to the lady to straighten out the conflicting claims of spirit and flesh, and she does it by a fine poetic sleight of hand which begs a dozen questions. Invoking the principle of complexity in harmony, she finds a necessity for the "contrapuntal serpent," and her verbal audacity satisfies us as much as the concept it evokes. A contrapuntal serpent, if he existed, would be a creature of both worlds, spirit and flesh; and sighing heaven, the cosmos reduced to humanity, equally satisfies both terms of the relation. This is the artful peacemaking that the lady indulges in. Yeats provides a much simpler reconciliation in the ballad when he has the three rose trees on the graves of poet, lady, and chambermaid intertwine so that now

None living can,
When they have plucked a rose there,
Know where its roots began.

Septimus, in *The Player Queen,* has grown resentful of his independent lady Decima, and has taken a mistress in her stead. The situation of "The Three Bushes" is repeated; Septimus's poems still envision Decima, his "daylight lady," but they are tapped out on Nona's shoulderblades. Nona senses that she possesses the least important part of Septimus's soul; Septimus knows that he is living in uneasy compromise; only Decima, independent, can cast off the past and look for a new lover. Noah's wife is not the part for her, so she will create a new play of her own. In one early draft she recalls that she has played the Queen of Sheba and Herodias; the present version has her announcing "The only part in the world I can play is a great queen's part . . . O, I would know how to put all summer in a look and after that all winter in a voice." It is this play-acting quality in Decima which Septimus vaguely mistrusts. Her chameleon transformations baffle and disturb him, so that he utters the classic wish for the domestication of the Muse: "Put off that mask of burning gold." The Muse reminds him that it was the mask which engaged his mind, not what lay behind it, and though he recognizes implicitly the truth of her reply, he makes one more effort:

> 'But lest you are my enemy
> I must enquire.'
> 'O no, my dear, let all that be;
> What matter, so there is but fire
> In you, in me?

The more Decima torments him, the more aloof she remains, the more beautiful she appears in his eyes, and the more powerful the poetry he writes to her becomes. The Image must remain sovereign and demanding, as Decima scornfully tells Nona when Nona accuses her of plotting to have Septimus cast into prison:

DECIMA. Would they give him dry bread to eat?
NONA. They would.
DECIMA. And water to drink and nothing in the water?
NONA. They would.
DECIMA. And a straw bed?
NONA. They would, and only a little straw maybe.
DECIMA. And iron chains that clanked.
NONA. They would.
DECIMA. And keep him there for a whole week?
NONA. A month maybe.
DECIMA. And he would say to the turnkey, 'I am here because
  of my beautiful cruel wife, my beautiful flighty wife'?

NONA. He might not, he'd be sober.

DECIMA. But he'd think it, and every time he was hungry, every time he was thirsty, every time he felt the hardness of the stone floor, every time he heard the chains clank, he would think it, and every time he thought it I would become more beautiful in his eyes.

NONA. No, he would hate you.

DECIMA. Little do you know what the love of man is. If that Holy Image in the church where you put all those candles at Easter was pleasant and affable, why did you come home with the skin worn off your two knees?

Lovers and poets (like nuns and mothers in another context) worship images, and images break hearts, as Yeats says in "Among School Children." Decima belongs among those images which Yeats apostrophizes as

> Presences
> That passion, piety or affection knows,
> And that all heavenly glory symbolise—
> O self-born mockers of man's enterprise.

There is no denying some autobiographical reminiscence in the treatment of Decima and Nona; it would be surprising if Yeats's Muse did not bear traces of the features of Maud Gonne. But by his fantastic allegory, Yeats has removed the play from the purely human sphere, and by his transparent allusions to poetry and plays, has made the transference to the aesthetic realm unmistakable. The two are interwoven: Decima throws away a part and throws away a man in one and the same gesture.

Once the rejection of Septimus is accomplished, Decima's headstrong and willful choice of a new lover becomes the motive force of the play, and Yeats's favorite symbol, the copulation of two worlds, begins to take shape. Though the players dance around Decima in their animal costumes, it is not among them that she will find her "beast or fowl." In fact, she suspects that any lover, human, bestial, or divine, is necessarily temporary.

> None has found, that found out love
> Single bird or brute enough;
> Any bird or brute may rest
> An empty head upon my breast.

She regrets losing Septimus, but her metallic personality is untouched by the breaking of his marriage vow: anger, not sadness, is her reaction. Her function is to break hearts, not to have her own broken, and in her cool acceptance of the ineffectual Prime Minister at the end of the play we see the temporizing of the Muse until the time is ripe for her new master, the elusive Unicorn, to possess her. She sings her song of invitation:

> Shall I fancy beast or fowl?
> Queen Pasiphae chose a bull,
> While a passion for a swan
> Made Queen Leda stretch and yawn,
> Wherefore spin ye, whirl ye, dance ye,
> Till Queen Decima's found her fancy.

Directly afterward, Septimus appears and announces "the end of the Christian Era, the coming of a New Dispensation, that of the New Adam, that of the Unicorn; but alas, he is chaste, he hesitates, he hesitates." Indeed the Unicorn hesitates, but not out of chastity. We sense that he is waiting for Septimus and the Players and the timid Queen to be gotten rid of before he takes possession of the kingdom through Decima. I think we are obliged to believe that Septimus' vision is accurate up to a point. After all, the old beggar's testimony corroborates his announcement, and if we are to distrust Septimus's vision of the Unicorn as the supplanting beast, the whole play collapses. In some way, Septimus realizes that he and the players minister to the Unicorn; irrelevant though they will be in the reign of the Unicorn, they are still in his camp, against the townsmen and their "bad, popular poets." Septimus can be defiantly gay in welcoming his own destruction: "I will speak, no, I will sing, as if the mob did not exist. I will rail upon the Unicorn for his chastity. I will bid him trample mankind to death and beget a new race. I will even put my railing into rhyme, and all shall run sweetly, sweetly." And though Septimus realizes his own imminent superfluity he yet defends the Unicorn passionately, and even mixes his own identity with that of the glorious beast: "Because I am an unforsworn man I am strong: a violent virginal creature, that is how it is put in 'The Great Beastery of Paris.' "

F. A. C. Wilson, in his discussion of *The Player Queen,* rightly says that the Unicorn "is perhaps the most celebrated of all emblems of alchemy as an image for the divinity"; and he mentions as well the esoteric significance of the unicorn in the Order of the Golden Dawn. He points out too that Yeats may have identified Noah with poetry. Blake had spoken of "Poetry, Painting & Music, the three Powers in Man of conversing with Paradise, which the flood did not Sweep away," and in Yeats's note on the passage, the three powers are identified as Noah, Shem, and Japhet. What Mr. Wilson fails to do is to take the necessary next step and identify divinity's converse with man (the Unicorn's proximate mating with Decima) as a symbolic description of the poetic process: though all men to some degree unite with images, the poet is the master of that act. The hint in the play itself is a broad one: Septimus announces that "Man is nothing till he is united to an image. Now the Unicorn is both an image and beast; that is why he alone can be the new Adam." We have already seen that Decima is both woman and image, making her fit to be the new Eve. Septimus recognizes the affinity between his wife and the Unicorn: "She is terrible. The Unicorn will be terrible when it loves."

The new images for poetry are incarnated in the Unicorn and Decima, and Septimus's grand gesture of saving the ancient images from destruction is futile. His images are irrelevant, though he speaks of them with pseudotragic bravado: "It is necessary that we who are the last artists—all the rest have gone over to the mob—shall save the images and implements of our art. We must carry into safety the cloak of Noah, the high-crowned hat of Noah, and the mask of the sister of Noah. She was drowned because she thought her brother was telling lies." But because the mask of Noah's sister reminds him of Decima, Septimus leaves it behind, and ironically enough the drowned sister is resurrected at the end of the play when Decima dons the rejected mask. Lost images are restored in the revolution of the cycles, and the old images become out of date. The timid Queen is an old image, too; if the Unicorn has been coupling with her in the night, the union has been barren, and she, representing the negation of all experience, is only too glad to be obliterated from the scene. Decima, symbolically the daughter of a harlot and a drunken sailor, assumes the gold brocade of the Queen, puts on a mask of burning gold, so to speak, and imposes her will on Septimus, the Players, the Prime Minister, and the people. She takes on her new role, foreseeing with liberty of impulse the destruction of her past, as she addresses the players: "You are banished and must not return upon pain of death . . . A woman player has left you. Do not mourn her. She was a bad, headstrong, cruel woman, and seeks destruction somewhere and with some man she knows nothing of; such a woman they tell me that this mask would well become, this foolish, smiling face! Come, dance." There is an echo in this speech of the original tragic ending, in which Decima is forced to drink poison; Yeats's comedy is never total.

If we ask, finally, what emerges from *The Player Queen* we can say dramatically, confusion; poetically, a few notable lines; symbolically, a vision of reality that is at best blurred. Yeats's late plays, when they are at all successful, are dramatized lyric pieces with the fewest possible characters.

The crowded stage of *The Player Queen* obscures the one essential relation Yeats is interested in presenting: the Decima-Septimus-Unicorn triangle. Muse and Poet, Muse and unknown Divinity of inspiration; at moments the three are, logically enough, indistinguishable. When Decima sings she is the poet; when Septimus can scarcely distinguish himself from the Unicorn he is allying himself with the source of inspiration; when Decima casts off Septimus she becomes "fierce" and "terrible" like the Unicorn. We are, in fact, justified in saying that Decima, Septimus, and the Unicorn form a Yeatsian Trinity; three natures and one substance. They are artistic principles at war with each other, and we acknowledge in turn their conflicting claims. Septimus's human attachment to Decima is played off against a sense of the mind's primary duty to the image conveyed by Decima's unfaltering progress to her enthroned niche. The overruling sovereignty and despotism of the poetic image, Decima's banishing of Septimus, the forsaking of old loyalties for the sake of art—these are contrasted with the charm of the players and the romantic gallantry of Septimus's obsolete mode.

This is material intrinsically better suited to reflective poetry than to comedy, at least given the cast of Yeats's mind, and *The Player Queen* shows a certain uneasiness in its rather deliberate high spirits. (*The Herne's Egg* suffers from somewhat the same uncertainty of direction, except that being in verse, it is more tightly constructed.) When Yeats has stripped his theme, given up his attempts at heavy-handed folk humor, and abandoned prose for verse, the poetic value of the plays increases, as [I discuss elsewhere] in *A Full Moon in March, The King of the Great Clock Tower,* and *The Herne's Egg,* all variants on the themes treated in *The Player Queen.*

PRISCILLA WASHBURN SHAW

"Leda and the Swan" as Model

Yeats can offer us, by way of conclusion, some measure of the distance which separates Valéry and Rilke. His work stands poised between that of the two other poets, because it communicates a feeling for the irreducible existence of both the world and the self. The eruptive, inescapable, energetic movement of reality often shapes the surface of his poems, as it did Rilke's. But this is now matched and completed by a similar awareness of the vigor of the self. Neither can totally overshadow or contain the other. There is at once continuity and discontinuity between the self and the world, a coming together as well as opposition, which ultimately creates the illusion of the independence of both. The pendulum swings, in Yeats's poetry, between these extremes, leading to poems which are sometimes complementary and even contradictory in their emphasis. But . . . let us turn to "Leda and the Swan," because it offers a particularly delicate and even balancing of the two elements:

> A sudden blow: the great wings beating still
> Above the staggering girl, her thighs caressed
> By the dark webs, her nape caught in his bill,
> He holds her helpless breast upon his breast.
>
> How can those terrified vague fingers push
> The feathered glory from her loosening thighs?
> And how can body, laid in that white rush,
> But feel the strange heart beating where it lies?

From *Rilke, Valéry and Yeats: The Domain of the Self.* © 1964 by Rutgers, The State University. Rutgers University Press, 1964.

> A shudder in the loins engenders there
> The broken wall, the burning roof and tower
> And Agamemnon dead.
>   Being so caught up,
> So mastered by the brute blood of the air,
> Did she put on his knowledge with his power
> Before the indifferent beak could let her drop?
>   (*The Collected Poems*)

The poem does not have the continuity of a story nor the complete presentation of a description; its organization is not a literary reproduction of the organization of external reality, yet it is also not a purely intellectual organization. The action interrupts upon the scene at the beginning with "a sudden blow," and again, in the third stanza, with "a shudder in the loins." It may seem inaccurate to say that a poem begins by an interruption when nothing precedes, but the effect of the opening is just that: It *is* an interruption for the poet. Nor does he stop to explain. We, too, are assumed to be familiar with "the great wings" and "the staggering girl." Or perhaps we also are too struck by the situation to become aware of the more conventional forms of identification such as naming. The exclamations continue, in a series of absolute constructions which give the progression, until the two beings are together. It is not until the last line of the stanza that time is taken for full syntax. After so many details which give only a partial view; which underline the birdlike qualities of the swan; which speak of the girl only in terms of motion, thighs, nape; the repetition of "breast" offers a kind of common denominator, linking the two beings and suggesting something closer to a full picture. Thus, the first bit of action is rounded off and the tempo relaxes with the line: "He holds her helpless breast upon his breast."

With this slowing down of the action, the poet's perspective shifts. The action does not of course stop completely, and the next stanza gives it indirectly in the word "loosening," as in the questions themselves, which could not be asked if the girl's attitude were not changing. But it is clearly subordinated; what is happening is now presented as incidental. The first stanza had stressed the out-thereness of the event; the physical detail was largely external, and none of it attempted to seize the event in its totality, nor to present either of the protagonists as a whole. The choice of detail suggested, above all, the movement in the scene and the movement of the eye, as one after another element in the situation attracted attention, and no time was given for a more total perception until the last line.

In the second stanza, on the other hand, we are made aware of the spectator and of the human mind which marvels at the event and tries to grasp and understand it. The shift in tone and perspective is recorded by the opening words "How can . . . ," which are further heightened by their repetition two lines later. At the same time, the stanza represents an attempt to give the inside of the event—for Leda—but in terms which parallel those of the first stanza and yet are still far from the conventional language for depicting emotion. For Yeats continues to spotlight parts of the bodies and to avoid the language of total perception. This technique very appropriately creates an impression of the terrified numbness, the dazed loss of control, and the succumbing to a greater physical force, which is all of Leda's reaction that we are permitted to see. In states of this sort, where it seems emotionally impossible to experience the situation as a whole because of partial shock, there is frequently fixation on detail, so that the stanza seems phychologically accurate as well as metaphorically effective.

But this is not all. In his minimal use of the possessive adjective, and the consequently greater use of somewhat unusual alternative forms, Yeats achieves effects which are curiously suspended between the concrete and the general. Thus, the stanza closes with a question which suggests not only an insight into Leda's reactions, but also some more general rule of human reaction:

> But how can body, laid in that white rush,
> But feel the strange heart beating where it lies?
> (The Collected Poems)

The linguistic suggestiveness of the absence of any qualifier for "body" is considerable. It brings to mind the treatment of proper names, and, with it, a touch of personification. At the same time, it echoes analogous treatment of undelimited substances—water, gold, flour—and of abstractions—honesty, life, chastity. (Cf. "Picture and book remain" from "An Acre of Grass" [*The Collected Poems*] for comparable effects.) This merging of the elemental, the abstract, the personal, and the concrete gives the line an unusual extension of meaning, and the same is true to a slightly lesser degree of the phrase "the strange heart," where again the possessive adjective is abandoned in favor of a more general and suggestive form. At the same time, the impact of the syntax is essentially not interrogative. If anything, it would seem that the question form was chosen because of its closeness to the language of exclamation. The effect on the reader is to force assent, to presume corroboration of something which is not totally understood, but which is experienced as overpowering, as precluding alternatives because of its sheer brute strength, and with this the possibility of a genuine question. The two lines really exclaim, "but how could it be otherwise," and this formulation is more emphatic than the conceivable declarative statement, "it could not be otherwise," if only because of the imperious appeal to the reader. There is thus suggested in the language itself an inevitability, which is mental, on the one hand, because it is formulated as a general rule, and real, on the other, because it records the irresistible forward movement of a single external event. We are made simultaneously aware of the reality of both mind and event. The two do not completely fall together; the mind does not reduce the event to an example or pretext, and yet the event does not totally absorb and contain the thought, because the latter is given more general extension than the event it encompasses. This is mind attempting to grasp event, and not, as in Rilke's *Neue Gedichte,* mind subservient to event, the object so completely understood on its own terms that the tension between the mental and the external is no longer visible. That tension is also absent in Valéry, although the nature of the accord that destroys it is different. In Valéry's poetry, the event suits the mind too well, dissolves into it too rapidly, in contrast to Rilke, where precisely the absence of such ready appropriateness leads to a largely single presentation of one or the other side of experience.

We sense in the Yeats the resistance of each to each, of mind to event and event to mind, and this in part because each is allowed its own movement, even while these movements overlap at times. Action will again interrupt the poem "Leda and the Swan," as the reflections of the second stanza are momentarily pushed aside at the beginning of the sestet with "a shudder in the loins." The lull which permitted reflection is broken with this new impetus from the outside, which then, much as in the opening stanza, leaps past the network of intervening action to the point where the motion subsides into state, and the future can be viewed as present or past. Each of these two stanzas, the first and the third, records the extreme limits of an event, the initial moment of eruption and then the moment at the other end, when the momentum has been dissipated and the effects of the action are spread out and become fully visible. The pattern is that of a projectile, with the focus of interest on the two end points—on the moment of greatest acceleration and then on the moment of stasis in which the motion terminates. The arc which connects these points is traced in the first stanza through the forward rush of the event; in the second, where the compression is even greater, it must be inferred, as the impulse is commuted directly into its result.

The question of the last lines opens the focus of the poem once more and immediately introduces another tempo which is no longer that of the event but of the human mind. As in the second stanza, the thread of the action is still visible through the reflections. The last line, although subordinated to the question, does bring the physical event to a close: "Before the indifferent beak could let her drop." But the focus is clearly elsewhere. The organization no longer suggests the pattern of an external occurrence, for the links are less causal and chronological than logical. The question opens with the reasons for which it is asked, the evidence which will suggest, depending on the interpretation, an affirmative or negative answer. The choice between the two—and it cannot be definitely made—hinges on the principle of reasoning implied: some law of extension or inclusion, or some law of contrasts. In the first case, the stanza asks: Since Leda succumbed to, and experienced so fully, the physical force of the god, did she share as well in his knowledge? The implication is that we might expect from such complete participation in one area, participation in another as well. The question, if so read, is not without a certain wistfulness, which is heightened by the last line with its reference to the "indifferent beak," as well as by the unconcern made explicit in the verb "drop."

Or these elements can be viewed as dominant, in which case the question arises from a feeling of resistance to the imposition of the supernatural, an attitude already potential in the second stanza of the poem. The reasons given at the beginning of the question, the description of the complete physical mastery, suggest then, by contrast, the absence of something other than brute force, some spiritual union. This feeling would then be confirmed by the indifference of the god to the human being which is made clear in the last line. The question can thus be read as a kind of protest: Was Leda allowed to participate more fully in the event, was she anything more than a mere vehicle? Or did the divine come, disrupt, accomplish its purpose, and leave, without considering precisely that which the poet presents in stanzas two and four—the feelings, the response, the meaning for the human being? Does the human have no significant place in the manifestation of the supernatural? What happens in the unimaginable conjunction of the human and the divine?

In both cases, however, the stanza clearly gives human reaction to an event. The attitude is one of attempting to understand or evaluate what has occurred. Accordingly, the laws of inference, rather than some more external kind of organization, determine the line of progression. Thought is clearly present as thought. The last stanza, as the whole poem, suggests a two-term relationship, in which both the human mind and the external event are given full reality. The poem is a confrontation of the two, in which neither the movement, nor the points of resistance of the one to the other, are allowed to dissolve and thus to be forgotten. When the two are brought together, as in the second stanza with "And how can body, laid in that white rush, / But feel the strange heart beating where it lies?," the coincidence of the external and the internal, of thought and event, acquires a new meaning because it is clearly felt as the coming together of two genuinely independent forces. These lines are more than an exclamation; they are almost a cry, wrung from the understanding as it wrestles with the world. It is the intensity of this encounter, the attraction and resistance between two poles, which distinguishes Yeats from Rilke and Valéry, and enables him to communicate the full reality of both personality and world.

THOMAS R. WHITAKER

Poet of Anglo-Ireland

Preserve what is living and help the two Irelands, Gaelic Ireland and Anglo Ireland so to unite that neither shall shed its pride.
—Pages from a Diary

I prefer that the defeated cause should be more vividly described than that which has the advertisement of victory. No battle has been finally won or lost.
—Wheels and Butterflies

When, in the late nineties, Yeats placed himself in a personal relation to Ireland, he not only moved toward a more autobiographical poetry and a dramatic relation to history but also took an important step toward a specific historical allegiance that would deeply affect his poetry. His early attachment to Sligo, his family heritage, his fruitful reliance upon Coole Park—all pointed toward the Anglo-Irish tradition. But the nationalism that had conflicted with his early provincial attachment yet more decidedly conflicted with any attachment to Anglo-Ireland.

As Yeats recalled in 1930, the question was complicated by his early romanticism. Anglo-Ireland was part of the eighteenth century and, though such nationalists as John O'Leary and J. F. Taylor praised that century and "seemed of it," Yeats himself had first "ignored it" because he wanted "romantic furniture" and then "hated it" because political opponents "used it to cry down Irish literature that sought audience or theme in Ireland."

From *Swan and Shadow: Yeats's Dialogue with History.* © 1964 by the University of North Carolina Press.

He turned away from Goldsmith and Burke because he considered them "a part of the English system," and he turned away from Swift because he acknowledged no verse between Cowley and Smart, no prose between Sir Thomas Browne and Landor. There were yet further complications. His early sympathy for the peasantry was not only nationalistic and romantic, but also religious and economic. At seventeen, "bored by an Irish Protestant point of view that suggested by its blank abstraction chloride of lime," he had sought out the peasant's pagan and Catholic lore. For him as for his father, Protestantism brought to mind the stereotype of the Belfast man, epitome of puritanical commercialism. Moreover, Yeats was then one who could praise the noble tradition which had made "neither for great wealth nor great poverty" and condemn the "new and ignoble" tradition of the vulgar rich, "perfected and in part discovered by the English-speaking people," which had made the arts all but impossible. He could also attack the wealthy as decayed gentry. In 1889, for example, he had criticized Robert Louis Stevenson's Chevalier Burke, in *The Master of Ballantrae,* as a false portrayal of the typical Irishman:

> He is really a broken-down Norman gentleman, a type found only among the gentry who make up what is called "the English Garrison." He is from the same source as the Hell Fire Club and all the reckless braggadocio of the eighteenth century in Ireland; one of that class who, feeling the uncertainty of their tenures, as Froude explains it, lived the most devil-may-care existence. . . . They are bad, but none of our making; English settlers bore them, English laws moulded them. No one who knows the serious, reserved and suspicious Irish peasant ever held them in any way representative of the national type.

By 1891, after much study of the eighteenth century in preparation for a historical essay never published, Yeats was only a little less antagonistic to the Anglo-Irish gentry. It is a class, he said, "that held its acres once at the sword's point, and a little later were pleased by the tinsel villany [sic] of the Hell Fire Club." Its existence had been "a pleasant thing enough for the world. It introduced a new wit—a humor whose essence was dare-devilry and good-comradeship, half real, half assumed." But for Ireland it had been "almost entirely an evil." Not the least of its sins had been "the creation in the narrow circle of its dependents of the pattern used later on for . . . 'the stage Irishman.' " The quality of the humor aside, Yeats agreed with William Carleton that the peasant "is not appeased because the foot that passes over him is shod with laughter." In the novels of Croker, Lover, and

Lever, Yeats saw the image of this gentry, usually with "a hospitable, genial, good soldier-like disposition," but with "no more sense of responsibility, as a class, than have the *dullahans, thivishes, bowas,* and *water sheries* of the spirit-ridden peasantry." That lack of responsibility explained why the Anglo-Irish had never had a poet: "Poetry needs a God, a cause, or a country." Maria Edgeworth was consequently the only novelist of the gentry to receive Yeats's full praise:

> She constantly satirized their recklessness, their love of all things English, their oppression of and contempt for their own coun-
> try. . . . Her novels give, indeed, systematically the mean and
> vulgar side of all that gay life celebrated by Lever.

It is no wonder that Yeats's *Representative Irish Tales,* which contains these comments, was reviewed by one periodical, as Yeats said later, "under the idea that it was written by a barbarous super-republican American."

But after the turn of the century, when Yeats began to formulate his own conservative synthesis, his view of the aristocracy changed markedly. He was both pursuing his anti-self and discovering his own heritage. By 1904 he treated with respect and admiration not only the ancient Irish and Norman-Irish aristocracy but also the Anglo-Irish of the eighteenth century. The stories retold in Lady Gregory's *Gods and Fighting Men,* he said,

> helped to sing the old Irish and Norman-Irish aristocracy to their
> end. They heard the hereditary poets and story-tellers, and they
> took to horse and died fighting against Elizabeth or against Crom-
> well; and when an English-speaking aristocracy had their place,
> it listened to no poetry indeed, but it felt about it in the popular
> mind an exacting and ancient tribunal, and began a play that
> had for spectators men and women that loved the high wasteful
> virtues.

He no longer saw foreign exploiters wearing the mask of harsh comedy. The English were at least trying to learn an ancient role from their conquered spectators.

> I do not think that their own mixed blood or the habit of their
> time need take all, or nearly all, credit or discredit for the impulse
> that made our modern gentlemen fight duels over pocket-hand-
> kerchiefs, and set out to play ball against the gates of Jerusalem
> for a wager, and scatter money before the public eye; and at last,
> after an epoch of such eloquence the world has hardly seen its

like, lose their public spirit and their high heart and grow quer-
ulous and selfish as men do who have played life out not heartily
but with noise and tumult. Had they understood the people and
the game a little better, they might have created an aristocracy
in an age that has lost the meaning of the word.

Yeats now criticized the Anglo-Irish primarily not for cruelty and irrespon-
sibility but for lack of depth and complexity in their passion. In order to
"create a great community," he would now re-create the old aristocratic
foundations of life—but "not as they existed in that splendid misunderstanding of the eighteenth century."

As he clarified his aristocratic ideal, he distinguished it from its debased
versions. Though he was pursuing an anti-self, that anti-self was no character
portrayed by Lever or Lover. Even in 1904 he saw the nineteenth-century
querulousness and selfishness as twice removed from the ancient ideal. And
when, during the 1920's, he finally accepted the Anglo-Irish tradition as
his own, he could define it all the more firmly. No longer was Chevalier
Burke typical of the gentry as a whole—broken-down Norman gentlemen,
eighteenth-century braggadocios, and nineteenth-century English Garrison.
A gulf had opened between the age of Swift and the gay and vulgar life
chronicled in the novels Yeats read in his youth. After the French Revolution,
he said, the "Protestant Ascendancy with its sense of responsibility" gave
place to the "Garrison, a political party of Protestant and Catholic landowners, merchants and officials." These "loved the soil of Ireland"—"the
merchant loved with an ardour, I have not met elsewhere, some sea-board
town where he had made his money, or spent his youth"—but

they could give to a people they thought unfit for self-govern-
ment, nothing but a condescending affection. They preferred
frieze-coated humourists, dare-devils upon horseback, to ordinary
men and women; created in Ireland and elsewhere an audience
that welcomed the vivid imaginations of Lever, Lover, Somerville
and Ross.

For the moment Yeats could dissociate even his immediate parental stock
from the Protestant Ascendancy with which he poetically identified himself.

Paradoxically, his complete allegiance to Anglo-Ireland was made possible by the establishment in 1922 of the Irish Free State. Nine years later
Yeats described its effect with his usual vivid oversimplification. The "mere
existence" of the new Irish state, he said, had delivered artists from "obsession." No longer distracted by political nationalism, they could now give
full attention to their work.

Freedom from obsession brought me a transformation akin to religious conversion. I had thought much of my fellow-workers— Synge, Lady Gregory, Lane—but had seen nothing in Protestant Ireland as a whole but its faults, had carried through my projects in face of its opposition or indifference, had fed my imagination upon the legends of the Catholic villages or upon medieval poetry; but now my affection turned to my own people, to my own ancestors, to the books they had read.

Though the transformation had really been long in developing, his memory stressed this essential truth: with Protestant Ireland now but a component of a free Irish state, he could change his allegiance without seeming, to himself or others, to desert the nationalist cause.

But political reasons had not disappeared from his mind. The Anglo-Irish, he thought, had much to teach a young state seeking political stability. Momentarily forgetting the praise O'Leary and Taylor had given the eighteenth century, his said: "Now that Ireland was substituting traditions of government for the rhetoric of agitation, our eighteenth century had regained its importance." And religion was still of political significance to him, though the "obsession" was different:

It seemed that we the Protestants had a part to play at last that might find us allies everywhere, for we alone had not to assume in public discussion of all great issues that we could find in St. Mark or St. Matthew a shorthand report of the words of Christ attested before a magistrate. We sought religious conviction by a more difficult research . . .

He was perhaps remembering that in 1925, after his speech on divorce in the Irish Senate, a passionate and ironic plea for tolerance, one senator had angrily retorted that the Gospel according to St. Matthew was historically accurate and, furthermore, should be the law of the land. Catholic censorship had of course plagued Yeats ever since the controversy over *The Countess Cathleen*. But before Irish Independence he had argued (with some reason) that such confusion of art with homiletics derived from English bourgeois puritanism and was therefore grotesquely out of place in Ireland under the apparent protection of the Roman Church. Now, as Protestantism came to mean the heroism of Parnell rather than the calculation of the Belfast man, and as Catholicism came to mean a crude intellectual tyranny in modern Ireland rather than a rich medieval culture, Yeats's historical analysis and his strategy changed. If, as he came to believe, in his country the Church *was* Babbitt, co-operation was impossible.

It is clear that Yeats had changed not his passion but its object. With rebellious pride the growing boy had defended the Catholic peasantry against the Anglo-Irish gentry; with that same pride the ageing man defended the heirs of those Anglo-Irish against the new Catholic rulers of the Irish Free State. The boy had learned, with his Fenianism, the righteous indignation and aristocratic integrity of John O'Leary; the man saw O'Leary's spiritual ancestry in the people of Jonathan Swift. In 1925, concluding his senate speech on the divorce question, Yeats said:

> I think it is tragic that within three years of this country gaining its independence we should be discussing a measure which a minority of this nation considers to be grossly oppressive. I am proud to consider myself a typical man of that minority. We against whom you have done this thing, are no petty people. We are one of the great stocks of Europe. We are the people of Burke; we are the people of Grattan; we are the people of Swift, the people of Parnell. We have created the most of the modern literature of this country. We have created the best of its political intelligence. Yet I do not altogether regret what has happened. I shall be able to find out, if not I, my children will be able to find out whether we have lost our stamina or not. You have defined our position and given us a popular following. If we have not lost our stamina then your victory will be brief, and your defeat final, and when it comes this nation may be transformed.

Nearly three decades before, Yeats had written to George Russell: "Absorb Ireland and her tragedy and you will be the poet of a people, perhaps the poet of a new insurrection." That counsel he had really directed to himself— and now, political circumstances reversed, directed to himself again. For one who continually sought emblems of adversity, who rejoiced in the fallen world from which he tried to escape, the repetition of the tragedy was not altogether matter for regret.

II

Such, in brief, was Yeats's revaluation of the Anglo-Irish heritage that he was to explore during the rest of his life. Establishing a possessive relation to that strand of history, he had in 1917 acquired the Norman tower at Ballylee, "a permanent symbol of my work plainly visible to the passerby." His theories of art, he said, depended upon just such "rooting of mythology in the earth." Partly because its main theme is not the Anglo-Irish heritage itself, "The Tower" (1925) illustrates how, uniting the pride of the two Irelands, Yeats had gradually rooted his own mythology in that soil of the past.

"What shall I do with this absurdity . . . ?" After the vigorous complaint against old age, posing the problem of the "Excited, passionate, fantastical / Imagination" that is "derided by / A sort of battered kettle at the heel," the speaker of "The Tower" enters upon a tortuous and elliptical reverie. Far from bidding the Muse "go pack," he invokes images and memories from the spiritualized soil, "For I would ask a question of them all." But he does not ask the question in this dialogue with history until ten stanzas later. Meanwhile we follow, with fascination and some perplexity, what seems but brilliant improvisation, a Yeatsian preponderance of means over ends like that apparent (but merely apparent) in "All Souls' Night."

The personages invoked, however, all testify to the richly varied past that is now the speaker's possession. Mrs. French is a figure from that cruel eighteenth-century comedy which Yeats once, with Carleton, utterly rejected. The ballad-poet Raftery had composed in the eighteenth-century tradition a tribute to one Mary Hynes, the remaining foundation of whose house the speaker has just stared upon. In *The Celtic Twilight* Yeats had recreated their story and its setting with quiet sympathy. There too he had mentioned the man "drowned in the great bog of Cloone" because of Raftery's song. Red Hanrahan is even more completely a possession: Yeats created him as Raftery had created the moonlit image of Mary Hynes, and "drove him drunk or sober" across the countryside as Raftery had driven the men bewitched by his song. But Hanrahan too came from the eighteenth century: the original name Yeats gave to that poet and hedge-schoolmaster, O'Sullivan Rua, suggests his prototype, the Irish peasant poet, Eoghan Ruadh Ó Suileabháin. Finally, the "ancient bankrupt master of this house" is (like the first founder in "Meditations in Time of Civil War") parallel to the speaker himself, save that he has "finished his dog's day."

These and some lesser figures now inhabit a common limbo. Accessible to the speaker's call, they are his present re-creations, who stand ready to instruct him. Both creatures and masters, they are possessed by the speaker and they possess him. That is so because they variously embody the power and the predicament of the excited, passionate, fantastical imagination: an outrageous power, maiming, blinding, maddening, murdering—the "horrible splendour of desire." If the farmer was Mrs. French's victim, so the drowned man was Raftery's, so Hanrahan was Yeats's; and perhaps the ancient bankrupt master of the Norman tower was, like Raftery, Yeats, Hanrahan, and all imaginative men, victim not only of circumstance but

also of that very imagination which now has made him "fabulous." Down
the centuries we see "Rough men-at-arms," images of that same "horrible
splendour of desire," who

> Come with loud cry and panting breast
> To break upon a sleeper's rest
> While their great wooden dice beat on the board.

It is precisely that splendor which the speaker himself now defiantly elects,
in full knowledge of its destructive power, as his highly traditional goal:

>   the tragedy began
> With Homer that was a blind man,
> And Helen has all living hearts betrayed.
> O may the moon and sunlight seem
> One inextricable beam,
> For if I triumph I must make men mad.

Only such triumph now seems possible to the ageing poet under "the day's
declining beam," deserted as the blind man is by all things belonging to
"the prosaic light of day," condemned to the moonlit realm of the imagination. Here, yet more violently than in "Meditations in Time of Civil
War," the predicament reverses that of Wordsworth's "Ode on the Intimations of Immortality," where the speaker is troubled by the fading of the
visionary light "into the light of common day."

If, when Yeats's speaker finally asks his question—

> Did all old men and women, rich and poor,
> Who trod upon these rocks or passed this door,
> Whether in public or in secret rage
> As I do now against old age?

—it now seems anticlimactic, that is because already the undeniable fact of
age pales before the splendor of the fantastical imagination that remains.
The embodied spirits stand before him, mute witnesses to his predicament,
yet witnesses now far more to the continuing power that resides within him.
And the calculated anticlimax is surmounted by a strange turn of events:

> Go therefore; but leave Hanrahan,
> For I need all his mighty memories.

The speaker retains out of that company the one who is most completely
his creature and his master. His own mighty memories are not enough; he

needs a memory's memory. Yet that paradoxical declaration of dependence
leads not to a genuine question but to a final taunt:

> Old lecher with a love on every wind,
> Bring up out of that deep considering mind
> All that you have discovered in the grave,
> For it is certain that you have
> Reckoned up every unforeknown, unseeing
> Plunge, lured by a softening eye,
> Or by a touch or a sigh,
> Into the labyrinth of another's being;
>
> Does the imagination dwell the most
> Upon a woman won or a woman lost?
> If on the lost, admit you turned aside
> From a great labyrinth out of pride,
> Cowardice, some silly over-subtle thought
> Or anything called conscience once;
> And that if memory recur, the sun's
> Under eclipse and the day blotted out.

As he evokes longingly the "great labyrinth" unexplored, he establishes a
precarious victory over the transcendent image of Hanrahan which he has
created. He tortures Hanrahan now as long ago with his own horrible
splendor of desire. Even for Hanrahan experience must have been limited;
he—like Homer, Raftery, and the speaker himself—is sentenced to the world
of the blind.

However, a strange though characteristic irony enters here. The speaker
is forcing upon Hanrahan, who has reckoned up or measured his experience,
a more disturbing self-measurement. Hanrahan's explorations and hence his
being have been limited by his own ego—directly through "pride" or "cowardice," or indirectly through the masks of intellect or conscience. He has
been limited by the "fear or moral ambition" which always threaten creative
activity, for desire—as this taunt obliquely recognizes—also demands surrender of self. We must, of course, see in the speaker's taunt to Hanrahan
his own self-knowledge and self-judgment. In other words, his own often
wildly egocentric celebration of desire here moves to a yet further recognition
of its pitfalls: the limitation of fulfilment inherent in the ego's anxious
possession of that world which it has created and known. Appropriately,
therefore, his phrasing approaches Blake's description of how "Los could
enter into Enitharmon's bosom & explore / Its intricate Labyrinths" only
when "the Obdurate heart was broken." The bearing of this recognition

upon his own problem of clinging to life and thus inhibiting the exploration of death will emerge implicitly in the rest of the poem.

Grasping the implications of this long review of images and memories, and moving on to the concluding testament, declaration of faith, and plan for the future, we may be struck by a similarity to another great dramatic monologue, by a poet whom the early Yeats admired. Despite many differences, Tennyson's "Ulysses" contains the same initially perplexing fusion of complaint, elegy, and defiant assertion—a fusion that renders, in heroic opposition to the finitude of human life, the infinitude of the creative and exploring mind. In both poems the selection of an ageing speaker heightens that contrast; the firm possession of a labyrinthine past makes more poignant the precarious tenure of the present and the vastness of all that is yet unexplored. Against all odds both protagonists try to project the achievements of the past into the present and on into an open future. But the speaker of "The Tower," himself a bitterly realistic poet for all his fantastic assertions, is explicitly concerned with the problem that Ulysses merely exemplifies—the problem that Yeats, in his long preparation for the poem, had once defined: "It may be," he had said in *The Celtic Twilight,* "that in a few years Fable, who changes mortalities to immortalities in her cauldron," will have changed blind Raftery to a perfect symbol of "the magnificence and penury of dreams."

In the second part of "The Tower" the speaker has evoked those aspects of his Anglo-Irish heritage which best symbolize the horrible splendor of the imagination wrought to its highest pitch. In his realism he dryly accepts, in his defiance he ironically exalts, Mrs. French, "Gifted with so fine an ear," as well as "beauty's blind rambling celebrant." Having dramatically vindicated the imagination in the face of all that is temporal, having seen also that anxious possession of the world created and known is a bar to further creation and exploration, he may now rest in a more serene faith in the independence of the imagination and in a "pride" that is not the ego's apprehensive desire to possess and dominate but the whole being's exultant sense of creative giving. He may therefore evoke without irony a quite different aspect of the Anglo-Irish heritage—that which Yeats had celebrated in his Senate speech of the same year:

> It is time that I wrote my will;
> I choose upstanding men
> That climb the streams until
> The fountain leap, and at dawn
> Drop their cast at the side

> Of dripping stone; I declare
> They shall inherit my pride,
> The pride of people that were
> Bound neither to Cause nor to State,
> Neither to slaves that were spat on,
> Nor to the tyrants that spat,
> The people of Burke and of Grattan
> That gave, though free to refuse—

If Houses of Lords and Houses of Commons are something other than human life, certain individuals who are politically active may yet be, as they are here, "what Blake called 'naked beauty displayed.' . . . The great men of the eighteenth century were that beauty; Parnell had something of it, O'Leary something . . ." Fisherman, fountain, dawn, with their connotations of natural richness and vitality, of Irish landscape and ceremony of innocence, help to define the beneficent pride of Anglo-Ireland, which is now (in an act consonant with its own nature) bequeathed at a moment of exultant self-giving to that new age for which Yeats had always hoped—an age "that will understand with Blake that the Holy Spirit is 'an intellectual fountain,' and that the kinds and degrees of beauty are the images of its authority." That "beauty" implies no mere aestheticism but rather what Yeats in 1902 had called "the pure joy that only comes out of things that have never been indentured to any cause" and that is a prerequisite for the "impartial meditation about character and destiny we call the artistic life."

As this phrase in "The Tower" moves toward its final sustained cadence, it introduces further images of the authority of that fountain which is the possession of no person; "pride" becomes yet more clearly impersonal—the pride of a natural largesse (of morn, horn, showers, hour) which works through individuals:

> Pride, like that of the morn,
> When the headlong light is loose,

—antithetical to that moment in "The Second Coming" which the line echoes: "The blood-dimmed tide is loosed"—

> Or that of the fabulous horn,
> Or that of the sudden shower
> When all streams are dry,
> Or that of the hour
> When the swan must fix his eye
> Upon a fading gleam,

> Float out upon a long
> Last reach of glittering stream
> And there sing his last song.

As the shower modulates into the song of the swan (which, like Tennyson's dying Merlin, follows the gleam), we recall that this very testament is such a shower or song in the arid landscape of decrepit age. The penury of the imagination, almost eclipsed by its magnificence, now appears only in such implications, or in the momentary defiance which the thought of the swan and his fading world brings:

> And I declare my faith:
> I mock Plotinus' thought
> And cry in Plato's teeth,
> Death and life were not
> Till man made up the whole,
> Made lock, stock and barrel
> Out of his bitter soul,
> Aye, sun and moon and star, all.
> And further add to that
> That, being dead, we rise,
> Dream and so create
> Translunar Paradise.

As the word "bitter" recognizes, these consciously defiant articles of faith are what in 1930 Yeats called "all that heroic casuistry, all that assertion of the eternity of what nature declares ephemeral." Yet in the poem they are truths of the imagination: "For if I triumph I must make men mad." The speaker is earning his right (declared in "To a Young Beauty") to attend that late but select dinner of which Landor once spoke, with Landor himself and with Donne, who also had proudly declared, "Death be not proud."

Turning to the future, he demonstrates through yet further shifts of tone, the imaginative validity of his argument. When Tennyson's Ulysses cast his thoughts beyond the sunset, he strangely merged death, a newer world, and a reliving of the past. But even more than for Ulysses, for this speaker penury and magnificence now meet and are reconciled in serene ambiguity:

> I have prepared my peace
> With learned Italian things
> And the proud stones of Greece,
> Poet's imaginings

> And memories of love,
> Memories of the words of women,
> All those things whereof
> Man makes a superhuman
> Mirror-resembling dream.

He has prepared his peace in the mirroring world of the imagination; but though he had referred to a future translunar Paradise, this peace is a present reality. The lines also state that he has made his peace with the things of the world which he must abandon. The slackening verse movement indicates that the speaker is beginning to rest after his orgy of creation, as Eternal Man rested on the seventh day, the mirroring imagination sufficient unto the moment. The simile that follows re-creates this moment, but with a difference. It moves from daws who "chatter and scream, / And drop twigs layer upon layer"—the life process of "preparing"—to the mother bird who

> will rest
> On their hollow top,
> And so warm her wild nest.

The simile further devalues preparatory life and the materials it accumulates, as opposed to the culminating moment; and it presents that peaceful and extended moment as one of brooding yet "wild" creativity.

A new vista of contemplative activity has opened. The speaker now must—and can—"leave both faith and pride" to others. It is, as he says, both a bequeathing and also now a quiet abandonment by one whose metal has been broken. From one point of view, we may say that, magnificence having been created, penury can be accepted. But penury has also been seen as a creative state itself. The obdurate heart broken, another labyrinth can be entered and explored. Hence there is little trace, in the final phrase of this testamentary song, of the proud credo uttered a moment before. The phrase begins by asserting the creative force inherent in any act of the imagination:

> Now shall I make my soul,
> Compelling it to study
> In a learned school . . .

But it modulates to something quite different from the last song of the defiant swan:

> Till the wreck of body,
> Slow decay of blood,

> Testy delirium
> Or dull decrepitude,
> Or what worse evil come—
> The death of friends, or death
> Of every brilliant eye
> That made a catch in the breath—
> Seem but the clouds of the sky
> When the horizon fades;
> Or a bird's sleepy cry
> Among the deepening shades.

The speaker approaches Keats's view that the world is the "vale of Soul-making," a "School" in which each soul learns its "Identity." But he leaves carefully unspecified the content of school and soul. He presents only, in all realism, the prospect of a fading world. More strictly, evil and loss no longer seem important; but as the metaphors suggest, with them fades all that is temporal. The lines render, in a quiet mode, the "tragic joy" which, Yeats had said in 1904, reaches its climax "when the world itself has slipped away in death." A similar thought had come to Yeats on the occasion of Synge's death: "He had no need of our sympathies. It was as though we and the things about us died away from him and not he from us." But in "The Tower" that darkening of the world of mirroring realities, that fading of the gleam on which the swan fixes its eye, is the final act of the eternal imagination. The poem has moved to the acceptance of death, and to the creation of death in that acceptance. The horrible splendor of desire—the creative and destructive, illuminating and blinding power of the imagination—here attains its final ethereal harmony: "a bird's sleepy cry / Among the deepening shades."

III

In re-creating history the speaker of "The Tower" moves beyond history. Following him, we have seen some ways in which Yeats was now grounding his concepts and symbols in the soil of Anglo-Ireland. But he wished to discover yet further relations between the people of Burke and the defiant swan, the Italian things, and the stones of Greece. In 1930 he wrote in his diary:

> How much of my reading is to discover the English and Irish
> originals of my thought, its first language, and where no such
> originals exist, its relation to what original did. I seek more than

idioms, for thoughts become more vivid when I find they were thought out in historical circumstances which affect those in which I live, or, which is perhaps the same thing, were thought first by men my ancestors may have known.

He was delighted to find Anglo-Irish prototypes for his own theory of history and his own conservatism. Swift's *Discourse of the Contests and Dissensions between the nobles and commons in Athens and Rome,* he thought, led up to Edmund Burke "so clearly that one may claim that Anglo-Ireland recreated conservative thought in one as in the other. Indeed the *Discourse* with its law of history might be for us what Vico is to the Italians, had we a thinking nation." In a moment of excitement he took a yet more extreme position. The *Discourse,* he said,

> is more important to modern thought than Vico and certainly foreshadowed Flinders Petrie, Frobenius, Henry Adams, Spengler, and very exactly and closely Gerald Heard. It needs interpretation, for it had to take the form of a pamphlet intelligible to the Whig nobility. He saw civilisation "exploding"—to use Heard's term—just before the final state, and that final state as a tyranny, and he took from a Latin writer the conviction that every civilisation carries with it from the first what shall bring it to an end.

Burke borrowed or rediscovered Swift's insight into historical process, Yeats concluded, while Coleridge borrowed "all but that inevitable end."

Discovering such English and Irish originals—studying "the rebirth of European spirituality in the mind of Berkeley, the restoration of European order in the mind of Burke"—Yeats found thoughts becoming more vivid not merely because he had established a historical relation to those thinkers but also because he was not studying "thought" alone. He would agree in part with the description of such study given by R. G. Collingwood, who also learned from Vico and Croce:

> I plunge beneath the surface of my mind and there live a life in which I not merely think about Nelson but am Nelson, and thus in thinking about Nelson think about myself. . . . If what the historian knows is past thoughts, and if he knows them by re-thinking them himself, it follows that the knowledge he achieves by historical enquiry is not knowledge of his situation as opposed to knowledge of himself. . . . He must be, in fact, a microcosm of all the history he can know.

But Yeats would go yet further. It is characteristic that, attributing a similar
Vichian theory of historical knowledge to Swift, he introduced a characteristically passionate complication: it is to Vanessa that Swift says, in *The
Words upon the Window-Pane,* "When I rebuilt Rome in your mind it was
as though I walked its streets." He was studying whole men—and learning,
in that study, about a microcosmic whole man in the present.

That is why he could say, "I have before me an ideal expression in
which all that I have, clay and spirit alike, assist; it is as though I most
approximate towards that expression when I carry with me the greatest
amount of hereditary thought and feeling, even national and family hatred
and pride." He elaborated that goal when revising these diary notations for
publication in *Wheels and Butterflies:*

> Swift haunts me; he is always just around the next corner. Some-
> times it is a thought of my great-great-grandmother, a friend of
> that Archbishop King who sent him to England about the "First
> Fruits," sometimes it is S. Patrick's, where I have gone to wander
> and meditate, that brings him to mind, sometimes I remember
> something hard or harsh in O'Leary or in Taylor, or in the public
> speech of our statesmen, that reminds me by its style of his verse
> or prose. Did he not speak, perhaps, with just such an intonation?
> This instinct for what is near and yet hidden is in reality a return
> to the sources of our power, and therefore a claim made upon
> the future. Thought seems more true, emotion more deep, spoken
> by someone who touches my pride, who seems to claim me of
> his kindred, who seems to make me a part of some national
> mythology, nor is mythology mere ostentation, mere vanity if it
> draws me onward to the unknown; another turn of the gyre and
> myth is wisdom, pride, discipline.

These eighteenth-century men—and especially Berkeley and Swift—
were therefore complex masks with whom Yeats might converse and from
whom he might learn of "what is near and yet hidden." Each stood before
him as both reflection and shadow: projection of his own consciously held
position and also of potentialities within himself that he had not yet fully
discerned. Each stood also as "cosmic" reflection and shadow: intimation of
an ideal passion and ideal unity, and embodiment of the tensions of the
fallen world. Early in the century, before his complete allegiance to Anglo-
Ireland, Yeats had suggested the use to which he would put these figures:
"There is scarcely a man who has led the Irish people, at any time, who
may not give some day to a great writer precisely that symbol he may require

for the expression of himself." But he had more fully suggested their meaning even earlier, in 1896, when Swift alone had seemed to him to transcend a fallen century. He had said then of Swift:

> He did not become . . . a great light of his time because of the utility of his projects or of any high standard of honest thinking— for some of his most famous projects were expressions of a paradoxical anger, while others he defended with arguments which even he could not have believed—but because he revealed in his writings and in his life a more intense nature, a more living temperament, than any of his contemporaries. He was as near a supreme man as that fallen age could produce, and that he did not labour, as Blake says the supreme man should, "to bring again the golden age" by revealing it in his work and his life, but fought, as with battered and smoke-blackened armour in the mouth of the pit, is to the discredit of "the century of philosophers": a century which had set chop-logic in the place of the mysterious power, obscure as a touch from behind a curtain, that had governed "the century of poets."

But even that fighting in the mouth of the pit—which Yeats was increasingly to see as a substantial part of his own vocation—was, he had said in 1896, a way of revealing "a more powerful and passionate, a more divine world than ours." For Swift had "given the world an unforgettable parable by building an overpowering genius upon the wreckage of the merely human faculties." The parable was of central importance to an admirer of *King Lear* who would later write "Sailing to Byzantium" and "The Tower" and would dramatize in *The Words upon the Window-Pane* the ageing Swift's dread of madness as a *hysterica passio* of historical dimensions.

That play itself is more than a spiritualist tour de force or an ingenious device for bringing historical drama into a modern setting. Like "The Tower," it renders the sense of a dramatic interpenetration of past and present. Indeed, the Swift who haunted Yeats, who was always just round the next corner, was audible to him also: "I can hear Swift's voice in his letters speaking the sentences at whatever pace makes their sound and idiom expressive. He speaks and we listen at leisure." Mediumship was an apt vehicle for what Yeats himself experienced as a psychological reality, a source of power "near yet hidden." Hence the scenario of the Anglo-Irish past, like that of *A Vision* or that of the early romances, might lend to the moods a voice. The dramatic perspective of *The Words upon the Window-Pane* recalls that of *On Baile's Strand*: the madness and death of the heroic are seen from

the vantage-point of the unheroic and utilitarian milieu which mirrors ourselves and which has helped to drive the hero over the edge of sanity. But
what once appeared in the context of Irish myth has now been discerned in
the experienced drama of history.

Like Swift, Berkeley was for Yeats a complex mirror of ideal and reality.
The great enemy of the abstract, he wished to "create a philosophy so concrete
that the common people could understand it." "Descartes, Locke and Newton
took away the world and gave us its excrement instead," said Yeats. "Berkeley
restored the world"—"the world that only exists because it shines and
sounds." In so describing a reparation of the fall presented in "Fragments,"
Yeats was not applauding Berkeley's idealism as it is usually conceived:

> Sometimes when I think of him what flitted before his eyes flits
> before mine also, I half perceive a world like that of the Zen
> priest in Japan or China, but am hurried back into abstraction
> after but an instant.

Similarly in *A Vision,* turning in reaction against his own abstract system
toward "a reality which is concrete, sensuous, bodily," Yeats recalled passages
"written by Japanese monks on attaining Nirvana." For Zen, Nirvana is no
escape from the wheel except as it is an immediate and concrete apprehension
of that harmony which the wheel merely symbolizes. It is no release from
individual consciousness except as it is a moment of enlightenment in which
the error of abstraction which posits cut-off individuals disappears. It is thus
cognate with the goal of spiritual alchemy and is an "affirmation" that
transcends the opposites, a "word" that cannot be refuted. Zen shares with
Yeats the view that "You can refute Hegel but not the Saint or the Song
of Sixpence."

"You ask me what is my religion and I hit you across the mouth."
That Zen retort might well have been uttered by the young Berkeley whom
Yeats envisioned, "solitary, talkative, ecstatic, destructive." Such a temperament, Yeats thought, Berkeley also showed in later years "though but
in glimpses or as something divined or inferred" behind the complacent
mask of the mature bishop, which he wore because, in a time "terrified of
religious scepticism and political anarchy," it "hid from himself and others
his own anarchy and scepticism." Yeats was here glimpsing a tension within
his own conservative "pose," though he had more complex dramatic and
psychological techniques for realizing and so transcending it. Thinking of
Berkeley's isolation, Yeats also thought of his own father "and of others
born into the Anglo-Irish solitude." Such men he saw as isolated from Ireland
("scattered men in an ignorant country"), isolated by their genius in a time

of imaginative ebb tide (for Berkeley the "first great imaginative wave had sunk, the second had not risen"), and isolated both physically and spiritually from England. Considering this last fact, Yeats saw in them the best elements of an Irish culture in which "solitaries flourish," a culture which has the "sense for what is permanent."

> Born in such community Berkeley with his belief in perception, that abstract ideas are mere words, Swift with his love of perfect nature, of the Houyhnhnms, his disbelief in Newton's system and in every sort of machine, Goldsmith and his delight in the particulars of common life that shocked his contemporaries, Burke with his conviction that all states not grown slowly like a forest tree are tyrannies, found in England an opposite that stung their own thought into expression and made it lucid.

Like Yeats himself, they were caught between contraries, goaded into passionate thought and action, and enabled to play a triumphantly liberating role—that of "hardship borne and chosen out of pride and joy." Their soil too had been spiritualized by tragedy. "The historical dialectic," Yeats said, "trampled upon their minds in that brutal Ireland, product of two generations of civil war . . .; they were the trodden grapes and became wine."

As a quasi-ideal culture, eighteenth-century Ireland suggested the Renaissance and Periclean Athens. Yeats saw "in Bolingbroke the last pose and in Swift the last passion of the Renaissance." Professionalism was not yet a curse. "Unity of being was still possible though somewhat over-rationalised and abstract, more diagram than body": the fall described in "Statistics" was just beginning. But when "Swift sank into imbecility or madness his epoch had finished in the British Isles." Thus far, Yeats's description suggests his Phase 18, from 1550 to 1650 (the picture of Europe after 1650 is much less favorable in "Dove or Swan"); but Swift's epoch was also a delayed and imperfect Phase 15:

> I seek an image of the modern mind's discovery of itself, of its own permanent form, in that one Irish century that escaped from darkness and confusion. I would that our fifteenth, sixteenth, or even our seventeenth century had been the clear mirror, but fate decided against us.

Hence a submerged analogy with Phase 15, that time when the shadow of history becomes a clear mirror, runs through Yeats's vision of the Enlightenment. Corbet, in *The Words upon the Window-Pane*, gives the conventional interpretation: "That arrogant intellect free at last from superstition." But

Yeats calls that "the young man's overstatement full of the unexamined suppositions of common speech," and he adds:

> I saw Asia in the carved stones of Blenheim, not in the pride of great abstract masses, but in that humility of flower-like intricacy—the particular blades of the grass; nor can chance have thrown into contiguous generations Spinoza and Swift, an absorption of the whole intellect in God, a fakir-like contempt for all human desire . . .; the elaboration and spread of Masonic symbolism, its God made in the image of a Christopher Wren; Berkeley's declaration, modified later, that physical pleasure is the *Summum Bonum,* Heaven's sole reality, his counter-truth to that of Spinoza. . . . Spinoza and the Masons, Berkeley and Swift, speculative and practical intellect, stood there free at last from all prepossessions and touched the extremes of thought . . .

That is the "horizontal dance" of opposites, *primary* and *antithetical,* Asiatic and European, which Yeats noticed in "Dove or Swan" only as Phase 15 approaches and recedes. It is the clear mirror, the mind's discovery of "its own permanent form"—a repetition of that self-discovery which, according to Hegel, took place in fifth-century Greece. For Yeats, Berkeley fought the "Irish Salamis," which resulted in the "birth of the national intellect."

Though the fusion of extremes was incomplete, though there was no real full moon when "all abounds and flows," it was a near miss. The Anglo-Irish would seem

> the Gymnosophists of Strabo close at hand, could they but ignore what was harsh and logical in themselves, or the China of the Dutch cabinet-makers, of the *Citizen of the World:* the long-settled rule of powerful men, no great dogmatic structure, few great crowded streets, scattered unprogressive communities, much handiwork, wisdom wound into the roots of the grass.

And the epoch passed, like that of Greece, with a sinking into the *primary.* The "mechanicians mocked by Gulliver" prevailed; the "moment of freedom could not last":

> Did not Rousseau within five years of the death of Swift publish his *Discourse upon Arts and Sciences* and discover instinctive harmony not in heroic effort, not in Cato and Brutus, not among impossible animals . . . but among savages, and thereby beget the sans-culottes of Marat? After the arrogance of power the humility of a servant.

Anglo-Ireland seemed thus to combine transcendental ideal and fallen reality. Yeats cast two crosslights upon it, revealing the virtues of Phidian Athens and the Renaissance as well as the tragic conflicts of modern Ireland. If, in his prose, the vision lacks complete coherence, it nevertheless testifies to his continual attempt to hold in a single thought reality and justice. The poetry itself brings that double vision into a single paradoxical focus.

IV

In the two poems celebrating Swift, Goldsmith, Berkeley, and Burke, that double vision is evident as a living tradition is viewed from the dramatic perspective. "The Seven Sages" begins with a trivial boasting, a parody of Yeats's own celebration of his family memories:

THE FIRST. My great-grandfather spoke to Edmund Burke
    In Grattan's house.
THE SECOND.   My great-grandfather shared
    A pot-house bench with Oliver Goldsmith once.
THE THIRD. My great-grandfather's father talked of music,
    Drank tar-water with the Bishop of Cloyne.
THE FOURTH. But mine saw Stella once.

Yet what is trivial? Tar water? Berkeley's *Siris,* as Coleridge said, "beginning with Tar ends with the Trinity, the omne scibile forming the interspace." Yeats himself said: "And the tar water, and the cures it worked, what a subject for a discourse! Could he not lead his reader—especially if that reader drank tar water every morning—from tar to light?" For these Anglo-Irish, logic is one with passion, and the loftiest intellectual achievement is rooted in the humblest biographical facts. The question of the fifth sage may then not arise from the inconsequence of senility:

THE FIFTH.   Whence came our thought?
THE SIXTH. From four great minds that hated Whiggery.
THE FIFTH. Burke was a Whig.
THE SIXTH.   Whether they knew or not,
    Goldsmith and Burke, Swift and the Bishop of Cloyne
    All hated Whiggery; but what is Whiggery?
    A levelling, rancorous, rational sort of mind
    That never looked out of the eye of a saint
    Or out of a drunkard's eye.
THE SEVENTH.   All's Whiggery now,
    But we old men are massed against the world.

Quite aware of the liberties he takes with history, the sixth sage praises both
an intensely subjective vision and the objective ability to share the unusual
vision of another. And though the seventh applies his redefined epithet much
as the old soldier in Tate's "To the Lacedemonians" applies another such—

> All are born Yankees of the race of men
> And this, too, now the country of the damned

—the sages embody a somewhat more dryly comic heroism. As the poem
proceeds, however, their "massed" opposition gains in dignity and richness.
They carry on the magnanimity of dissent in "Burke's great melody," the
love for the common life in what "Oliver Goldsmith sang," the savage
indignation chiseled on the "tomb of Swift," and the persuasive utterance
of Berkeley, leading "from tar to light":

> a voice
> Soft as the rustle of a reed from Cloyne
> That gathers volume; now a thunder-clap.

Once more an apparently inconsequent remark leads us back to origins:

> THE SIXTH. What schooling had these four?
> THE SEVENTH.   They walked the roads
> Mimicking what they heard, as children mimic;
> They understood that wisdom comes of beggary.

Though the poem returns to the apparently trivial, the last word has the
resonance of a tradition maintained in spite of, and because of, adversity.
It has the resonance, too, of the understanding in "The Tower" that magnificence arises from penury, and the understanding in "Meditations in Time
of Civil War" that the honeybees may "build in the crevices / Of loosening
masonry." "Beggary" is the state of "fruitful void," known by the wise fool
or by the visionary poet who has become again "unaccommodated man" and
stands "naked under the heavens." It is here celebrated by minds magnan-
imous in victory, heroic in defeat, firm in apparent eccentricity, yet humble
before the simplest facts of experience.

   In "Blood and the Moon," because the speaker is no simple sage but
the owner of the tower, the double vision is more complex, and a more
painful wisdom comes of a more extreme beggary.

> Blessed be this place,
> More blessed still this tower;
> A bloody, arrogant power

Rose out of the race
Uttering, mastering it,
Rose like these walls from these
Storm-beaten cottages—
In mockery I have set
A powerful emblem up
And sing it rhyme upon rhyme
In mockery of a time
Half dead at the top.

In Vichian manner he re-erects the tower that rose out of the race, para-doxically both expression and master of Ireland. As he blesses that tower, his emblem joins spirit and blood in a fruitful if precarious marriage that mocks his own less vital, more incoherent time.

Then, after recalling towers that variously combined wisdom and di-recting power, he sings his own symbol of the compelling harmonies of life:

I declare this tower is my symbol; I declare
This winding, gyring, spiring treadmill of a stair is
                    my ancestral stair:
That Goldsmith and the Dean, Berkeley and Burke have
                    travelled there.

That firm pronouncement, with its relish for the bitter and salt of effort and repetition on the winding path of nature, gives body to the nostalgia of the narrator of "Rosa Alchemica," who had boasted of his "wide staircase, where Swift had passed joking and railing, and Curran telling stories and quoting Greek." In various ways the following triplets balance wisdom and power, spirit and clay:

Swift beating on his breast in sibylline frenzy blind
Because the heart in his blood-sodden breast had dragged
                    him down into mankind,
Goldsmith deliberately sipping at the honey-pot of his mind,

—prophetic illumination because of enforced suffering and compassion, bal-anced by judicious mental delectation—

And haughtier-headed Burke that proved the State a tree,
That this unconquerable labyrinth of the birds, century
                    after century,
Cast but dead leaves to mathematical equality;

—proud logic supporting the organic richness and force of a body politic
that transcends the dead level of rationalist structures—

> And God-appointed Berkeley that proved all things a dream,
> That this pragmatical, preposterous pig of a world, its
> > farrow that so solid seem,
> Must vanish on the instant if the mind but change its theme;

—a magical, whimsical power of the mind to annihilate the gross solidity
of flesh. From sibylline frenzy to subjective mind's ascendancy, it is a rich
chord: Anglo-Ireland "free at last from all prepossession" and touching the
"extremes of thought." The precarious harmony is that of the "winding,
gyring, spiring treadmill" of life itself, with its continual shifts and
counterstresses:

> *Saeva Indignatio* and the labourer's hire,
> The strength that gives our blood and state magnanimity
> > of its own desire;
> Everything that is not God consumed with intellectual fire.

Far more precarious, however, than the unity of that blessed and bloody
tower is the speaker's possession of it. Hence, indeed, the note of forced
rhetoric in his mocking and his celebration; for, despite his declaration, he
is of the time which he mocks. His emblem is at most a passionate mental
re-enactment of that eighteenth-century power. It is proper, therefore, that
his series was climaxed not by Swift but by Berkeley, whose consuming
intellectual fire leads toward the more extreme perception of the speaker
himself. Stepping now outside his mentally possessed tradition, he returns
to his own time. The opposites so variously unified begin to fall apart in
his mind:

> The purity of the unclouded moon
> Has flung its arrowy shaft upon the floor.
> Seven centuries have passed and it is pure,
> The blood of innocence has left no stain.
> There, on blood-saturated ground, have stood
> Soldier, assassin, executioner,
> Whether for daily pittance or in blind fear
> Or out of abstract hatred, and shed blood,
> But could not cast a single jet thereon.
> Odour of blood on the ancestral stair!
> And we that have shed none must gather here
> And clamour in drunken frenzy for the moon.

Spirit and blood no longer meet and interpenetrate in the miracle of various life. The lunar shaft is inviolable; on the ancestral stair is blood shed for base motives. The speaker, now barred from the realm of physical power, can but clamor in drunken frenzy for that of spirit. His stair is no longer the gyre of life but a deathly limbo between blood and the moon. It is as though the sequence hoped for in "The Magi" were reversed.

As the speaker now turns his gaze upward from the bestial floor toward the sky, the opposites fall further apart. A Blake engraving captioned "I Want! I Want!" depicts a ladder leaning against the moon, a small figure at the base beginning its climb; Yeats's "John Sherman" mentions a brooch in the form of "a ladder leaning against the moon and a butterfly climbing up it." Symbols of the soul's impossible ascent, they may have led Yeats to use here the dying butterflies in the waste room atop Thoor Ballylee, as the speaker's clamor for the moon leads to a half-mocking perception of beauty in death:

> Upon the dusty, glittering windows cling,
> And seem to cling upon the moonlit skies,
> Tortoiseshell butterflies, peacock butterflies,
> A couple of night-moths are on the wing.
> Is every modern nation like the tower,
> Half dead at the top?

He then turns upon his argument and denies the wisdom of Swift's heart, of Goldsmith's honeypot, of Burke's haughty head, even of Berkeley's mind, which fully controlled a living world:

> No matter what I said,
> For wisdom is the property of the dead,
> A something incompatible with life; and power,
> Like everything that has the stain of blood,
> A property of the living; but no stain
> Can come upon the visage of the moon
> When it has looked in glory from a cloud.

That abrupt and arrogant reversal is tinged, he knows, with "drunken frenzy" and bitter mockery. It is as though he would justify both the separation of the opposites which he must endure and his own deathly yearnings. He is still caught, like his modern tower, in a realm that is neither blood nor moon. But is his frenzy utterly different from that which emerged from Swift's middle state? As the victim of his historical moment, he has at least the wisdom appropriate to his condition: half-dead, barred from full life or death, he knows himself. And in knowing himself, in holding reality and justice in a single thought, he does in fact take another step on the winding stair of life.

The strength of this poem, like that of "Meditations in Time of Civil War," could not exist without the speaker's vigorous honesty. Despite a rather common critical assumption based upon our usual blindnesses, self-dramatization does not preclude self-knowledge. Hence, though the detailed conflicts of "Blood and the Moon" derive from a historical predicament, its final meaning is of the Dantesque order that Yeats saw in all art worthy the name: "the disengaging of a soul from place and history, its suspension in a beautiful or terrible light to await the Judgment, though it must be, seeing that all its days were a Last Day, judged already."

V

Beginning with a direct personal relation to Ireland, moving in widening circles through the re-experienced drama of the past, Yeats could reach a universal history—the Renaissance, Phidian Athens, all the antinomies of *primary* and *antithetical* or of blood and the moon. Fleetingly in personal meditation, enduringly in the poems, he merged dramatic experience and panoramic vision in a full-bodied yet comprehensive reality.

> Now that I am old and live in the past I often think of those ancestors of whom I have some detailed information. Such and such a diner-out and a charming man never did anything; such and such lost the never very great family fortune in some wild-cat scheme; such and such, perhaps deliberately for he was a strange, deep man, married into a family known for harsh dominating strength of character. Then, as my mood deepens, I discover all these men in my single mind, think that I myself have gone through them all at this very moment, and wonder if the balance has come right; then I go beyond those minds and my single mind and discover that I have been describing everybody's struggle, and the gyres turn in my thought.

The experienced and re-experienced drama leads toward the panoramic vision. That statement of 1938 alludes to a richness of content that results from years of meditation, and it conforms to Yeats's understanding of Vico's theory of historical knowledge. But the basic technique of the meditation itself, like so many of his "truths," had been with Yeats since his twenties.

He had presented it in his Blake study as the means of redeeming fallen man, of creating the apocalypse through the power of imagination:

> The mood of the seer, no longer bound in by the particular experiences of his body, spreads out and enters into the particular experiences of an ever-widening circle of other lives and beings, for it will more and more grow one with that portion of the mood essence which is common to all that lives. The circle of the individuality will widen out until other individualities are contained within it, and their thoughts, and the persistent thought-symbols which are their spiritual or mental bodies, will grow visible to it. He who has thus passed into the impersonal portion of his own mind perceives that it is not a mind but all minds. Hence Blake's statement that "Albion," or man, once contained all "the starry heavens," and his description of their flight from him as he materialized. When once a man has re-entered into this, his ancient state, he perceives all things as with the eyes of God.

But that "truth" possessed so early was now tested by passion and reinforced by the experience of others. Whether or not Yeats had noted Emerson's remark that "Dante's praise is that he dared to write his auto-biography in colossal cipher, or into universality," he himself saw others do much the same thing:

> Swift seemed to shape his narrative of history upon some clair-voyant vision of his own life, for he saw civilisation pass from comparative happiness and youthful vigour to an old age of vio-lence and self-contempt, whereas Vico saw it begin in penury like himself and end as he himself would end in a long inactive peace.

Hegel and Balzac, he thought, also "saw history as a personal experience." He knew, of course, that each personal vision must, to some degree, be unique: "When I allow my meditation to expand until the mind of my family merges into everybody's mind, I discover there, not only what Vico and Balzac found, but my own particular amusements and interests." History as vision is limited by one's own mental breadth and depth; history as dramatic experience is limited by the extent to which one has, in one's own life, gone over the whole ground. But to seek history in any other way, Yeats believed, is to compile anatomies of last year's leaves and not to see or create a living forest.

That understanding of history informs most of Yeats's major poems. But one, "Coole Park and Ballylee, 1931," shows with unusual clarity the meditative process widening out from immediate personal experience toward the panoramic vision. Its rapid yet oblique movement depends upon Yeats's gradually developed "universalism" or "seeing of unity everywhere," attained through the "glove" of intimately possessed particulars. The emblems of the poem are not postulated so much as discovered, for the speaker meditates upon a concrete world that presses in upon him, demanding significant articulation.

> Under my window-ledge the waters race,
> Otters below and moor-hens on the top,
> Run for a mile undimmed in Heaven's face
> Then darkening through "dark" Raftery's "cellar" drop,
> Run underground, rise in a rocky place
> In Coole demesne, and there to finish up
> Spread to a lake and drop into a hole.
> What's water but the generated soul?

Though recalling Porphyry on the cave of the nymphs, or Yeats on the streams of Shelley's Alastor and the Witch of Atlas, the stanza does not flatly apply some neo-Platonic system. The final question expresses the sudden illumination toward which the specific meditation has moved. The abstract equivalence is but the simplest and most certain part of that illumination—enough to focus tentatively its matrix of particulars. ("I prefer to include in my definition of water a little duckweed or a few fish. I have never met that poor naked creature H_2O.") We go over the course again in retrospect: the soul's pristine vigor, the strange doubleness of its psychic life (moor hen and otter), its swift youthful accomplishment; then adversity or seeming death (the darkness of Raftery's "cellar" suggesting that of the "dark man" himself), forcing the soul downward into the realm of otters but not preventing its eventual creative victory as it rises "in a rocky place" (which recalls, among other things, the "place of stone" in "To a Friend Whose Work Has Come to Nothing"); there, finally, its serene fulfilment and death. But to spell out must not be to limit this "clairvoyant vision"— to deny, for example, a longer temporal course depicted, which prepares for the poem's later widening of focus: the stream which moves past the Norman tower, past the "strong cellar" of the ballad-poet Raftery, to Coole demesne, the residence of Lady Gregory. Though the subject of the meditation will not achieve final definition until the end of the poem, its area is already clear: the accomplishment and the transience of a soul and of a tradition.

The complex stream has led the speaker from his post of observation, his window ledge, to Coole demesne and its suggestions of imminent death. He turns from that thought, but cannot turn from either the mood or the site, both of which seem engendered by the thought.

> Upon the border of that lake's a wood
> Now all dry sticks under a wintry sun,
> And in a copse of beeches there I stood,
> For Nature's pulled her tragic buskin on
> And all the rant's a mirror of my mood:
> At sudden thunder of the mounting swan
> I turned about and looked where branches break
> The glittering reaches of the flooded lake.

The "dry sticks" suggest the end of a life and of an era, the arriving of the "wintry sun" of solar *primary*. The immediate Yeatsian response, where such "branches *break* / The glittering reaches," is tragic "rant": the soul's defiant effort to "rise in a rocky place," to transmute a final hole to a temporary cellar. As in "Nineteen Hundred and Nineteen," the "thunder of the mounting swan" echoes that response. Yet even that image must in turn be altered by the overwhelming sense of transience:

> Another emblem there! That stormy white
> But seems a concentration of the sky;
> And, like the soul, it sails into the sight
> And in the morning's gone, no man knows why;
> And is so lovely that it sets to right
> What knowledge or its lack had set awry,
> So arrogantly pure, a child might think
> It can be murdered with a spot of ink.

An emblem of what? Yeats, in an often-cited letter, said, "a symbol of inspiration, I think." But we should not ignore his own uncertainty: here as elsewhere the poem refuses to be caught in the net of any simple abstract equivalent. Stormy, even divine power and beauty, arrogant purity—yet seemingly more transient than the soul itself: whether it is that soul, comes to the soul, mirrors the soul, or is created by the soul, it suggests the momentary fulfilment of spirit that redeems the imperfect temporal world.

Twice in this stanza the stream of thought carries the speaker toward the idea of death; once he pulls back, with a third "And," to start his celebration anew—but again, irresistibly, a quality suggests its negation. The oblique rendering of the transience of poetic power, human life, and historical tradition can no longer be maintained. The unstated cause of the "mood," evaded repeatedly, demands utterance. The fact to be confronted is not "sudden thunder" but "dry sticks":

> Sound of a stick upon the floor, a sound
> From somebody that toils from chair to chair . . .

The theme of personal mortality finds its specific focus, crucially unnamed, and the earlier implications of the end of an era, the end of a period of artistic accomplishment, begin to unfold:

> Beloved books that famous hands have bound,
> Old marble heads, old pictures everywhere;
> Great rooms where travelled men and children found
> Content or joy; a last inheritor
> Where none has reigned that lacked a name and fame
> Or out of folly into folly came.

After describing further that spot where persons as well as trees and gardens were rooted, that placid lake filled by the turbulent stream of time, the speaker turns to the rootless and superficial present, and his mood deepens. This is a more complex adversity—"all that great glory spent." The "glittering reaches of the flooded lake" of history too are dimming. The only glory now possible would be that song celebrated in "The Tower," when the swan fixes his eye upon a fading gleam; but the swan can no longer sing:

> We were the last romantics—chose for theme
> Traditional sanctity and loveliness;
> Whatever's written in what poets name
> The book of the people; whatever most can bless
> The mind of man or elevate a rhyme;
> But all is changed, that high horse riderless,
> Though mounted in that saddle Homer rode
> Where the swan drifts upon a darkening flood.

As the "Last Arcadian" once mourned the death of the "woods of Arcady," one who *was* a last romantic now mourns "dry sticks" on Coole estate. But the gain in richness and depth is considerable. The growing boy knew that the intimately possessed particulars of life might lead toward the universal; but John Sherman, standing by the riverside of his youth, saw little more than "familiar sights—boys riding in the stream to the saddle-girths . . ., a swan asleep." The ageing man, standing in imagination by the final lake, looks through such sights, transmuted, upon the landscape of the past. That "darkening flood"—which so marvelously widens and deepens the water imagery—is not the lesser adversity, the "darkening" drop into Raftery's cellar which helped to create "dark" Raftery's "book of the people"—or helped "dark" Milton "build the lofty rhyme." No stream rises; no swan mounts. Pegasus is riderless, and we see no wings. The stream of generation has moved from that double image of youthful vitality, "Otters below and moor-hens on the top," to a double image of its dying fall, drifting swan upon shadow.

The speaker, ostensibly surviving his own significant life, looks back from a "last inheritor" at Coole Park into an indefinite past, from himself and others who were the last romantics to Raftery, Milton, and Homer. It seems a vision not of the cycles of history but of a radical fall. Yet winter does lead to spring, a riderless horse may be ridden, a drifting swan may mount. Even in despair the emblems cannot deny the force of life that produces a continual dialogue between Yeats and the temporal world. Indeed, in this final stanza the meditation itself rises to great lyricism as it claims its impossibility. No more than Lycidas does this swan of a past era float upon his watery bier unwept. Song mourning the lack of song belies itself. Yeats, who knew that no battle has ever been finally lost, knew also that tradition may live in the lament for its passing.

IAN FLETCHER

Rhythm and Pattern in Autobiographies

The title of *Autobiographies* is accurate. The single volume contains approaches to the past made at distinct times in differing modes, ranging from the mosaic of *Trembling of the Veil* to the *journal intime* structure of *Estrangement*, a man talking to himself after the day's work and bitterness with a kind of vivid formality. I want to touch only on *Reveries, Trembling of the Veil* and *Dramatis Personae*, not because I believe that *Estrangement, The Death of Synge* or the 1930 Diary are less important, but because they are less consciously historical, more disjunct, aphoristic, the raw material for composed autobiography.

Of all Yeats's prose *Autobiographies,* though sometimes occasional and often polemical, are the most sustained. The aphoristic and fragmentary sections were possibly intended as prolegomena to that "new autobiography—1900 to 1926" which Yeats thought of as "the final test of my intellect, my last great effort," which he kept putting off. There are problems about the three parts of *Autobiographies* that are my concern. *Dramatis Personae* was largely composed from Yeats's letters to Lady Gregory, but the history of the composition of *Reveries* is obscure: it probably went through several drafts. Richard Ellmann informs us that an earlier draft of *Trembling of the Veil* was completed in 1916–17. Comment on *Autobiographies* must be provisional.

The first mention of *Reveries* in Yeats's letters belongs to November 1914. From this it is clear that Yeats had been engaged with the book from about the late summer on. The seven years before this date had been both painful and frustrating, and *Reveries* was composed in their shadow: schisms

From *An Honored Guest: New Essays on W. B. Yeats.* © 1965 by Edward Arnold (Publishers) Ltd.

in the Abbey, the mere success of esteem of his own plays, the *Playboy* controversy of 1907, Synge's death in 1909 and the controversy with the Dublin Council and populace over the proposed Lutyens Gallery for Lane's pictures. In 1908 the appearance of Yeats's *Collected Works* must have seemed to the poet to mark off an era, as though his achievement were already in the past. At this time we find him in letters referring to himself as "belonging to the fabulous ages" and "becoming mythical even to myself": we find an increasing identification with the past and with his dead friends of the 1890s in particular. Such backward looking was a symptom of general discouragement. His own personal life had become random and in his spiritual life there was a void. By 1914 he had broken his connection with the rump of the Golden Dawn that remained after the schisms of Mathers and Waite. We find him resorting to spiritualism and trying somewhat pathetically to verify the historicity of the spirits who "came to him through mediums."

The pressures in such circumstances were towards the organisation of an attitude; documentation and self-clarification; an attempt to stabilise the present—an aim that makes its first positive appearance in his volume of poems *The Green Helmet* of 1910. It is here that the process of mythologising himself and his friends begins. Recent history is frozen, stylised. Maud Gonne becomes the emblem of his present despair—a *femme fatale,* still making a traditional appearance as an Irish Helen, but now associated directly with Dublin: "Was there another Troy for her to burn?"

It is rather in *Poems Written in Discouragement* of 1913 and in *Responsibilities* that the mythologising becomes explicit and past and present are consciously poised against one another. Addressing in the opening poem of *Responsibilities* his burgess ancestors of the late eighteenth and early nineteenth centuries, Yeats writes:

> Although I have come close on forty-nine,
> I have no child, I have nothing but a book,
> Nothing but that to prove your blood and mine.
> (The Collected Poems)

In this volume the events of the last seven years are mythologised: the epigrams of *The Green Helmet* edge into dramatic lyric. Synge, Lady Gregory, John O'Leary, and Hugh Lane are poised against the Dublin of the present which fumbles in a greasy till by the light of a holy candle. Aristocrat, noble Fenian, and poet equally represent a heroic and defeated past.

Placing himself in history and tradition was indeed one of Yeats's "responsibilities" at this time, but it conflicted with a "responsibility" to the present: he needed to associate himself with Lady Gregory and Hugh

Lane; the enemy being a textbook burgess capitalist such as William Murphy or those petty-burgess Paudeen enemies of Synge and Lane. His own impeccably burgess ancestors have to be dignified with "the wasteful virtues" that "earn the sun," credited with spontaneity and "personality." But what we can accept in *Responsibilities* as dramatic speech (even so amusingly defiant a line as "Blood that has not passed through any huckster's loin") will be harder to accept in a prose account; we accuse the historian of self-interest. In the poems the "personal ego" (J. B. Yeats's phrase) has evaporated, a role in contemporary history can be enforced and acted out.

In the Preface to *Reveries,* dated Christmas 1914, Yeats wrote:

> I have changed nothing to my knowledge; and yet it must be
> that I have changed many things without my knowledge; for I
> am writing after many years and have consulted neither friend,
> nor letter, nor old newspaper, and describe what comes oftenest
> into my memory.

But the past remains the possession of others and he fears that "some surviving friend may remember something in a different shape and be offended with my book." The frankness is partly ingenuous: he is attempting to transcend his past self by presenting a selective image of that self, and he wishes to trust what has survived by impressing itself most deeply, though he is aware that memory not only shapes the past but actually imposes meanings. And re-enacting the past not only changes the past, it changes the present.

A recently published letter of 20 November 1914 to Lady Gregory indicates how Yeats wished to see himself:

> That is a wonderful letter of my father's. It came at the right
> moment for I am writing an account of Dowden (I shall wind
> up with the Rhymers' Club). I think we shall live as a generation
> as the Young Irelanders did. We shall not be detached figures.
> I think it is partly with that motive I am trying for instance to
> improve my sisters' and publish my father's letters. Your biog-
> raphy when it comes will complete the image.

Here Yeats explicitly associates himself with his friends, the tragic actors of *Responsibilities,* as "a generation," and associates his friends as a group with Young Ireland. As D. J. Gordon has put it, "an acute, exacerbated sense of his own historicity comprehended the historicity of others, sharpened and nourished by the awareness that he and his friends were part of the history of modern Ireland." Implicitly he also associates himself with the

Rhymers' Club—another "generation" whose defeat substantiates and extends the defeat of the artists of J. B. Yeats's and Yeats's own "tragic" generation. The pressure here is towards overcoming a tragic determinism.

Lady Gregory was still very much alive, while the Rhymers (with the exception of Symons, whose career had been broken by madness) were dead and so historically perfect. Poetry demonstrated its classic superiority over history: it could mythologise the living as though they were not themselves still part of an emerging historical process. This mode was not to be abandoned. Yeats continued to write poems, consciously conceived as historical acts, on persons, and on the places associated with them. Writing these, he was deliberately creating a version of the modern history of Ireland, "an Ireland the poets have imagined terrible and gay," a version he wished to transmit as a document to posterity. But as the letter to Lady Gregory shows, Yeats was not averse to documentation of another kind. It is in this light that his father's unfinished and his own achieved autobiography must be seen. And while he was engaged on *Reveries,* Lady Gregory was concluding her chapter of autobiography, *Our Irish Theatre,* with its selective extracts from Yeats's letters and its heroic portraiture of O'Leary and Synge.

Yeats's original plan had been to conclude *Reveries* with an account of the Rhymers' Club; that the Rhymers were much in his mind at this time we know from *Responsibilities,* where Johnson and Dowson are given tragic status. Like the Young Ireland writers, the more prominent Rhymers possessed a much greater historical than aesthetic importance, even though the Rhymers' devotion to art was altogether opposed to Young Ireland's subordination of art to rhetoric and politics.

Young Ireland had been an attempt on the part of a few to realise a nation's soul, in contrast to O'Connell's flattery of the mob. The Rhymers also attempted, in a different way, to realise in themselves the historical spirit, and they rejected popular culture. Both groups survive as groups rather than as individuals: the Rhymers partly because they were to be memorialised by Yeats in much the same way as Gavan Duffy had memorialised the Young Ireland figures in *Young Ireland* and *1845–1849.* Yeats's intention was to follow Duffy as the historian of a generation that had realised itself historically because "it thought the same thought" and created its own history. And Duffy's historical record had itself been an attempted reshaping of history.

Yeats's portrait of Duffy looks forward to the graceful malice of *Dramatis Personae.* It presents him as the anti-type of O'Leary among the Young Ireland generation, living on like some Latimerian fish to abash the new age. It is one version of history competing actively with another, though the ground disputed is narrowly literary:

Sir Charles Gavan Duffy arrived. He brought with him much manuscript, the private letters of a Young Irish poetess, a dry but informing unpublished essay by Davis, and an unpublished novel by William Carleton into the middle of which he had dropped a hot coal, so that nothing remained but the borders of every page.

A fussy short sentence is swallowed by a long sentence, whose gyre concludes with the exquisitely emblematic case of the burning coal and so acts out Duffy's dry-fingered antiquarianism; his incapacity to sustain whatever was genuinely creative in Anglo-Irish literature. Yeats's position in the quarrel with Duffy may have owed something to Arnold, but it was immediately influenced by the beliefs of the Rhymers.

The Rhymers—as Yeats saw them—were, unlike Young Ireland, concerned not merely with personal art but with collapse and disintegration, and they wished to enact this in themselves sacrificially. Yeats's association of Young Ireland with the Rhymers, and of J. B. Yeats's generation of artists and poets with his own, is not simply because (contingently or not) they formed part of his own drama. It sprang from the need to find what Yeats termed "rhythm" in history (a rhythm of heroic failure). As his early interest in Joachim de Flora's Four Ages showed, this had been one of his preoccupations in the 1890s. Such "rhythm" had to be recognised in the multiplicity of the self before it could be recognised in history; it determines the structure of *Trembling of the Veil* rather than that of *Reveries*.

Reveries is concerned with heroes and sacred places. The book's polarities are Ireland and England: Sligo, Dublin and London. Yeats as child and young man is involved in his father's uneasy shifts between these places: a rootlessness symbolic of the modern imaginative artist (it predicts the rootlessness of Simeon Solomon or Dowson), and also of the decline of true nationalism. Places for Yeats have a quality of *mana* that owes little to patient visual detail (it is hardly "Pre-Raphaelite"). It is the *interaction* of places and persons that he particularly evokes. "He was probably always moved more by the human image than the painter's." Yet he still saw that human image partly in terms of the painter's eye. From his father, he had caught an eye for pose and gesture, for the unselfconscious stance that reveals the intimate self, the ground of this perception being that gathering of the "moment" in J. B. Yeats's impressionist portraiture.

With Yeats, physical image creates narrative, is both cause and symptom: what actually happens becomes metaphorical. In *Autobiographies* people tend to be arrested in moments that reveal "a fragment of the divine life," an instant which has the effect of a complete statement, both stylised and spontaneous. Yeats owes this, however, less to his father's portraits than to his letters.

Just as *Dramatis Personae* wins immediacy from the dialogue *outre tombe* with George Moore, *Reveries* wins immediacy from its dialogue with Yeats's father:

> Someone to whom I read [*Reveries*] said to me the other day 'If
> Gosse had not taken the title you should call it "Father and Son".'
> I am not going to ask your leave for the bits of your conversation
> I quote.

Father and son influenced one another and one of John Butler Yeats's gifts, that of aphorism, was clearly passed on. Between 1912 and 1914 he wrote his son a number of remarkable letters which had much to say on the subject of "personality," the essential self freed from accidents of time and habit; on the necessary solitude of the artist and the need for dramatising one's experience to avoid a purely personal art. "Personality" for J. B. Yeats was "love":

> *neither right nor wrong*—for it transcends intellect and morality,
> and while it keeps to being pure personality we love for it is *one*
> with our very selves, and with the all *pervasive* Divine.

In precisely these terms the "personalities" of Yeats's *Autobiographies* are presented as parts of his "very self." At a moment of indecision Yeats was using his father as a mentor, as he had previously used other mentors (Johnson, Ricketts, etc.).

Practising his father's advice to dramatise experience, Yeats began with J. B. Yeats himself. His father's crisis, a crisis in romantic art and literature, is presented in *Reveries* through an argument in terms of "personality" between Pre-Raphaelite imagination, intensity, on the one hand, and Positivism and an Impressionism defined as "Realism" on the other. J. B. Yeats's betrayal of Pre-Raphaelite principles is associated with the treason of his other friends.

The material here is derived from J. B. Yeats's letters. The elder Yeats's friends were a pathetic rather than a tragic generation. Some, to be sure—Page, Wilson, Potter—die without a choice being offered. They are solitaries, without an audience. Others like Nettleship or Dowden survive by compromise. All are caught in emblematic gestures that lead one from the work to "personality." The crippled genius of Nettleship enacts its own mutilation: the enormous cup he drinks from contains—cocoa, so that Edwin Ellis's remark that Nettleship "drank his genius away" has vibrations the speaker barely intended. Dowden's ironic calm and O'Leary's moral genius, passionate, Roman, Hebraic, confront one another.

Dowden may be taken as characteristic of Yeats's problems. His subject had died only a year before, and J. B. Yeats had been Dowden's "intimate enemy," but after Dowden's death Yeats was not prepared to adopt his father's gentlemanly attitude. J. B. Yeats wrote that it was better to be illogical than inhuman, and accused his son of presenting Dowden deliberately and exclusively from a personal and didactic point of view; of submitting Dowden to a contrived biographical pattern. After the publication of *Reveries* W. B. Yeats returned to the question, admitting that he was nervous about the Dowden section, but arguing that it could not be omitted, since the book was "a history of the revolt, which perhaps unconsciously you taught me, against certain Victorian ideals." And as though admitting his father's accusation of being inhuman, Yeats observed in the following year that "in my account of Dowden I had to picture him as a little unreal, set up for contrast behind the real image of O'Leary." The juxtaposition is not really dramatic, but drama enters in the presentation of the divided self common to both Dowden and O'Leary. O'Leary's noble head, his intransigence, his sense of political morality as style and his love of literature are poised against the flatness of the autobiography on which he lavished such effort. Dowden's romantic face and his earlier poetry that hints at passion, though passion renounced, are poised against his over-reliance on intellect.

J. B. Yeats's relationship with Dowden has a subdued parallel in his son's relationship with J. F. Taylor, obscure great orator, ugly, solitary, flashing into high speech; a disappointed though pertinacious lover of women. The image of Taylor is important in several ways. It enacts that opposition between poetry and oratory that J. B. Yeats believed was inevitable; but explains Taylor's greatness by presenting him in *O altitudo* moments as altogether solitary, unaware of the blind crowd, a poet. Taylor is also a man divided in himself—his jealousy of Yeats's friendship with O'Leary is more than a Young Ireland Fenian distrust of the new "literary" nationalism. The encounter is presented less definitively than it would have been in *Trembling of the Veil*. Taylor's motives, his inner life, remain unpredictable, mysterious. He is viewed from a distance, and this precisely catches the "point of view" of the young Yeats of the late 1880s and 1890s, a young man who was a late comer to an Irish scene which he found already peopled by powerful figures. He shows himself here as always intensely aware of the difference between his own generation and theirs. The enmity between himself and Taylor is constructive: to choose one's intimate enemies objectifies one's limitations.

Such stringency hardly seems reflected in the record. The prose of *Autobiographies* is often thought of as Paterian, lushly mantic, salted with some good Irish stories. Yet if *Reveries* owes anything to Pater, that influence is less of cadence and vocabulary than attitude, and of an attitude that reinforces the influence of Yeats's father. In *Style,* Pater had distinguished between the debris of fact and the writer's personal sense of fact. Analogously he had distinguished the "moment" as the unit of experience, isolated, absolute, flexible, in protest against the "positive" fiction of a stable world. The creative role of contemplation and, particularly, memory in Pater's work and his influence on Proust and Virginia Woolf are well known. For Pater, memory constitutes an identity which can be redeemed from time by re-enacting moments of sensuous significance: ". . . the finer sort of memory, bringing its object to mind with great clearness, yet, as sometimes happens in dreams, raised a little above its self and above ordinary retrospect" (*The Child in the House*). In Pater's words, this is a substitution of the "typical" for the "actual"; memory operates discontinuously, if vividly, and is recognised by the sense of loss. But substitution of "typical" for "actual" is distancing, and few of Pater's evocations of childhood have any eager directness of detail or sense of the jaggedness of recall. Similarly, Yeats's account of family, schools, holidays, adolescent awakening to sex, and ideals is distanced by a meditative style—as Mr. Ellmann has pointed out, anger is "adroitly excluded." But the arrangement of *Reveries* with its sharp sections (rather than the "chapters" Yeats termed them) is intended to enact discontinuousness. The sections vary in length (xviii and xx by contrast with xi) resembling (in intention at least) that lyrical dissolution of event in Romantic historians where rapid sections and sentences echo the pulse of what is re-enacted and the historian's excitement in re-enaction. Yeats's rhythm of anti-climactic reflection in *Reveries* is naturally slow and even. (He uses the Carlylean historic present only for the first page or two of *Reveries,* in Section xv of *Ireland after Parnell* and in Section xx of *Trembling of the Veil* to evoke the "crack up" of the '90s.) His early memories leave the impression of being recorded solely because they are remembered; but each "spot of memory" relates to such themes as: I, the poet, William Yeats, Ireland, romantic past and sordid present.

We have seen that what is acceptable as dramatic speech in *Responsibilities* might become suspect in autobiography. In prose Yeats stresses heroism, nobility of personality rather than aristocratic value connected with property; despite a mild flourish of ancestors in the third section, *Reveries* are surprisingly devoid of social context. What emerges is Yeats's sense of being "Irish" in the English Babylon.

In *Reveries,* many of the connections, as in *Responsibilities,* are carried by syntax. Style in courage and platonic courtesy is mediated through asyndeton, punctilious subjunctives, magniloquent "buts," yet the sentence-structure is rarely overelaborate. Where we find elaboration of rhythm it is, like the imagery, functional, as in this passage on George Eliot where style itself rebukes:

> She seemed to have a distrust or a distaste for all in life that gives
> one a springing foot. Then, too, she knew so well how to enforce
> her distaste by the authority of her mid-Victorian science or by
> some habit of mind of its breeding, that I, who had not escaped
> the fascination of what I loathed, doubted while the book lay
> open whatsoever my instinct knew of splendour.

The second is an unusually long sentence for *Reveries*. The histrionic pauses, contours almost of the breathing mind, the anxious poise between authority and instinct, the final freed tune with its faint Pauline echo fully realise the inwardness of the experience. (The experience has perhaps little to do finally with George Eliot.)

"Now that I have written it out," Yeats wrote in his preface, "I may even begin to forget it all." A middle-aged bore, bowed down with the weight of "a precious, an incommunicable past," he may stop buttonholing strangers. But the deeper meaning suggests the cathartic; final responsibility to the past involves not rejection, but transcendence: liberation from guilt, self-pity, historical necessity, the inescapable folly of art, multiplicity and indirection, that "wilderness of mirrors," whether of Wilde's competing gifts or Magian temptations. Writing is the act of self-criticism that detaches the poet from the composed image, even if the composure issues from anticlimax, "a preparation for something that never happens."

In *Reveries*, Yeats's past self is realised, painfully encountering and addressing others, socially clumsy, morally naive. This book ends not with the Rhymers' Club but with Yeats's return to London in 1887, giving the volume a severer shape. He stands at the beginning of his career as an Irish poet, at the moment when he realises himself as an exile, and in this light the final judgment on himself in 1914 is ironic rather than self-pitying. The title *Reveries* is not an escape into the past, it signifies an attempt to distinguish pattern. At the point of painful disengagement from spoiled aspirations the conditions have been fulfilled for the narrator's "epiphany": a synthesis, as often in Yeats, has been proclaimed at the point where it is rejected.

II

Writing to his father on 26 December 1914, Yeats indicated that when he carried his memoirs beyond 1887 he would be liable to further difficulties of the type already encountered in treating of Dowden:

they would have besides to be written in a different way. While
I was immature I was a different person and I can stand apart
and judge. Later on, I should always, I feel, write of other people.
I dare say I shall return to the subject but only in fragments.

Often one of his best critics, Yeats has defined the limitations of *Trembling
of the Veil.* Far more ambitious, eloquent, and richly detailed than *Reveries,
Trembling of the Veil* is tonally and structurally puzzling. The second draft
was composed during the period of the Anglo-Irish and Irish Civil wars,
when Yeats was clarifying the material of *A Vision.* The period described
lies between 1887 and 1897, the death in 1891 of the political Messiah,
Parnell, marking an important division. Formally "Four Years" is the most
satisfying section; the remainder was written to contract (60,000 words) and
Yeats more than once expressed uneasiness as to whether the years between
1891 and 1897 could be stretched to the agreed length.

Writing to Olivia Shakespear on 22 December 1921, he observed that
the book was likely to seem inadequate, since "I study every man I meet
at some moment of crisis—I alone have no crisis." And in another letter of
28 February 1934 he reveals that the problem of omission was still with
him when he came to compose *Dramatis Personae:* "I am just beginning on
Woburn buildings . . . alas the most significant image of those years must
be left out." The reference is to the *enmenagement* with Mrs. Shakespear in
1896 or that of 1903. And since the unrecorded crises are the heart of much
of his later poetry, the loss is severe. If there is little sense of the author's
presence in *Trembling of the Veil,* little self-criticism and self-clarification,
the abstention is clearly deliberate.

In addition to reticence about his deepest emotional experiences, there
were other difficulties. "Whenever I have included a living man I have
submitted my words for his correction. This is specially important . . . I
want to show that though I am being published by Moore's publisher I do
not accept Moore's practice." That he still had doubts is indicated by this
passage from a letter to Mrs. Shakespear: "[The book] needs the wild mystical
part to lift it out of gossip, and the mystical part will not be as clear as it
should be for lack of diagrams." "Mysticism" was beyond Moore, that
"precious thing" that Moore, like a passing dog, "defiled."

It is Moore's version of history which Yeats's autobiographies challenge.
In *Trembling of the Veil* Yeats uses something of Moore's approach not to the
living but to the dead. The distinction lies between Moore's malice and
Yeats's didacticism; the similarity lies in the thematic and apologetic elements. As Arthur Schumaker has pointed out, *Hail and Farewell* uses distinct

thematic devices derived from Wagner's *Ring,* all leading to the climax where Moore discovers himself as Siegfried "given the task of reforging broken weapons of thought and restoring Ireland to thought and responsibility." His stated intention was to represent the past moment as a passing *now:* "To take a certain amount of material and model it much as [one] would do in a novel." The persons in Moore's trilogy become types of human character, representative of a fallen Ireland; transitions are concealed, meditation modulates into speech, chronology is fluid; manipulation of the past is added to selection of event and, as is not the case with *Trembling of the Veil,* there is a high incidence of direct speech. The similarities to Yeats's work, and the contrasts, are plain.

Another passage from a letter to Mrs. Shakespear reveals how in *Autobiographies* even energising hatred of the dead was to be muted. Tenderness to the living can be exemplified by Yeats's treatment of Johnson, who was Mrs. Shakespear's cousin and to whom she had been deeply attached: he was to be shown "as the noble tragic figure that he was . . . those who follow me are likely to take their key from what I have written." But the effect was to puzzle rather than convince. Charles Ricketts found the memoirs in general persuasive, but the presentation of Johnson surprising:

> It is singular that he should have impressed himself on you, doubtless it was the attraction of the *opposite,* he struck me then, and in recollection, as a typical 'Fruit sec' of his class, time and training. I caught him making a lamentable howler in a translation of Baudelaire. He said or did something else which I have forgotten and never created that bogus atmosphere with which he impressed you.

Where *Reveries* had been the record of self-discovery through others, in *Trembling of the Veil* all sequence of cause and effect is fractured by a new teleology, the invasion of the "supernatural," the most violent force in history. Gossip and mysticism collide, but do not coalesce. Another sophisticated form of determinism results, though not the positivists' mere aggregation of fact against which the whole structure of *Trembling of the Veil* is a protest. The relatively firm chronology, the questing quality of *Reveries,* is dissolved and the book given a sense of omen fulfilled: the validation of his own insights and those of his generation of poets and occultists, "the things wild people half scholars and rhapsodical persons wrote about, when you and I were young." With Parnell's death in 1891 *Four Years* comes to an end; 1892, the year Yeats began from in his *Oxford Book of Modern Verse,* the year of the *First Book of the Rhymers' Club,* ushered in the poetry of what he came to see as the last phase of the historical cycle. The insights of his friends and their rejection of the vulgar dream of progress was to be more violently corroborated than either he or they had anticipated.

Yeats shared with his generation a sense of history that expressed itself as an acute, even exacerbated sense of contemporaneity, of the moment defined only in its relationship to past and future. Scholarship, revolution and the natural sciences had conspired to induce in late-nineteenth-century artists and intellectuals what was often an anguished sense of the moment as isolable, definable, an unstable ridge between abysses. It is in the nineteenth century that the sense of belonging to a decade, to a generation, was developed. Not until the 1890s could Lord Henry Wootton have said to Dorian Gray "fin de siècle" and have received the antiphonal answer "fin du globe." Such tremors are common to ends of centuries, but the 1890s have more in common with the year 1000—a year of perfect numbers—or with the year 1600, than with the shrugging dismissal of, say, Dryden's *Secular Masque*. As the blank zeros of the calendar figure approached, the temporal uncertainties of the century merged in a diffuse, an irrational chiliasm.

The sense of Apocalypse, of the new age heralded by some terrible annunciation, was substantiated by Madame Blavatsky, Mathers, and the Symbolists. Against this was posed the possibility of unity of culture: the symbol, to be achieved like Stalinism in one country, Ireland. But the historical pattern faltered into anticlimax: the "Tragic Generation" immersed themselves in the flux, dying "as soon as their constitutions would permit," and the attempt to achieve unity of culture through Societies, through the more literate Unionists and Landowners, and finally—transcending tragic individualism—through a Symbolist theatre, failed. The Easter Rising forced Yeats to redefine the past, in Morton Zabel's words "to discover the laws of character, of creative power and of history." The last three sections of *Trembling of the Veil* break off into a "bundle of fragments," into the incoherence of an historic present without a future tense, which requires *A Vision* for its clarification.

"In art rhythm is everything," Arthur Symons had declared in a Symbolist manifesto published in *The Dome* of 1898. Yeats assumed Symons's phraseology of "pattern" and "rhythm" and applied them (in an article published also in *The Dome*) to the Symbolist designs of Althea Gyles and subsequently to poetry and to Symbolist "total" theatre and history. The words themselves imply "image" (rather than naturalist "subject"), the non-rational, the visionary. The Symbolist reaction towards trance is accompanied by a reaction against the tyranny of fact: a supernatural "rhythm" against which personality (the individual in tragic passion) defines itself.

The search for both "rhythm" and "pattern," recurrence in time and space (the artist's isolation and the dilemma of a generation) manifests itself in the search for a cyclical view of history. This Yeats began to wish to substitute for the notion of history as chaos or as chiliastic. He was already reaching towards this in the 1890s, though the members of the Tragic Generation are without it. When he came to write *Trembling of the Veil* such a view becomes a category for the interpretation of personalities, individualities. The Tragic Generation merely re-enact more violently and self-consciously the experiences of J. B. Yeats and his friends.

Yeats's 1890s are hardly those of history, or of literary history. To the sober historian the imposition of Death Duties in 1894 appears more significant than the trials of Wilde in the following year; the continuous economic depression of 1890–6 than the sputtering history of the Rhymers. Yet Yeats focuses on two of the major characteristics of the decade: Ireland, and the climax of the revolt against Victorianism, the so-called normality that was sick. We get the flavour of a London that was now dominating the provinces, imposing its own centralised cultural pattern; and we even have some vague sense of the brooding, almost iconic figure of Victoria herself, ageless, it seemed, the dignified if dowdy incarnation of a people's dream. But Yeats's 1890s may still seem altogether too narrow, since we now associate the decade's revolt with figures who seem more relevant to the twentieth century, with Ibsen, Zola, Shaw, Butler and Gissing, rather than with the denizens of the Cheshire Cheese. Yet the *fin de siècle* mood was startlingly diffused: in James's *Altar of the Dead,* in Wells's early fables, for example. And the themes of *Trembling of the Veil,* the sense of isolation and alienation and the confrontation of artist and audience, remain valid comment beyond Yeats's circle.

For Yeats's '90s include (if somewhat obliquely) many pressures common to all schools. There are, for example, the temptations of placating and securing an audience through the new publicity media, "the interview and letter to the press"; what Yeats calls Moore's "immediate sensational contact with public opinion." Again, we find the Imperialists' self-destructive energies of aggression realised in the image of Henley and his "regatta" of young men. Much of Yeats's comment is gossip, but it remains if not actual, typical: his image of Beardsley as Huysmanish saint conforms to the image John Gray gave when he edited Beardsley's letters. Johnson (in *Mors Janua Vitae* and *Mystic and Cavalier*) and Wilde had both mythologised themselves. With Dowson, however, the case was different. Yeats followed Symons, who had presented Dowson in 1900 as a conventional *poète maudit,* "a demoralised Keats," though understandably Symons makes little attempt to associate Dowson with his contemporaries. Dowson, however, had also done his mythologising and this ran counter to Symons, and to Yeats's association of the "Tragic Generation" with the protest against Positivism. Submitting to the Huxley-Tindall world-view, Dowson's ethic of "drift" was culled from the negative side of Schopenhauer's philosophy: a willed will-lessness.

Yeats had then every excuse for mythologising his friends, for, like all young poets, they mythologised one another, and Yeats was performing a service similar to Gautier's history of Romanticism, where the generation of 1830 is aggrandised by gossip. The Tragic Generation insisted on suffering and dying mythologically: they were always trying to invent themselves, such was their sense of the individual's isolation in history, their distrust of "generalisation." And Yeats's mythologising begins as always from physical appearance: Henley, the paralysed viking; Johnson, the suave ambiguous Hellenistic head over the figurine body tapering away to vanishing-point; the uneasily bewigged Davidson; suggesting verdicts on lives and art.

Moreover, the process by which the notion of a "Tragic Generation" was elaborated can be studied. Yeats had mythologised Johnson during Johnson's lifetime in a brief essay in Brooke's and Rolleston's *A Treasury of Irish Poetry* (1900). He associated Johnson with Villiers's *Axël* in his tower, wavering in solitude between two dreams: of Ireland and the Catholic Church. But Johnson was a special case—his life had by that time passed already into a "mythic" phase, a living death of illness, terror, remorse, whisky, and isolation. Yeats had not associated Johnson with a generation. In 1908 Symons suffered the nervous collapse that virtually ended his career and in 1909 Davidson walked into the sea. In a lecture given at the Memorial Hall, Manchester, on 31 October 1910 Yeats reveals that by this time he was placing his own generation historically, but in a manner that was strictly limited. His account anticipates strikingly the account of the Rhymers' programme given in *Trembling of the Veil*. He begins with the Renaissance discovery of Academic Form (against which Pre-Raphaelitism had rebelled) and proceeds to the rejection of "subject" in painting and its parallel in poetry. It is the version of "dissociation of sensibility" which Yeats offers elsewhere. The hero-villain Milton is "the Raphael of traditional morality" and the expression of classical morality alternately ennobled and dulled Wordsworth's genius and chilled Tennyson's *Idylls*. The 1890s witnessed "the revolt of my own fiery generation" and "the man who first proclaimed it was the younger Hallam who invented the phrase 'the aesthetic school in poetry.'" The new type of poet was one who did not aspire to teach, eschewing popular morality and easy anecdote, but simply gave one "his vision."

Yeats, his lecture goes on, had come to recognise that "we have thrown away the most powerful of all things in literature—personal utterance." What he had thought of as a purely personal insight was, he now saw, "the thought of his generation . . . One thing I had not foreseen and that was if you make your art of your personality you will have a very troubled life. Goethe said, 'We know ourselves by action only; never by contemplation.' The moment you begin the expression of yourself as an artist your life in some mysterious way is full of tumult." It was a lesson explicit already in Hallam's essay on Tennyson which had been reprinted by one of the Rhymers, Le Gallienne, in 1893. "To me it meant Irish leagues and movements and all kinds of heterogeneous activities which were not good for my life, as it seemed to me at the time. To the others it meant dissipation; that generation was a doomed generation . . . I believe it was that they made their nature passionate by making their art personal." And of Johnson and Dowson, Yeats spoke in terms that closely resemble those in *Trembling of the Veil*, concluding that when he thought of that "doomed generation I am not sure whether it was sin or sanctity which was found in their brief lives."

It is an interpretation which has not been strictly touched by notions of "personality." The tone is far more tentative than that of *Trembling of the Veil*, where Yeats is more assured about sin and sanctity, while the doctrine looks back to *Ideas of Good and Evil*. Of Dowson Yeats had written that his art "was curiously faint and shadowy. I believe that the art of any man who is sincerely seeking for the truth, seeking for beauty, is very likely to be faint and hesitating. The art that is entirely confident, or the speaking and writing . . . entirely confident, is the work of the kind of man who is speaking with other men's thoughts." That hint as to false certainty provides the only crystallisation of what the Rhymers—in Yeats's presentation of them—were reacting against; not anecdote, but the formalism of English Parnassians such as Gosse, Dobson and Lang. In an article published in the *Providence Journal* of 1892 Yeats had attacked the foreign forms of these Parnassians, though the main target was the false "objectivity" of attempting to rid a poem of any taint of its author. The attack on exotic forms seems to consort with the churchwarden pipes, ale, and Dr. Johnson's Cheshire Cheese.

Yeats's presentation of himself in *The Tragic Generation* sharply illustrates the process to which his material was being subjected, and perhaps some of the limitations, even the inadequacies, which this treatment resulted in. In the 1910 lecture, as in *Autobiographies*, Yeats claims that he founded the various societies with which he was connected in the 1890s to make substantive the moral of the artist losing himself in toil that is not sedentary

(Yeats's unhappy emotional life at this time had affinities with the passive Dowson's). It remains difficult, however, to determine whether his inaccuracies are due to stylisation or simple forgetfulness. But two examples are certainly central. Yeats obscures the origins of the Rhymers' Club which he claims to have founded with Rhys in 1891 and which, in fact, gradually cohered out of informal readings at 20 Fitzroy Street, "Whiteladies," the house Arthur Mackmurdo had bought in 1889. For Yeats, this process is not sufficiently dramatic. If on the one hand his own account is false to the young man of *Reveries,* feeling his way, on the other it dramatises, legitimately perhaps, that young man's latent decisiveness: he presided over the moment of coherence. There is little sense in *Trembling of the Veil* of the Rhymers' miscellaneous muster, ranging in age from the fifties down. Consequently, the Rhymers tend to be confused with the "Tragic Generation." The "pattern" that Yeats is distinguishing applies not merely to the Rhymers and to Henley, but to naturalists like Crackanthorpe, whose unhappy love affair and suicide make him severely exemplary.

Similarly, although there was a preliminary meeting of the Irish Literary Society at the Yeats house in Bedford Park, Yeats's assertion that he was the Society's founder was challenged by the secretary, Michael Macdonagh, in an unpublished account of the Society's archives, and Yeats's claim is not supported by the Society's early historian, W. P. Ryan. To be sure, Yeats admits that the Society cohered out of the Southwark Club, but it is clear that he is presenting himself in a way that is not altogether usual in this section of *Autobiographies.*

For other reasons, Yeats's relationships with women in the 1890s are subjected to "pattern." The counterpart of the male artist is the "new" woman who tends to assume male characteristics: Althea Gyles (the redheaded girl in AE's settlement in Dublin and one of Smithers's repertoire of mistresses), Florence Farr, Maud Gonne. Apart from the luminosity of her first visit to Bedford Park, Maud Gonne scarcely appears as the object of Yeats's "barren passion." That she should appear at all is perhaps remarkable, though she is confined to her agitator's role, particularly to the male role of orator (there is no account of her interest in the occult). Metaphor carries a narrative force when she is glimpsed *en passant* with her regalia of bird-cages and canaries (though once with a Donegal hawk) rather as she appears with a more conventional monkey in Sarah Purser's oil. Cruelty and triviality are hinted—Yeats's usual defensive assertion of the Fatal Woman theme.

Yet the very elaboration of *Trembling of the Veil* defeats its own purpose. It muffles the book's climax. What we seem to be fundamentally concerned with is the relation between artist and audience. This is resolved most nakedly by the artist's counter-attack through the theatre. In the theatre the dramatist encounters that audience under conditions of sharp excitement. When he belongs to a generation self-consciously in revolt, the hostility between himself (making a customary first-night appearance) and his audience is almost ritually enacted (the disapprobation of plays was distinctly less inhibited then). Moore in *Ave* tells us that Yeats believed that the author should be present at first nights: only by watching the effect of his play could he learn his trade.

The Tragic Generation opens with a theatrical episode—the staging of Todhunter's *Sicilian Idyll* at the Bedford Park Club House.

It was Todhunter's practice that had given Yeats his earliest model for emulation, as we gather from an unpublished letter of 24 April 1885 to Todhunter from J. B. Yeats:

> I am most grateful to you for your kind letter and your interest in Willie—but did not write because I suppose painting devours everything—yet I have been wanting to tell you that Willie on his side watches with an almost breathless interest your course as dramatic poet—and has been doing so for a long time—he has read everything you have written most carefully.
>
> —he finished when at Howth your Rienzi at a single sitting—'the' sitting ending at 2 o'clock in the morning . . .
>
> That Willie is a poet I have long known—what I am really interested in is seeing the dramatic idea emerge and I think before this present drama . . . of his has finished, you will see evidence of his dramatic instinct.

The whole account of Todhunter in *Trembling of the Veil* is manipulated with such firm economy that nothing sways the reader from the definitive image of Todhunter sitting in his box at the Avenue Theatre, surrounded by his family, enduring the crass cries of gallery and pit, without gesture though with dull courage, as his *Comedy of Sighs* staggers to its fiasco.

"Petulant and unstable, he was incapable of any emotion that could give life to a cause." Todhunter refuses to act out the drama of the passionate artist confronting the enemies of art; artistically he dies in his bed. Successful at Bedford Park, Todhunter had been tempted to conquer the commercial theatre, but to conquer the managers he abandoned poetry for Ibsen, or more precisely, Pinero. Of Todhunter's *Helena of Troas* (1886) Yeats wrote that "I had thought (it) as unactable as unreadable," though in 1892, following second-hand accounts of its production: "its sonorous verse united to the rhythmical motions of the white-robed chorus, and the solemnity of burning incense, produced a semi-religious effect new to the modern stage."

Nothing could more firmly relate to the theme of symbolism triumphing over positivism and naturalism. What seems to have struck Yeats most was the "mood" of E. W. Godwin's production in 1886, "acting, scenery and verse were all a perfect unity." But the account of Todhunter has to submit to its climax. His experience at the Avenue Theatre in 1894 predicts that of Synge, though it was Yeats himself and his father who actually faced the audience when the *Playboy* challenged their clichés. There is a brisk contrast with Wilde (or Shaw) cajoling the audience with the play and mocking them in person. When James faced a hostile crowd on the first night of *Guy Domville,* history obliged with an exemplary episode: the solitary artist extending the dramatic ritual by appearing as scapegoat (Dickens's public readings which so shortened his life provide the anti-type).

The most famous of the scapegoats was, of course, Wilde. In Yeats's account of him the artist's life becomes itself a play; though Wilde's genius balked at tragedy, "that elaborate playing with tragedy was an attempt to escape from emotion by its exaggeration." The trial is only obliquely mentioned, but for Yeats it was clearly Wilde's last and greatest play. Wilde played it as comedy, but its note turned tragic, and when he was convicted "the harlots in the street outside danced upon the pavement," a tousled maenadic parody of the tragic chorus, or the Furies on the roof-top of Agamemnon's palace.

G. S. Fraser has best defined Yeats's attitude to Wilde as one of "Platonic tolerance":

> Thrasymachus and Protagoras are archetypal figures of intellectual comedy, they are there in the dialogues to be destroyed, yet they represent something in human nature—the bully or the sophist in all of us—that is indestructible. Yeats's Oscar Wilde is (given another scene, another set of weapons) as indestructible an archetype as Plato's Alcibiades. His life should be a great tragedy, or a horrid melodramatic warning; but his temperament is irrepressibly that of what Yeats, in another connection, called 'the great comedian'. And his Mask dominates his Body of Fate. . . . What should be appalling becomes farcical, and what should be ignoble farce is magnificently lent style.

Of this the brothel episode in Dieppe is the most graphic instance. Dowson and Wilde pool funds to teach Wilde "a more wholesome taste." A crowd attends them to the brothel and awaits the event. Wilde appears:

He said in a low voice to Dowson, 'The first these ten years, and
it will be the last. It was like cold mutton'—always, as Henley
had said, 'a scholar and a gentleman', he now remembered that
the Elizabethan dramatists used the words 'cold mutton'—and
then aloud so that the crowd might hear him, 'But tell it in
England, for it will entirely restore my character.'

The episode is conceived dramatically and Wilde disappears with an exit-
line that is both pathetic and funny.

The section on *The Tragic Generation* which began with the account of
A Comedy of Sighs ends with the meeting with Synge and with Yeats and
Symons witnessing Jarry's *Ubu Roi* at Lugne Poe's symbolist *Théâtre de
l'oeuvre*. In Jarry's play, from a distance of twenty years, he can see only
comedy and the return of the objective cycle. The reduction of human beings
to marionettes, where the self-conscious and the primitive come full circle,
the point where "the painter's brush consumes his dreams," provides a
faltering finish before the onset of "the Savage God," confirming the circular
and determinist structure of the whole book.

III

On 28 February 1934 Yeats referred to "the drama I am building up
in my Lady Gregory." The material taken from his own letters was to be
transformed into an epitaph on the conflict of personalities that preceded
the founding of the Abbey Theatre and into an exaltation of Lady Gregory
as aristocrat and prose artist over Moore and Martyn. Himself the only
survivor, Yeats approached the past in a manner at once detached and
involved: "things reveal themselves passing away." The years between 1897
and 1902 assumed coherence: "It is curious how one's life falls into definite
sections—in 1897 a new scene was set, new actors appeared." But the
dramatic metaphor at once pays tribute to the excitement of those years and
distances them: Yeats himself, or rather his idea of himself, is a puppet
among puppets. If the national theatre is to be judged, he wrote, "what
[Moore] is and what I am will be weighed and very little what we have said
and done."

Yet much of *Dramatis Personae* is concerned with what Moore said and
did. Through a pretended auditor, it is a dialogue with Moore. Before
composing it, Yeats was reading Moore "that I may write"; and the writing
was designed to overgo Moore in his own art, impressionist autobiography,
an art based on Paterian "style," self-transparency. "Style" is indivisible,
and what one says or does or writes flows from what one is.

Moore's side of the dialogue had begun in 1898 with *Evelyn Innes,* dedicated to Yeats and Symons, "two writers with whom I am in sympathy." Moore cast Yeats as the poet and magician Ulick Dean, and a letter to Olivia Shakespear suggests that Yeats was both pleased and amused. *Hail and Farewell* appeared long after the quarrel between the two men. In *Ave* Moore hesitates between two images of Yeats. The poet's operatic appearance suggests an image close to Katharine Tynan's: "an Irish parody of the poetry I had seen all my life strutting its rhythmic way in the alleys of the Luxembourg gardens, preening its rhymes by the fountains, excessive in habit and gait." The other image suggests latent strength, and Yeats's slippery dialectic is accorded appreciation. Yeats did not take ridicule kindly and the breach between himself and Moore was final, though Moore carried his ingenuousness into old age and complained that when Yeats came to London he never visited Ebury Gardens.

Although *Dramatis Personae* attempts to surpass Moore in his own art, Yeats is no Messiah. Under the relaxed surface, however, the book focuses Yeats's version of history, the game or play which every literary achievement imposes more firmly on the past, even if it is a past that has now a splendid irrelevance.

We begin with the three Galway "great houses," Coole, Roxborough, Tulyra (and by implication we think of Moore Hall in County Mayo). The relaxed quality of *Dramatis Personae* owes something perhaps to the fact that Yeats had already written the poems that celebrate Lady Gregory and the part she and Coole played in modern Irish history. There is none of the "spilled poetry" and spilled mythology of parts of *Trembling of the Veil.* Yet *Dramatis Personae* itself clarifies the ground for "The Municipal Gallery Revisited" and supremely the "painted stage" of "The Circus Animals' Desertion." In *Dramatis Personae,* after judging Moore and Martyn, Yeats implicitly judges himself.

The judgements on Moore and Martyn are full of malicious insight. Yeats proceeds to use them, as Moore had used Martyn and Yeats, for copy. A mutual contempt binds Moore and Martyn and a common self-esteem. Martyn, the saint, warms himself with his own sanctity in the presence of the sinner, Moore, and the sinner feels more self-importantly wicked in the presence of the saint. The judgement is framed through a peasant saying which reduces both men to a very ordinary humanity. Indeed, both Moore and Martyn reduce themselves to the peasant. Yeats's note here is one of malice discovered through the questing rhythms of talk—Martyn's mother is of dubious class and Moore's education was not at Urbino but in the stables. Physical appearance promotes, as usual, mythologising: Moore's face is carved out of that sour and vulgar vegetable, the turnip. The most inconsequential narrative serves the theme: "One evening . . . I heard a voice resounding as if in a funnel, someone in a hansom cab was denouncing its driver, and Moore drove by." This is sinewy talk: frustration and aggression are suggested by the simile, and the final resonant anticlimax turns Moore into a one-man juggernaut, "not a man, but a mob." Moore's lack of style, of the aristocratic values, is tangentially but convincingly demonstrated by his treatment of cabmen and waiters. Yeats's "style" emerges simply through talk and once only by reference to "my great-grandmother Corbet, the mistress of Sandymount," where the resonance is well-manneredly casual. Yeats's values are again obliquely asserted. His insistence on Moore's gross frankness about women recalls his own reticence; the frankness is even dismissed as compensation for ugliness: "he never kisses and always tells." His own love for Maud Gonne, Yeats distances as he distances his mystical circus animals, "which I have discussed too much elsewhere." His own platonising view of one man, one woman, whether wife, mistress or obsession, he treats without pomp. The auditor is invited to distinguish.

There are connections with the method of *Trembling of the Veil*. History assumes a metaphoric role in the account of the emblematic fire at Tulyra which divides the present from its roots in the past and reinforces the image of Martyn as mule. Indeed, the presentation of Martyn is queerly harsh compared with Moore's genial contempt. Differences in politics and the schism of the Theatre of Ireland in 1907 may have rankled, and Martyn's rather public conscience irritated Yeats as it had irritated Moore. Counterpointing Moore's account in *Ave*, Yeats's account of Gill's dinner to himself and Martyn is conducted through the familiar dialectic of "images." Moore speaks first, inaudibly, badly, succeeded by Taylor, who is below his best. But physical description distinguishes the two men. Taylor's body, as the tense phrases record, "was angular, rigid with suppressed rage, his gaze fixed upon some object, his clothes badly made, his erect attitude suggested a firm base"—a firm base in the Ireland whose provinciality condemned him to obscurity. Moore, the failed cosmopolite, is hit off in one comprehensive sentence: "Moore's body was insinuating, upflowing, circulative, curvicular, pop-eyed." The lack of physical definition is brilliantly suggested by the use of near-synonyms, each purporting to catch at the oddity, the absence of style, and after the rise into the mock-pompous "circulative" and "curvicular" the word "pop-eyed" forces its way artlessly out and the image collapses into finality. Both Taylor and Moore are placed by the image of O'Grady who speaks with such a drunken majestic sweetness that his Unionist opponent applauds the Nationalist sentiments. "Their torch smoked, their wine had dregs, his element burned or ran pure." O'Grady's oratory is the purest symbolism, includes but transcends logic.

For both Yeats and Moore final judgement on their respective styles, their respective self-transparency, is a literary judgement. Moore had learned the necessity for style in the later 1880s under the influence of Pater, but the books that most satisfied their author, *Heloise and Abelard* and *The Brook Kerith*, though written after *Hail and Farewell*, had their roots in the trilogy and in *The Lake.* Yeats's shrewdest stroke is the suggestion that the painful limpidities of the later Moore were based on some "silly youthful experiments" of his own. (Susan Mitchell's suggestion that Moore owed to Yeats the notion of revising and re-revising his earlier work is instantly plausible.) Yeats does not underestimate Moore's force, but praise is polemical. Moore's work is a triumph of will, not the effect of grace, and the effort shows. Apparent magnanimity is frequent in *Dramatis Personae.* Episode is balanced against episode and Yeats's side of the *Where There is Nothing* encounter, with its sputter of threats and telegrams, is prepared by the reference to Moore's plagiarism that reveals both shamelessness and courage.

The structure of *Dramatis Personae* moves towards the exaltation of Lady Gregory, and Yeats's own talk is taken up into her translation of Grania's lullaby over Diarmuid in that "musical caressing English which never goes far from the idiom of the country people she knows so well." This has been ushered in by the compunction of the last reference to Moore ("I look back with some remorse"), by the brief account of Hyde's ease of style in the Irish language and a reflection on Synge, the inheritor. Our thoughts are swayed deliberately to "Coole" and "Coole and Ballylee"; and by the comic sparagmos of the tinkers after the performance of Yeats's and Lady Gregory's *Unicorn from the Stars* to the *Playboy* and its consequences both on stage and off, to riots and the superior fictions that cause them. The subject of the lament, Diarmuid and Grania, indicates that more than a requiem over the episode of the National Theatre is intended, for its subject symphonically associates Lady Gregory with Yeats and with Moore, since all were concerned in writing a play of that title that was finished to no one's satisfaction and whose comic history is recorded in Moore's *Ave.* It remains a final comment on *Dramatis Personae* also, on the fiction that does not deceive its author, but whose unity of tone makes it the most artfully achieved of Yeats's essays in self-transcendence.

ALLEN R. GROSSMAN

"The Moods": Tradition as Emotion

The mind or imagination or consciousness of man may be said to have two poles, the personal and impersonal, or, as Blake preferred to call them, the limit of contraction and the unlimited expansion. When we act from the personal we tend to bind our consciousness down as to a fiery center. When, on the other hand, we allow our imagination to expand away from this egoistic mood, we become vehicles for the universal thought and merge in the universal mood.

    —W. B. YEATS and EDWIN J. ELLIS, *The Works of William Blake*

The archetypal self-finding on which poetic knowledge is based arises, as we have pointed out, in a single experiment which Yeats never ceased repeating: the comparison of the imaginal content of mind as autonomous subject with the imaginal content of world as the object of mind and the origin of experience. The discovery to which this experiment leads is that images which arise in the individual consciousness are also images in the great resource of collective representation which constitutes historical culture. The last and absolute version of this assertion is that mind and world are symbolically identical. This gigantic assumption was beyond Yeats's intention, though not beyond his capacity for fantasy. Such a cosmic man would possess as an account of his origins the origins of being itself. This would be the absolute or "divine" version of poetic knowledge, and we have already seen traces of this idea in the course of our exposition. In the essay on "Magic" Yeats elaborated his notion that "our memories are part of one great memory." The purpose of this assertion is to enable the poetic speaker

From *Poetic Knowledge in the Early Years, A Study of* The Wind Among the Reeds. © 1969 by the Rectors and Visitors of the University of Virginia. The University Press of Virginia, 1969.

95

to exercise his traditional powers as the vehicle of immortal language by declaring that individual experience and universal or collective experience are the same thing. This is *mutatis mutandis* a conventional version of poetic knowledge or what we have somewhat too formally called archetypal self-finding. The problem with which Yeats is dealing is a form of the question of tradition. The essay on magic despite its explicitness is rather a description than a way of working. The major theory which Yeats promulgated in the nineties to account for the relationship between the content of the individual mind and the content of the collective representations of Western culture was what he called "the Moods."

Yeats's early poetry offers in effect two solutions to the problem of the relation of the mind to history. The first is the transmigrant mind exemplified in Irish mythology by the universal presence of the wonder-working magician. The second is the symbol or multitude of symbols which are themselves omnipresent in history, and which come into relation to the mind of the poet through emotion, the element common to the mind in history and the mind in eternity. Transmigration in one or the other of these forms is necessary to Yeats' conception of the Romantic and post-Romantic worlds, in order to account for the accessibility in the present of the mythologies of the past. Accordingly, the notion of literary tradition as a purely historical phenomenon, that is, as a universe of models for imitation, is alien to Yeats's sensibility.

By and large, he invokes the first of our two alternatives, that of the transmigrant mind, when referring to the ideal poet who is also the ideal man; and the second, that of the transmigrant symbol, when referring to that tradition of symbols which is the exclusive and dangerous resource of humanity in terms of power and beauty. There is no harmony between these two positions. Yeats alternates between the notion that the mind is itself eternal and the notion that the mind, like the reeds which the wind visits, is merely the host of the imagination and suffers inevitably the anguish of the human "amphibion," who is reluctantly man and reluctantly God.

If the whole symbolic resource of the human imagination is equally present at all times in history as a distinct cosmological entity such as the Neoplatonic *anima mundi,* then the significant history of the human mind can be understood as a whole through literature, and the function of literature is to organize and expose the eternal imagination. If on the other hand the mind is itself eternal, the business of the poet is that of the Socratic teacher, namely, the liberation of the eternal from the temporal man. Throughout his career Yeats is concerned, both with the ideal organization of history through poetry, and with the ideal organization of the human mind, which takes place first in the act of creation and then in the experience of art. Both aspects of the enormous poetic ambition suggested by these concepts require the suppression of personality in any recognizable definition of that quality and value the poet insofar as he is a vehicle of something which as a man he is not.

On the whole, Yeats is certain about his symbols but uncertain about their relation to himself. He conceives of them, both as a welcome asylum from the nineteenth century and as a scourge demanding of humanity more reality than it can endure. We see this in his ambiguous treatment of the mythology of the wind. He alternates between the use of the wind as a symbol of the Transcendental in the Neoplatonic sense and its use as an expression of lost but entirely human potentialities of sentiment. His insight demands that, even in the nineteenth century, the psychology of the poet be transcendental, but he is uneasy in the face of that demand as a real moral possibility. As a result his imagination, like Blake's, proliferates entities representative of mind (the host, the fairies, the stars, the everlasting voices) the semantic nature of which is unstable, to some degree dependent on whatever aspect of the poet's real unconsciousness is at any given moment engaged.

Yeats's first didactic poem is "The Moods." He presents it at the beginning of *The Wind among the Reeds,* as a statement of the problem of tradition. In 1899 "The Moods" appeared as follows:

> Time drops in decay,
> Like a candle burnt out,
> And the mountains and woods
> Have their day, have their day;
> What one in the rout
> Of the fire-born moods,
> Has fallen away?

This poem is not only very slight conceptually but of negligible aesthetic value. It was, however, reprinted by Yeats in all collected editions of his poems after 1899 and, in a somewhat different form, in all editions of *The Celtic Twilight* (1893), in which it first appeared as an epigraph. Further, it is cited in the Tenth Section of *Per Amica Silentia Lunae* (1917) as an illustration of a cosmological system which is still important to him.

"The Moods" exists in at least two discrete versions, the earlier associated throughout all printings with *The Celtic Twilight* and the later occurring in all other contexts. The last three lines in the earlier version are as follows:

> But kindly old rout
> Of the fire-born moods
> You pass not away.

Between the version of 1893 and that of 1899 Yeats disposed though not completely of the trivializing diction of the fairy convention ("kindly old moods") and introduced the terror of a world not susceptible to the control of the mind (his characteristic grammar of query). The superseded convention represents the childhood fantasy of a secret world which supplies the affection that the real world withholds. Yeats valued the supernatural because it gave evidence of possibilities of feeling unavailable to him as a natural man.

The term "Mood" first appears in Yeats's poetry in the poem in question, and an examination of the literary community around 1893 suggests that it had a very limited currency in Yeats's sense. In Edwin J. Ellis's poetic drama "Fate in Arcadia" (1892) we find the moods assimilated momentarily to the fairy convention as impersonal transmigrant emotions.

> MAID: Who lives in Fairyland?
> FAIRY: Only the Moods,—a strange and wandering band.
>   They come like travelling maskers for their day
>   And house them here, and grief and laughter play
>   Until their service being done,—on—on
>   They, leaving the heart's door open, are gone.

The irrelevance of this systematic intrusion into the otherwise arbitrary symbolism of Ellis's play suggests that the psychology of the Moods was not indigenous to Ellis's mind. Clearly Yeats and Ellis developed the notion between them in the course of their collaboration on the problem of Blake. In the Yeats-Ellis *Blake* Mary Green is described as a "mood expressed, a State, and as such of more universal importance and artistic significance than an individual." Of *The Book of Urizen*, the editors say,

> This is the story of one of the eternal states or moods of man,
> which are from everlasting. The individual enters these Moods
> and passes on, leaving them in the Universal Bosom, as travellers
> leave in space the lands through which they go. The name of the
> Mood is Urizen.

Whatever the source of the Moods as Yeats understands them, it is clear that he has in this case as in others constructed his symbolism by the addition of an occult to a Romantic attitude. Yeats himself has suggested that nearly all the "popular mysticism" of his youth derived ultimately from Spinoza and that the "modes" of Spinoza are related to the cabalistic *sephiroth* which come into Latin as *affectiones.*

In order to understand Yeats's dependence on the notion of Moods it is necessary to refer to his uncollected contributions in English periodicals, where he deals more extensively than anywhere else with the problem of tradition. In July 1895 the first of a series of three articles dealing with "Irish National Literature" appeared in the *Bookman:*

> Englishmen and Scotsmen forget how much they owe to mature traditions of all kinds—traditions of feeling, traditions of thought, traditions of expression—for they have never dreamed of a life without these things. . . . In a new country like Ireland—and English speaking Ireland is very new—we are continually reminded of this long ripening by the immaturity of the traditions which we see about us.

In reviewing the recent past of Irish literature Yeats finds that

> the Irish national writers who have bulked largest in the past have been those who, because they served some political cause which could not wait, or had not enough of patience in themselves, turned away from the unfolding and developing of an Irish tradition and borrowed the native English methods of utterance and used them to sing of Irish wrongs and preach of Irish purposes.

From the first half of the century he paradoxically selects Moore, Davis, and John Mitchell, as having dealt substantively with the problem of tradition, although it is only for Mitchell that he has any real admiration.

> These were the most influential voices of the first half of the century and their influence was not at all the less because they had not a native style, for the one made himself wings out of the ancient Gaelic music, and the other two were passionate orators expounding opinions which were nonetheless true because the utterance was alien; and were not poets or romance writers, priests of those immortal Moods which are the true builders of nations, the secret transformers of the world, and need a subtle, appropriate language or a minute, manifold knowledge for their revelation. John Mitchell, by the right of his powerful nature and his penal solitude, communed indeed with the great Gods, now and always none other than the Immortal Moods . . . but

he gave them no lengthy or perfect devotion, for he belonged to
his cause, to his opinions.

It is only when he comes to consider William Allingham that he is able to
praise with less qualification.

In him for the first time the slowly ripening tradition reached a
perfect utterance; and the Immortal Moods, which are so impatient of rhetoric, so patient of mere immaturity found in his
poetry this one perfect ritual fashioned for their honour by Irish
hands.

I have quoted from this article at considerable length in order to show
the peculiar complexity of Yeats's attitudes toward the problem of tradition
in general and Irish authors in particular. First of all "tradition" consists in
the whole environment of the mind, involving not only "expression" but
also received capacities of "feeling" and "thought." Secondly, it seems to
have nothing to do with a native style in any comprehensible sense, since
if Mitchell did not have it no objective observer could discover that Allingham did. Thirdly, it involves a subjectification of reality inconsonant
with political cause or with the arbitrary relation to the external world which
Yeats, like Plato, calls opinion. Although the Moods seem to be universal
as they are immortal, the degree to which a writer serves them is the measure
of his achievement with respect to the *Irish* tradition. Tradition therefore is
universal, and "Irish tradition" as Yeats conceived it in 1895 simply expressed the degree to which Irish writers participated in that universal well
of resource. On a psychological level the Moods allowed Yeats to express
his early sense of the infinity of his emotions by translating them out of the
limiting context of time. From a literary point of view the Moods liberate
him from the temporal restrictions of nationality.

The most remarkable thing about the addiction of Irishmen to Theosophy in the early years of the Celtic Revival is that Theosophy is a dog-
matically universalist movement. When Mohini M. Chatterjee came to
Dublin in 1886, he published an article in the *Dublin University Review* for
May of that year called "The Common Sense of Theosophy," in which he
sets forth doctrines basically the same as those which Yeats enunciated fifteen
years later in his essay "Magic." In November of that year Yeats published
his first critical article in the same periodical showing the effect of theosophical universalism on his aesthetic theories. He is speaking of Ferguson,
whom of all the Anglo-Irish writers he seems never to have ceased to admire.

Ferguson's poetry is truly Bardic, appealing to all natures alike,
to the great concourse of the people, for it has gone deeper than

the intelligence which knows of difference—of good and evil, of the foolish and the wise, of this and that—to the universal emotions that have not heard of aristocracies, down to where Brahman and Sundra are not even names.

Further, without using the term "Mood" he speaks of legends in the sense that was to become his custom ten years later.

Legends are the mothers of nations. I hold it the duty of every Irish reader to study those of his own nation. . . . If you will do this you will perhaps be saved in their high companionship from that leprosy of the modern—tepid emotions and many aims. Many aims, when the greatest of the earth often owned but two— two linked and arduous thoughts—fatherland and song. For them the personal perplexities of life grew dim, and there alone remained its noble sorrows and noble joys.

Ireland is a new country from the point of view of tradition, and the Moods are old. As in the passage above, Yeats frequently equates the Moods with legend. Legends belong to antiquity. Because antiquity in Yeats means virtually the same thing as subjectivity, legends confirm emotions which in the modern world are no longer credible.

Emotions which seem vague or extravagant when expressed under the influence of modern literature cease to be vague and extravagant when associated with ancient legend and mythology, for legend and mythology were born out of man's longing for the mysterious and infinite.

The success of any movement which could give Ireland a tradition in the sense in which Yeats described it in 1895 would be marked by its capacity to come to terms with the past as history and as mind, according to the canons of total subjectivity and extravagant emotion. In the Celtic Revival as characterized by Nora Hopper and George Russell, Yeats felt that he perceived the beginning of such a movement.

Whatever the cause we have for the first time in Ireland and among the Irish in England a school of men of letters united by a common purpose . . . and it is my hope some day in the maturity of our traditions to fashion out of the world about us, and the things that our fathers have told us, a new ritual for the builders of peoples, the imperishable moods.

In Europe the old movement as Yeats conceived it (*In Memoriam,*

"Locksley Hall," "Bishop Blougram's Apology," "Les Châtiments," Matthew Arnold) was "scientific and sought to interpret the world"; the new movement (*The Well at the World's End, Parsifal,* "Aglavaine and Selysette," *Axel*) "is religious and seeks to bring into the world dreams and passions which the poet can but believe to have been born before the world and for a longer day than the world's day." For the poet the subjectivity must necessarily be eternal. The agony of the fundamental paradox must be undergone, and though the resources for idealism are as many as the religions of the world, none in Yeats's early verse unified the mind sufficiently to mitigate the pain.

Before 1900 Yeats sought to express his sense of the rising tide of emotion in relation to Ireland through the establishment of a cult of Irish Heroes, after 1900 through the establishment of an Irish theater. But the sources of his poetry were too various, and his emotions too strong, to admit of any successful reassociation of poetry with the Ireland of history under the conditions of his early inspiration. In the notes to his Irish anthology of 1895 he shows his contempt for Tom Moore by praising first a French translation of one of Tom Moore's lyrics and then assigning even higher praise to Bridges's English translation of the French. In this way the poem as Mood passes from country to country seeking a tradition of style competent of it. Similarly when Yeats and George Moore undertook their collaboration on "Diarmuid and Grania," Yeats's program for the development of a stylistically mature product involved a planned transmigration. Moore was to go to Paris and do the scenario in French; thence it was to pass to a second party who would translate it from French into Gaelic; Lady Gregory would translate the Gaelic to vulgar English; and Yeats would "put style on it." Whether or not this is an exaggeration of the fact, the point is clear. The modern literary impulse must undergo a refinement including the discipline of France, where Yeats felt the new movement to have arisen, and of ancient Ireland, from which it derives its power and specificity. Only then could it receive the last mark of transfiguration, "style," and become Irish in the sense that the Moods as a concept of tradition demand.

The Moods are not one, like the Judaeo-Christian deity, but many, like the pagan gods. As a symbol of inwardness they represent a fundamental disunity which Yeats continuously attempts to resolve and yet cherishes as a symbol of mysterious power. The only conventional resolution of the multiplicity of emotions is "abstraction" or the dreaded withdrawal from feeling. The Moods are the "true builders of nations," the source of power both in history and the mind, and to lose through abstraction a direct relation to these powers would be to lose all. In personality the Moods are the sources of motivation. Raised to the level of history (for they are also metaphysical entities), they account for the manner in which poetry, as mediate between eternity and time, forms nations and individuals. But if we pass beyond Yeats's own capacity to comment on his predicament, we must observe that so long as emotional reality remains multiple and unrelated to consciousness, personality cannot emerge. Just as Yeats, in embracing the cosmic psychology of the Moods, disavows true nationality, so also he disavows true identity. Archetypalism, like nonrational psychology, bypasses identity by locating value above or below consciousness. Personal identity was the abstract unity which Yeats felt it necessary to abolish, and the style of *The Wind among the Reeds* is exactly oriented to convey the sense of the extinction of personality in the process of transformation.

Yeats in this period will accord unity neither to deity nor to the self, as if in the dispute for power between God and man, father and son, neither force can be allowed to emerge victorious. Further, the notion of the transcendental character of the Moods literally accords power only to the gods, for clarity is achieved only by the abolition of mechanisms by which time and eternity can mingle. The dispute as to whether the Rose is white or red, the possession of the father or the son—whether reality is occult and generated in the self or Neoplatonic and irrecoverably beyond the self—is one of the irreducible "obscurities" of the Yeatsian text.

The notion that salvation would be achieved by a new resort to the emotions was a common possession of Yeats and his age. In general, it took the contrary form of realism with respect to the external world and the sexual object. The poetry of Symons, Dowson, and Richard Le Gallienne began in the music hall. The new poet like the new woman was undertaking the "larger latitude." Messages were being received from the London East End as well as the Hindu East. Dowson was not only the votary of Cynara but also the lover of Adelaide and the translator of Zola. Edwin Ellis, with whom Yeats seems to have developed the Mood psychology, attracted the young poet by his stories of sexual escapades on the continent as well as by his knowledge of Blake, so that the sexual initiation and the occult became simultaneous. Leonard Smithers, who presided over the *Savoy*, was a notorious publisher of pornography. Decadence in the sense of emotional extravagance was a commonplace.

> Oh! our age-end style perplexes
> All our elders time has tamed.
> On our sleeves we wear our sexes
> Our diseases, unashamed.

> Have we lost the mood romantic
> That was once our right by birth?
> Lo! the greenest girl is frantic
> With the woe of all the earth.

Thus John Davidson, not the least member of the "Tragic Generation," introduces his *Earl Lavender*. The typical solution to the problem was, as in the case of Wilde and Dowson, the complete dissociation of the sexual from the ideal content, a solution worked out in all the bitterness of its moral destructiveness in Hardy's *Jude the Obscure* (1895). But Yeats never allowed his idealism entirely to lose its psychological ambiguity. His symbol of the decadent imagination was the whore who gave birth to a unicorn, "most unlike man of all living things, being cold, hard and virginal," and who cries out after her child in terms of oxymoron expressing the paradox of body and soul, "Harsh sweetness, Dear bitterness, O Solitude, O terror." In *The Wisdom of the King* the hawk-headed youth woos his mortal love (the Ireland of history) with his richest gifts "for he could not believe that a beauty so much like wisdom could hide a common heart." The gift of wisdom which he offers and she refuses are words which tell

> How the great Moods are alone immortal, and the creators of
> mortal things, and how every Mood is a being that wears, to
> mortal eyes, the shape of Fair-brows, who dwells, as a salmon,
> in the floods; or of Dagda, whose cauldron is never empty; or of
> Lir, whose children wail upon the water; or of Angus, whose
> kisses were changed into birds; or Len, the goldsmith from whose
> furnaces break rainbows and fiery dew; or of some other of the
> children of Dana.

The discovery of the hawk-headed youth is that "wisdom the gods have made, and no man shall live by its light, for it and the hail and the rain and the thunder follow a way that is deadly to mortal things."

RICHARD ELLMANN

Oscar and Oisin

Yeats came to know Oscar Wilde during that period when he was obliged, and disposed, to respond to a new literary society. His family moved to London in April 1887, his twenty-first year. He could not afterwards regard Ireland in quite the same way. In Dublin he had made one of a company of young mystics, but these seemed virginal in comparison with the great hermeticists Madame H. P. Blavatsky and MacGregor Mathers whose orders he entered in London. In Dublin, nationalism was the movement to stir the hopes of the young, while in London this was three hundred years out of date and among young Englishmen anarchism and socialism had the cry. Writers like William Morris, whom Yeats quickly came to know, were more various than writers of his acquaintance in Dublin. Not that he succumbed to what he saw: his letters home, his "dreamladen" poems and tales about the west, his editions of Irish poets and storytellers, his sense of himself as an Irish writer indicate how he clung to what, in a sense, he had left forever. His point of view could never again be simple, and for many reasons, not all of them conscious, he held just as hard, until late in life, to his rooms in Woburn Buildings near Euston Station. "To an Irishman," he explained, "England is fairyland." When Hugh Kingsmill asked him if Wilde was not a snob, he gave an answer made indulgent by his own experience, "No, I would not say that. England is a strange country to the Irish. To Wilde the aristocrats of England were like the nobles of Baghdad."

Already settled in this Persian scene were, besides Wilde, two other literary compatriots, George Moore and Bernard Shaw, also a generation

From *Eminent Domain: Yeats Among Wilde, Joyce, Pound, Eliot, and Auden.* © 1965, 1966, 1967 by Richard Ellmann. Oxford University Press, 1967.

ahead of him. Moore was the most established, having won an audience
with his early novels; Shaw and Wilde were still eyeing success. Both were
none the less conspicuous on the London foam, Wilde in particular having
been painted, caricatured, and parodied for a decade. Among the three,
Yeats was to have most to do with Moore, though they met some years
later. He met Shaw and Wilde at a time when he did not yet know his
way.

The encounter with Shaw took place at William Morris's house, and
was promptly recorded in Yeats's letters and in Shaw's journal. Yeats could
not deny Shaw's wit but he could question Shaw's depth and consider him
"cold-blooded," an estimate to which, in spite of many *pro forma* compli-
ments, he afterwards kept. To Shaw, Yeats's interest in another world was
an exploitation of Irish weaknesses, though he conceded later that Yeats
"was always careful not to act nor romance or otherwise try to impose on
me as he did on his Rosicrucian fans." It was quickly clear that the two
were headed for a lifelong argument. But if Shaw, or for that matter Moore,
had never lived, Yeats would have come round to the same view. Wilde,
however, obtruded further into his consciousness.

In his *Autobiography* Yeats said that at the time of their first meeting,
Wilde had already reviewed *The Wanderings of Oisin* and praised it without
qualification. He was cavalier about time and attitude, the date being later,
the attitude more reserved. His sense of Wilde's generosity improved a little
upon the two reviews, kind as they were, which Wilde devoted to the book.
They were grounded on Wilde's illusion that his own, and late nineteenth-
century art in general, might alternate between the "sunlit heights" of
Athenian classicism and the Aeolian harp of English romanticism. Measuring
Yeats accordingly, he found elements of both present, yet still inchoate; the
title poem had something of the epic's largeness of vision but lacked the
epic's grand simplicity. (It was still good enough for Wilde, in conversation,
to compare Yeats's storytelling ability to Homer's.) Some of the poems were
fragmentary and incomplete, lacking in that architectonic quality for which
Matthew Arnold had made everyone look. As for the romantic temper, Wilde
admired the blend of Celt and Keats, of "very naive and very primitive"
ingredients along with richness and delicacy. On the other hand, he noted
some danger of "outglittering" Keats with "strange crudities and irritating
conceits." He complained that Yeats was "more fascinated by the beauty of
words than by the beauty of metrical music," a friendly way of noting a
number of lapses in the latter. Yeats deferentially corrected these as soon as
he could. Wilde also objected to the word "populace" in the line,

And a small and feeble populace stooping with mattock and spade;

he said it was "somewhat infelicitous." Yeats changed it to "race" for twenty years; then a certain amount of infelicity began to seem desirable to him, and he changed it back. Wilde, after registering these strictures, prophesied that Yeats would do work of "high import." He added shrewdly, "Up to this he has been merely trying the strings of his instrument, running over the keys." Yeats cannot have forgotten this remark, since when he in turn criticized the poems of the twenty-year-old Joyce in 1902, he wrote that they were "the poetry of a young man who is practicing his instrument, taking pleasure in the mere handling of the stops."

Before Wilde ceremoniously heralded Yeats's advent to London, the two men knew about each other through Lady Wilde, Oscar's mother. On 25 July 1888 she first invited Yeats to call, and after that he came often, to be greeted each time as "My Irish poet." He was delighted with "Speranza's" revolutionary past and with her folklorist present, demonstrated the year before by her book *Ancient Legends, Mystic Charms and Superstitions of Ireland*. From it he was to borrow the wooden plot of his play, *The King's Threshold*. In his own *Fairy and Folk Tales of the Irish Peasantry*, published late in September 1888, he praised her book for divulging "the innermost heart of the Celt in the moments he has grown to love through years of persecution, when, cushioning himself with dreams, and hearing fairy-songs in the twilight, he ponders on the soul and on the dead." This praise was filially quoted by Wilde when he reviewed this book of Yeats as well.

In his *Autobiography* Yeats describes how he met Wilde first, not at Lady Wilde's house but at William Ernest Henley's. The place enables him to contrast Henley, busy and imperial, with Wilde, indolent and subversive. The time was evidently September 1888, for that was the month when Henley took up Wilde (he threw his stick at him later), and when Yeats referred to Wilde in a column for an American newspaper as "the most finished talker of our time." What made this first meeting "an astonishment" was that Wilde spoke in perfectly formed sentences, unparalleled even among the eloquent Irishmen and Englishmen whom Yeats knew. The air he wore of having successfully assumed a new, rarefied personality (the opposite of the stage Irishman)—an effect enhanced by the likelihood that some of his conversation had been rehearsed—was for Yeats an allegorical victory of imagination over environment and heredity. He voiced something of this thought to Wilde, "I envy those men who become mythological while still living," and received in return a prescription for conduct, "I think a man should invent his own myth." This remark of Wilde's is quoted in the first draft of Yeats's *Autobiography,* and it is central to his own views. Much of his work is a gloss on it, like his early essay on Shakespeare which says that "there is some one myth for every man, which, if we but knew it, would make us understand all he did and thought." The sense of living a myth was implicit in Yeats's defense of Wilde against the charge of being a poseur; he told George Russell, an exponent of being true to the depths of one's being, that posing "was merely living artistically, and it was the duty of everybody to have a conception of themselves, and he intended to conceive of himself." Wilde's remark was in fact simmering in his mind, to be encompassed into a system.

At Henley's, Wilde pleased Yeats also by his manner of commending Pater's *Studies in the History of the Renaissance* to that unPater-like company. "It is my golden book," he said, "I never travel anywhere without it; but it is the very flower of decadence; the last trumpet should have sounded the moment it was written." "But," someone interjected, "would you not have given us time to read it?" and Wilde answered, "Oh no, there would have been plenty of time afterwards—in either world." Wilde was at once admiring Pater and making him faintly ridiculous, freeing himself by professing outlandish bondage. He did in fact regard Pater's style as too bookish, lacking "the true rhythmical life of words," while Pater rejoined that Wilde's style was too lifelike, that he wrote like an excellent talker.

Yeats's most memorable meeting with Wilde was on Christmas Day, 1888. Wilde invited him for dinner pretending that Yeats was alone in London, a pretense Yeats was glad not to embarass by truth. Having heard the gossip about the untidy house of Wilde's parents in Dublin, and about the dirty fingernails of Sir William Wilde, the eye-and-ear surgeon, he was unprepared for what he found in Tite Street. The drawing room and dining room were done in white, not only the walls but furniture and rugs too. The only exception was the red lampshade suspended from the ceiling; this cowled a terra cotta statue which stood on a diamond-shaped red cloth in the middle of the white table. The effect of theatrical simplicity was like a Beardsely drawing.

There were, with all Wilde's suave goodwill, difficult moments. He started at his young visitor's shoes, which, like his poems, were found to be "very naive and very primitive" in their yellowness, a botched attempt to comply with the vogue for undyed leather. Yeats's effort to tell one of Wilde's children a story about a giant frightened the child to tears and earned a reproachful look from the father, whose own stories of giants dwelt upon their amiability rather than their monstrosity. Flustered by his gaucherie, Yeats was not wholly at a disadvantage. He knew that in poetry, the one kind of literature where Wilde had so far, by publishing a whole book, staked out a definite claim, his own powers were greater. Wilde's muscleless poetry was in fact an example of what not to do. "Overshadowed by old famous men he could not attack, for he was of their time and shared their admirations," Wilde had exaggerated "every Victorian fault." "He thought he was writing beautifully when he had collected beautiful things and thrown them together in a heap. He never made anything organic while he was trying to be a poet." Something of this verdict must have conveyed itself to Wilde at the Christmas dinner, for he converted the muted disparagement into articulate victory by saying, "We Irish are too poetical to be poets; we are a nation of brilliant failures, but we are the greatest talkers since the Greeks." This distinction Yeats was willing to allow, and he came to defend Wilde's best work as a kind of aristocratic oral literature, the educated counterpart of the oral tradition among the Irish peasantry. In keeping with this idea, he later, for the *Oxford Book of Modern Verse,* pruned "The Ballad of Reading Gaol" until it had lost almost all its "foreign feathers" and was close to a folk ballad.

After dinnner Wilde brought out the proofs of his essay, "The Decay of Lying," which was to be published the next month in the *Nineteenth Century.* It had an immediate and lasting effect on this first auditor. Yeats did not share the then fashionable aversion to critical theory, but until this time his own principal literary ideas were derived from occultism and nationalism. He needed an esthetic which would take account of the intense speculation about the nature and function of art that had been going on since the pronouncements of the romantic poets. This Wilde provided, summing up the disdain for experience of writers from Gautier to Mallarmé, the disdain for morality of Poe and Baudelaire, the disdain for content of Verlaine and Whistler. Wilde saw that such views might gather new vitality if counterposed against conventional theories of sincerity and verisimilitude. The most original aspect of his own essay came from its dialogue form, which enabled him to shift stance and emphasis as the conversation turned, sharpening the central paradox with all its dialectical possibilities.

As the title indicated, "The Decay of Lying" began as a mockery of the current talk of Neronian decadence. Wilde spoke of a club called "The Tired Hedonists," and explained, "We are supposed to wear faded roses in our buttonholes when we meet, and to have a sort of cult for Domitian." To the suggestion that the members must be a good deal bored with each other, he agreed, "We are. That is one of the objects of the club." So Wilde smiled decadence away. He had also as target the essay by Zola published nine years before, *Le Roman experimental,* which minimized imagination and style, and made the artistic labyrinth into a scientific laboratory. The true and lamentable decadence, Wilde said, was this Zolaesque encroachment of life upon art.

The esthetic he propounded was to be less ethical, less salvationist than that of Matthew Arnold, whose recent death seemed to give warrant to a new esthetician. Wilde accordingly premised the superiority of the imagination to the faculties of reason and observation. This being granted, then lies are better than truths, whims than sobrieties, masks than faces. The truest poetry is the most feigning. These opinions are developed in Yeats's writings, for example, in his verse dialogue, "Ego Dominus Tuus," where Hic and Ille are very like Wilde's Cyril and Vivian, one pleading for the self-realization that goes with sincerity and veracity, the other for the self-transcendence that accompanies fabrication of a mask embodying all one is not. In the poem, however, the discovery of what Yeats calls the anti-self is the occasion for a sudden unleashing of energy; the anti-self is more than a synthetic mask, it is a daimonic counterpart, willed unconsciously as well as consciously, which when evoked proves to have powers beyond those of the evoker. Wilde did not present the fitting on of a mask as so culminative or preternatural; he thought of it as a kind of gambling with one's public aspect rather than as a half-voluntary searching for a new being with which the old being could fuse.

The preference for fabrication led Wilde to endorse the trend of nineteenth-century painting toward Orientalism. The conventions of art should be so powerful as to envelop the work's ostensible occasion. He joked about the vogue of Japan, saying that "the whole of Japan is a pure invention. There is no such country, there are no such people." While he was touting the glory of art divorced from life, he was also adroitly mocking the British disconnection from other cultures. Yeats shifted from Japan to Byzantium: in the large, Byzantium too is a pure, or at least an impure *invention*—a state of mind conjurable by an ageing Irishman looking for a magnificent "instead" for his own and Western decrepitude. Japan and Byzantium are not areas but conceits, the one propelling Wilde to witty excursions as the other propelled Yeats to pernings in a gyre. Yeats pursued the meaning of Orientalism more studiously: in half-Asiatic Byzantium he saw an imaginative triumph of formalism over random agitation, but in India he recognized something else, a denial not only of life but of form as well: "Grimalkin crawls to Buddha's emptiness." This renunciatory aspect of the East did not interest Wilde; he liked Japanese painting rather than Sankara philosophy; for Yeats, however, Asia was capable of supplying a continent-sized symbol of that will to erase, to demolish, which he saw to be as native—at least latently—even in the West, as the will to indite, to create.

Up to a point Wilde patronizes life for its inferiority to art, but "The Decay of Lying" has a second declension, which maintains that art inseminates life with its images. It brings color to what would otherwise be neutral gray. "Think of what we owe to the imitation of Christ, of what we owe to the imitation of Caesar." Yeats kept this phrase in mind, quoting it in his *Autobiography*. It spurred him to two complications of the idea: according to the first, history might be chronicled in terms of the degree to which men's minds have been possessed by images or have been dispossessed of them. In *Per Amica Silentia Lunae* Christ and Caesar are masks worn by new actors, St. Francis and Caesar Borgia:

> Some years ago I began to believe that our culture, with its doctrine of sincerity and self-realisation, made us gentle and passive, and that the Middle Ages and the Renaissance were right to found theirs upon the imitation of Christ or of some classic hero. Saint Francis and Caesar Borgia made themselves over-mastering, creative persons by turning from the mirror to meditation upon a mask.

In most subsequent considerations Yeats disjoined the Middle Ages, which he saw as breaking down distinctions between men and so attenuating their respective images, from the Renaissance, which magnified such distinctions and gave each its most defined expression.

Out of the same antithesis he framed a theory of psychological types. Men could be divided into two great categories, those who assumed and those who denied images. The first seek, through form, a means of control over "mere anarchy," the second practise submission, either by eliminating all deliberate effort or by accepting a "passionate intensity" dictated by others. These contraries are spelled out in "The Second Coming," but they can be found much earlier, as in this draft of a passage for *The Player Queen*:

> Queens that have laughed to set the world at ease,
> Kings that have cried 'I am great Alexander
> Or Caesar come again' but stir our wonder
> That they may stir their own and grow at length
> Almost alike to that unlikely strength
> But those that will not make deliberate choice
> Are nothing or become some passion's voice
> Doing its will, believing what it choose.

The contrast is continued in later poems like "A Dialogue of Self and Soul" and "Vacillation," though in them a *tertium quid*, a possible blending of these opposite urges within art, is envisaged.

Wilde was not capable of this rather Talmudic development of his own idea, and he was more concerned with the oscillation from Christ to Caesar than with putative reconciliations of them. He had at any rate enough to do in illustrating that men envisage the world in conformity with what artists have prescribed. Just as a geographical area may be considered a figment of the imagination, so with a temporal span: "The nineteenth century, as we know it, is largely an invention of Balzac." The word "largely" is breezy enough to put down question. In a sentence greatly admired and often quoted by Proust, Wilde said, "One of the greatest tragedies of my life is the death of Lucien de Rubempré." Likewise Hamlet, though only a character in a play, has had his effect upon two centuries: "The world has grown sad because a puppet was once melancholy." Yeats cavilled at Wilde's lax substitution for "sad" of "melancholy," and did not accept the defense that the sentence needed a full sound at the close; but he had no objection to the content. In "The Gyres" he invokes and extends Wilde's epigram:

> Irrational streams of blood are staining earth;
> Empedocles has thrown all things about;
> Hector is dead and there's a light in Troy;
> We that look on but laugh in tragic joy.

Philosophers may affect the world as strongly as poets; Empedocles' image of the world as Strife was sealed by his suicide. He was himself like the volcano into which he plunged, and men and events could not choose but to break into hostile fragments in conformance with his view of them. The Trojan war was a historical event, but history can do nothing except offer its detailed conformation of the power of imagination over life.

Wilde applied this theory of art as first cause to other arts besides literature. Corot's paintings created the fogs that they were thought merely to depict, an idea which Proust echoed when he said women began to look like Renoir's images of them. As for sculpture, Wilde said, "The Greeks . . . set in the bride's chamber the statue of Hermes or Apollo, that she might bear children as lovely as the work of art she looked at in her rapture or her pain. They knew that Life gains from Art not merely spirituality . . . but that she can form herself on the very lines and colours of art, and can produce the dignity of Pheidias as well as the grace of Praxiteles." To Yeats the images are not only cosmetic but, in their effects, military. As he writes at the end of his life in *On the Boiler,* "Europe was not born when Greek galleys defeated the Persian hordes at Salamis, but when the Doric studios sent out those broad-backed marble statues against the multiform, vague, expressive Asiatic sea, they gave to the sexual instinct of Europe its goal, its fixed type." This classical world is much more Dionysian than Wilde had conceived it.

The principal theme in "The Decay of Lying" develops from overturning the conception of imitation. That art is an imitation of life, that life is an imperfect imitation of a supernal world of forms, were theories of famous men which Wilde was ready to revise. By his lights Plato had needlessly suggested that the forms were extraterrestrial, when in fact they were terrestrial, and could be found in the world of art. Art makes life imitate it. Whether the forms of art have any source or sanction beyond the human Wilde chose not to consider, sensing that metaphysical speculation would land him back in the romantics' camp. In modifying Plato's cave he does some dexterous sidestepping:

> Remote from reality, and with her eyes turned away from the shadows of the cave, Art reveals her own perfection, and the wondering crowd that watches the opening of the marvellous many-petalled rose fancies that it is its own history that is being told to it, its own spirit that is finding expression in a new form. But it is not so. The highest art rejects the burden of the human spirit, and gains more from a new medium or a fresh material than she does from any enthusiasm for art, or from any lofty passion, or from any great awakening of the human consciousness. She develops purely on her own lines.

Wilde allows art to take up the burden of neither the divine nor the human spirit. The "many-petalled rose" which festoons the passage is an image that might imply some transcendent origin, but is not allowed to do so; when Wilde speaks of the "highest" art he associates it with a change of technique, not of content or aspiration. We have grown accustomed today to what was then still unfamiliar doctrine, that new methods bring new meanings.

Just here Yeats asserted himself. With great self-restraint he did not take over the image of the rose, though he used it often in his verse; instead he assimilated from Rossetti an image equally rusty and romantic, but solider sounding: "The beryl stone was enchanted by our fathers that it might unfold the pictures in its heart, and not to mirror our own excited faces, or the boughs waving outside the window." He agrees with Wilde that art is neither confessional nor photographic, neither wholly subjective nor wholly objective. The beryl stone is what he usually calls Anima Mundi, a sublime lexicon of the imagination which stores old images and the potentialities of new ones. From it men draw, without necessarily meaning to, the models for their creations, creations which may be deeds as well as works of art. Because images give direction to conduct as well as to artifice, Yeats was able in *A Vision* to conceive of human destiny as a panorama of images and men, sometimes mixed congenially, sometimes not. At moments men achieve more or less reality because they are more or less at one with their images, incarnating or failing to incarnate. One of the great subjects of art becomes the tension of this relation, and another is the remission of tension either by total embodiment, or by an Asiatic rejection of all images, though Yeats sometimes implies that such a rejection is itself an imaginative feat.

Yeats needed the word symbolism to bind together particular symbols in the larger lexicon. Wilde spoke occasionally about symbols but had no interest in the kind of integration which Yeats developed. He did, however, dwell upon the way that symbols may lose as well as gain power over us, and said that they were "as limited in extent and duration as the forces of physical energy." Because Wilde conceived of the images as discontinuous rather than, as Yeats announced, processional, he thought life to be by nature dilettantism. When Yeats offers the same idea,

> Love's pleasure drives his love away.
> The painter's brush consumes his dreams,

it is to suggest a common source for both creation and destruction. Nonetheless, he was quick to see possibilities in Wilde's conception. One day Wilde said he had been inventing a new Christian heresy. Christ was crucified but did not die, and after burial managed to escape from his tomb. He lived on as a carpenter, the one man upon earth who knew the falsehood of Christianity. Once St. Paul visited his town and he alone in the carpenters' quarter did not go to hear him preach. Henceforth the other carpenters noticed that, for some unknown reason, he kept his hands covered. Yeats's mind smouldered with this fable for twenty years before he exalted it into his poem, "The Magi," where not Christ but "the pale unsatisfied ones" suffer from the diminution of an image that once possessed them.

Another fable, which Wilde called the best short story in the world, impressed Yeats also with its "terrible beauty." Christ came from a white plain to a purple city, and as he passed through the first street, he heard voices overhead, and saw a young man lying drunk upon a window-sill, "Why do you waste your soul in drunkenness?" He said, "Lord, I was a leper and You healed me, what else can I do?" A little further through the town he saw a young man following a harlot, and said, "Why do you dissolve your soul in debauchery?" and the young man answered, "Lord, I was blind, and You healed me, what else can I do?" At last in the middle of the city he saw an old man crouching, weeping upon the ground, and when he asked why he wept, the old man answered, "Lord, I was dead and You raised me into life, what else can I do but weep?" From Yeats's point of view this grief was too diffuse—he didn't like weeping in art anyway—so when he took over Lazarus for his play *Calvary* he dried up the tears and replaced luxuriance in sorrow with truculence:

> For four whole days
> I had been dead and I was lying still
> In an old comfortable mountain cavern
> When you came climbing there with a great crowd
> And dragged me to the light.

Lazarus is in rebellion against Christ's love, and he exhibits a homely desire to live and die on his own terms. In the same play Judas is represented as betraying Christ not for gain but for freedom from God's power and mercy. Out of Wilde's promptings Yeats framed a battle between secular efflorescence and spiritual constriction, between the pluralism of images in life and art, and the imageless monism of religion. It is Anima Hominis, not Anima Dei, which he serves as prophet, though the other is a necessary countersign.

Wilde's most sustained retelling of a Biblical episode, *Salome,* dealt with his theme of spent images. The legend had been much worked by writers in France, but Wilde borrowed brazenly, knowing that it would assume a different expression through his mind. His old antithesis of Christ and Caesar appears here as John the Baptist against Herod and Salome, all three aroused by strange loves. Their ardors, sacred and profane, are strident. The first turns John into a sterile scold, the second turns Herod into a fool, Salome into a necrophile. Wilde's quite astringent theme is that their respective excesses, of renunciation and self-indulgence, are equally repulsive and ill-starred. There was much in this play for Yeats to dislike: he found the dialogue "empty, sluggish, and pretentious," and the action lacking in tension. He went reluctantly to a performance of it in 1905 and afterwards wrote a friend, "The audience was curiously reverential, and as I came away I said to somebody, 'Nothing kept us quiet but the pious memory of the sainted author.' " On the other hand, he wrote a friend in 1911 that *Salome* was very much a part of our time, and in the 1930s he reconsidered it in *The King of the Great Clock Tower* and later in *A Full Moon in March.* He replaced the atmosphere of morality and immorality alike gone fetid with a quite energetic notion of "the slain god, the risen god." The poet's head is severed but still sings because, in Auden's words, the death of the poet is kept from his poems, or, in language more like Yeats's, because images fructified by human passions survive physical destruction, their human embodiments being in fact temporary residences for animators more than human in origin and strength. Here as elsewhere, Yeats imposed a metaphysical dimension, which could be called imaginative though he, like Blake, considered *imaginative* a synonym for *eternal,* upon Wilde's less haunted scene. For Yeats the preternatural is enwoven with the natural. He imposed also a systematic symbolism upon what Wilde left improvisatory. A difference in temperament prevented his sharing Wilde's interest in the *failings* of character; Yeats's personages are always gathering strength, even when misguided. So *Salome* was reconstructed to make the king strong, the queen profound, the poet-prophet right.

At the time that Wilde's fame turned to infamy, he came himself to constitute a kind of image of the abused artist. His career was, he thought, as archetypal as Byron's. Yeats was entirely in accord with what he regarded as Wilde's decision not to escape, since escape would only blur the image. At the same time, the passage from scapegrace to scapegoat was not altogether simple for Wilde. "Even when disaster struck him down," Yeats said, "it could not wholly clear his soul." Though on release from prison Wilde promised to redeem his name, "his heart was shallow." Yeats summed it up in a note after Wilde's death, "He was an unfinished sketch of a great man." The "good things" in his works are most lifted from his conversation, where he could test them by immediate reaction. Avid for applause, he moved from emphasis to emphasis. What was best in him stemmed from a recklessness which Yeats compared to that of an Irish eighteenth-century rake or gambler, or to "an audacious Italian fifteenth-century figure." Only in *The Importance of Being Earnest* did he completely accept this quality in himself and so achieve, for the first time, unity.

As Wilde gained and then lost his public, Yeats struggled toward his own position. He elaborated the esthetic theories Wilde had imparted to him, and nourished the images. But he also began to regard himself as belonging to a brotherhood of symbolists as well as of occultists and patriots. There were other esthetic theories around him, but they lacked solidity. Walter Pater's impressionism was one of these; whatever its usefulness in painting, when applied to literature it attached too much value to what Yeats disliked as "isolated lyrical moments." Another theory, decadence, was for a time espoused by Arthur Symons, with whom Yeats shared rooms in the middle 'nineties. Symons spoke of decadence warmly as "really a new and beautiful and interesting disease," and, in an essay on "The Decadent

Movement in Literature" (1893), he exalted it until it sounded like health: "To fix the last fine shade, the quintessence of things, to fix it fleetingly, to be a disembodied voice, and yet the voice of a human soul: that is the ideal of Decadence." Yeats felt that this was a fainthearted and precious misconception. In 1898 he declared that what many called "the decadence" he, because he believed "that the arts lie dreaming of things to come," preferred to call "the autumn of the flesh." To Symons's notion that decadence might be considered the trunk of modern literature, and impressionism and symbolism its two branches, Yeats responded that the trunk was symbolism. He had spent three years, from 1892 to 1895, in bringing Blake's symbolic system out of its supposed eccentricity and into the main stream of European culture. Then, for Symons's magazine *The Savoy,* he wrote three essays on Blake, relating him to Mallarmé and Villiers de l'Isle-Adam, and offering a theory of symbolist art. He contributed to *The Savoy* also his stories, "The Tables of the Law" and "Rosa Alchemica," in which the narrator declares that for his mind "symbolism was a necessity," and also several ostentatiously symbolic poems like "The Secret Rose." Under this pressure, reinforced by much discussion in the rooms they shared in Fountain Court, Symons had to change his theory. He decided to publish a book on *The Symbolist Movement in Literature* instead of on the decadent movement as he had planned. Instead of being all decay, it was all recrudescence. This was one of the swiftest changes of face in literary history. Appropriately the book was dedicated to Yeats.

Symons's book drifted genially among various interpretations of symbolism, and had minimal force as a literary polemic. Yeats wanted to declare himself emphatically, and he did so in 1900 in an essay entitled "The Symbolism of Poetry." He began by defending the value of an esthetic, corroborating here Wilde's essay on "The Critic as Artist." Then, after discussing the indefinable symbolism in style, he took up the theme of the relation of art to life, trying to anatomize more precisely the way in which symbols, emotional and intellectual, gather their force and spread their influence throughout the world:

A little lyric evokes an emotion, and this emotion gathers others about it and melts into their being in the making of some great epic; and at last, needing an always less delicate body, or symbol, as it grows more powerful, it flows out, with all it has gathered, among the blind instincts of daily life, where it moves a power within powers, as one sees ring within ring in the stem of an old tree. This is maybe what Arthur O'Shaughnessy meant when

> he made his poets say they had built Ninevah with their sighing;
> and I am certainly never sure, when I hear of some war, or of
> some religious excitement, or of some new manufacture, or of
> anything else that fills the ear of the world, that it has not all
> happened because of something that a boy piped in Thessaly.
> . . . I doubt indeed if the crude circumstance of the world, which
> seems to create all our emotions, does more than reflect, as in
> multiplying mirrors, the emotions that have come to solitary
> men in moments of poetical contemplation.

The statement is tender in a way that Yeats later would not have permitted, but with all its gracious qualifications it insists, as strongly as Wilde and with more subtlety, on the conception of life modeling itself upon art "as in multiplying mirrors." Here Yeats has poets alone in command of symbols, but in his later work heroes, as artists of action, may also be in command of them, as may lovers. We cannot fail to be symbolists to some degree. The material world is not solid but molten, with symbols in various states of realization.

This essay, published just before Queen Victoria's death, consolidates the esthetic thinking of Wilde and Yeats and, with whatever caution or freedom it was reinterpreted, summons into being such writers as Eliot, for whom the unreality of the modern city derives from its loss of animating images, or Pound, whose *Cantos* offer unexpected substitutes such as Confucius and Malatesta for the images of Christ and Caesar, or Wallace Stevens, who finds like Wilde that "life is the reflection of literature." Long after Wilde had passed out of fashion, he was still fulfilling indispensably the role of precursor.

HAROLD BLOOM

Toward A Vision:
Per Amica Silentia Lunae

ANIMA HOMINIS

Yeats first intended to call this "little philosophical book" of 1917 *An Alphabet,* as though he meant it to be a key to the rudiments of his imaginative work, or to the convictions upon which that work was founded. Starting with the poem "Ego Dominus Tuus" (1915) as extended motto, the book divides itself into two reveries, "Anima Hominis" and "Anima Mundi," the first dealing with the Mask and the second with the relation of the Mask to the spiritual world, realm of *daimons* and the dead. In the total structure of Yeats's work, *Per Amica Silentia Lunae* serves as introduction to the visionary center, to the later poems in *The Wild Swans at Coole,* and to *Michael Robartes and the Dancer, Four Plays for Dancers,* and *A Vision* itself.

The cover design for *Per Amica Silentia Lunae,* done by Sturge Moore at Yeats's suggestion, is the Rose, now a symbol of the Mask, and thus a mark of deliberate continuity between the earlier and later Yeats. In this surpassingly beautiful little book, Pater and the Cambridge Platonist Henry More are made to join hands, as though the creator of Marius had his true affinities not with the second Renaissance of Romanticism but with the *Theologica Germanica* and related works. *Per Amica Silentia Lunae* is a masterpiece in the tradition of the marmoreal reverie, worthy to stand beside Browne's *Urn Burial* and *Garden of Cyrus* or most of Pater. Except for the *Autobiographies,* it is Yeats's great achievement in prose, a book to be read and re-read, unlike *A Vision,* which we are compelled to study, but so frequently with regret.

From *Yeats.* © 1970 by Oxford University Press, Inc.

The book begins with a brief, charming Prologue addressed to "Maurice," Iseult Gonne, with whom Yeats was, perhaps, half-in-love. Tone dominates here; the book, Iseult is told, completes a conversation her Persian cat interrupted the previous summer. There follows "Ego Dominus Tuus" [discussed elsewhere], a poem on the image of desire or Mask, the starting point for *Anima Hominis* even as the essay, "Swedenborg, Mediums, and the Desolate Places" is the starting point of *Anima Mundi*. The poem ends with a reference to a secret doctrine, which "the mysterious one," the double and anti-self, will read in the subtler language of the Shelleyan characters written on the wet sand by the water's edge, and which he fears to communicate to "blasphemous men." This suggestion of the hieratic is taken up in the opening sentence of "Anima Hominis," where Yeats comes home "after meeting men who are strange to me." He fears to have caricatured himself, being unfit to move among what he calls, in Blakean language, "images of good and evil, crude allegories."

What follows is an eloquent prophecy of what Yeats was to call "The First Principle" of his aesthetic, written years later as part of a general introduction for a projected edition of his complete works. A poet always writes out of the tragedy of his personal life, but never directly to the reader, for "there is always a phantasmagoria." It may be mythology, history, or romance, but even poets as personal as Shelley or Byron never write as what they and we are, bundles of accident and incoherence. They have been "reborn as an idea, something intended, complete." But note, in this age of Eliot, Auden, and the New Criticism, that there is *no* escape from or evasion of personality in this phantasmagoria, which is indeed precisely what Blake and Pater called "vision" and the other major Romantics the Secondary or creative Imagination. The artist becomes "part of his own phantasmagoria and we adore him because nature has grown intelligible." Nature is a power separated from our creative power, until the poet makes nature intelligible to us, "and by so doing a part of our creative power." There follows the most powerful and self-confident proclamation of the High Romantic imagination made in our time, and surely one that the host of anti-Romantic Yeats critics ought to have pondered. Yeats's Romanticism, Tate asserted, would be invented by his critics. Yeats has forestalled us, grandly: "The world knows nothing because it has made nothing, we know everything because we have made everything." So much for nature and God, and their merely Primary worlds.

Twenty years earlier, in "Anima Hominis," Yeats was no less confident, but he was then a little warier at identifying himself with his anti-self, of being made one with his own phantasmagoria. Yet the wariness, even then, was poetic strategy, a crucial element in the vacillation necessary for Paterian style. The phantasmagoria is there as "an heroic condition," vision, justly compared to Dante's *Vita Nuova* where the "Lord of Terrible Aspect" says to Dante: *ego dominus tuus,* or to the landscape of the Lower Paradise in Boehme. Yeats makes a hieratic withdrawal from life, and finds himself as the poet-visionary proper, enjoying a heroic condition. He calls this a "compensating dream," but he means compensation in a Coleridgean rather than a psychoanalytic sense, judging by the major instances he gives, beyond himself. He admits cases of compensation, like that of Synge, who in ill-health delights in physical life, but his interest is in art as "an opposing virtue" rather than a therapy. Most profoundly, this idea of the "opposing virtue" creates a pattern of heroic desperation, which may be the most moving design in the mature Yeats. Though the pattern exhibits familiar elements— a withdrawal from experience into the *antithetical* quest, identified with Shelleyan poethood, the occult way, the war between men and women—a new clarity defines itself also. Against whatever he knew of Freud and what he knew of the Pre-Socratics, whose view that character is fate Freud shared, Yeats implicitly urges the contrary view that personality is fate, the *daimon* is our destiny. The purpose of this exaltation of self over soul is not to evade the tragic reality of the Freudian and Pre-Socratic view, but to oppose it with another conception of freedom, one necessarily not available to more than a handful of artists, men whose work is a flight from their horoscopes, their "blind struggle in the network of the stars." On the simplest level of his deliberate illustrations of the "opposing virtue," Yeats is hardly convincing; he gives us the "irascible" William Morris as following "an indolent muse," the genuinely violent Landor pursuing calm nobility, and Keats, "ignorant, poor, and in poor health" thirsting for luxury. Not only are all of these quasi-mechanical compensations, but the Yeatsian notion of Keats is too absurd to be interesting. But in passing to Dante, who with Shelley is to dominate the description of Yeats's own Phase 17 in *A Vision,* Yeats returns to the true depths of his own *antithetical* conception. Thinking back to Simeon Solomon, painter and broken monument of the prelude to the Tragic Generation, Yeats remembers a Shelleyan phrase of Solomon's: "a hollow image of fulfilled desire." In Book iii, *Hodos Chameliontos,* of *The Trembling of the Veil,* Yeats distinguishes between the Mask or Image that is fated, because it comes from life, and the Mask that is chosen. Though in "Anima Hominis" he says that all happy art is but Solomon's hollow image, he means by this that tragic art is happy, yet expresses also the "poverty" of its creator, this use of "poverty" being strikingly similar to Stevens's use of it to mean "imaginative need," or a need that compels the

imagination to come into full activity. Dante, like Shelley, fights a double
war, with the world and with himself. Yeats touches the heights of his true
visionary argument, truer than any he makes in *A Vision,* when he praises
an ideal poet for choosing the Mask as an opposing virtue, and so attaining
the "last knowledge." When the poet has seen *and foreseen* the image of all
he dreads, while still seeking the image of desire to redress his essential
poverty, then he will have his reward:

> I shall find the dark grow luminous, the void fruitful when I
> understand I have nothing, that the ringers in the tower have
> appointed for the hymen of the soul a passing bell.

The enormous plangency of this magnificent (and Paterian) sentence
gains terrible poignance when set in the context of its genesis, February
1917, when Yeats was moving toward his fifty-second birthday, still un-
married, and not knowing he was to be married before the year was out.

Having attained to this "last knowledge," Yeats is free to explore the
hollow image or *antithetical* self, and find there (with Plutarch's help) the
figure of the *daemon,* who whispers in the dark with the poet's beloved, as
Yeats's own *daemon* (hardly Leo Africanus, but the Spirit that Denies) whis-
pered in the dark with Maud Gonne. Hence, "the desire that is satisfied is
not a great desire," a harsh judgment that goes back to the values of
"Alastor," and to Blake's early engraved tracts. There rises from this the
doctrine that Yeats insists the true poet shares with saint, hero, martyr:
that only the *antithetical* man is not deceived, and so finds reality, "a contemplation in a single instant perpetually renewed," a privileged moment
or pulsation of the artery, a time of inherent excellence, epiphany not of
the Divine shining out of a natural babe, but of the mind's own power over
everything that is merely given.

When Yeats has reached this point, at the close of the ninth section
of "Anima Hominis," his reverie would appear to be accomplished, his
warfare done. But in four more sections, the subtlest in the book, the subtlest
indeed that he wrote in prose, he passes inevitably to the problem of poetic
originality, which is the problem of poetic influence.

Poet or sculptor, Yeats says, cannot seek originality; he will sing or
mould after a new fashion anyway if he expresses *antithetical* emotion. This
is unfortunately an evasion, and Yeats does not rescue himself from it by a
bitter wit, when he finely insists that "no disaster is like another." So it
seems to the lover, but hardly to the reader. Yeats is firmer when he implies
that no originality can be sought deliberately, since the *daemon* is our enemy,
and is interested only in our disaster, and not in what he can make of it.

The *daemon* must be held off (he cannot be overcome) through the poet's true originality, which is the strong poet's creative misinterpretation of his strongest precursor. This is the burden of Section XI, which follows, and finds an image for Yeats's freedom by a *clinamen* that uses Blake as point-of-departure. Mentioning Balzac and "the Christian Caballa" as sources, but not Blake, the section transforms a Blakean image of apocalypse from Plates 97–98 of *Jerusalem*. The dialectic of the transformation was sketched in Section VI of *Anima Hominis,* which itself develops convictions that dominated "Adam's Curse," and emerged again in "Ego Dominus Tuus." The anti-self, which leads the poet to at least the possibility of his fuller self, leads also to an uncovering that promises release from time's burden, including the embarrassments of poetic tradition. So Section VI associates St. Francis and Caesar Borgia (a delightful conjunction) with the old nonchalance whose decay is lamented in "Adam's Curse." Saint and man-of-power alike make their creativity by turning from a lesser to a greater mode of imitation, "from mirror to meditation upon a mask," the *daimonic* Will they meet in *antithetical* reverie. In Section XI the mirror is "the winding movement of nature" or "path of the serpent," and the meditation upon the mask is the straight line of an arrow shot into the heavens, aimed at the sun. The winding path is associated with Blake's vision of Milton's Shadow, the Covering Cherub, the burden of time including the sinister beauty not only of the historical churches but of Milton's own poetry, and of the beauty of all cultural tradition, Scripture included, when Scripture is used to help cover our creativity, to block the path to paradise. The arrow shot at the sun is the Cherub's uncovering, the originality of each strong, new poet, and in Yeats's view is fired only by the poet who meditates upon a mask.

On Plate 97 of *Jerusalem* a revived Albion stretches his hand into Infinitude and recovers his Bow. His fourfold flaming Arrow finds its target in "A sun of blood red wrath surrounding heaven on all sides around," a Sun composed of "the unnumerable Chariots of the Almighty," of the contraries reconciled, "Bacon & Newton & Locke, & Milton & Shakespeare & Chaucer," the empiricists and the visionaries at last together. In Section XI of "Anima Hominis" Yeats speaks of "we who are poets and artists," unable to reach into Infinitude, "not being permitted to shoot beyond the tangible," and who are therefore subject to the endless cycle of desire and weariness, while living only for the sudden epiphany, the vision that comes "like terrible lightning." Prophesying the mystical geometry of *A Vision* (before the revelation made through Mrs. Yeats by ghostly Instructors), Yeats speaks of the winding mathematical arcs that prick upon the calendar the life-span of even the greatest men. Beneath these Urizenic heavens we are condemned to "seek reality with the slow toil of our weakness and are smitten with the boundless and unforeseen." Our efforts, in feeling or in thought, are doomed unless we learn to meditate upon the Mask, which means we must renounce mere *primary* experience, even with its saving epiphanies, "leave the sudden lightning," give up nature or "the path of the serpent" and thus take on the state of Blake's apocalyptic Man: we must "become the bowman who aims his arrow at the centre of the sun."

We confront here Yeats's *clinamen* in regard to his precursor, Blake; a creative misinterpretation overcomes poetic influence. In Blake's vision, to meditate upon a mask is only to be a Spectre vainly pursuing an elusive Emanation; this is natural religion, the worship of each day's unfulfilled desire. Here Blake is close to Freud, and Yeats opposed to both, even as Jung is opposed. Yeats begins Section XII of "Anima Hominis" by granting that the doctors are right in regard to certain dreams; unfulfilled desires and censoriousness can end in mere dream and nightmare, if they do not undergo the "purifying discouragement" that allows passion to become vision. But (whether we wake or sleep, in explicit echo of Keats) vision sustains itself by rhythm and pattern, and makes of our lives what it will. "Anima Hominis" ends, after this defiance of analytic reduction, with the poet's warning to himself. The imagination can wither, as in Wordsworth, most terrible of instances; rhythm and pattern, once found, are not enough. There must be fresh experience: "new bitterness, new disappointment," for the finding of a true mask, and prolonged meditation upon it, does not make suffering less necessary. It is Yeats's highly individual contribution to the Romantic Sublime, this insistence that continued loss is crucial. Without fresh loss, the Sublime becomes the Grotesque, and the poet only a pretender to the Mask.

ANIMA MUNDI

"Anima Hominis" succeeds where Book I, *The Great Wheel*, of *A Vision* will fail, in giving a persuasive account of the necessity for finding a mask. Similarly "Anima Mundi" is more coherent and appealing than the later books of *A Vision* are, in showing us how the *antithetical* self can be related to the world of the dead. Partly, this superiority of *Per Amica Silentia Lunae* over *A Vision* is due to the extravagant over-elaborations of the later work, as contrasted with the simplistic reveries of a poet closer to his earlier thought. But I judge the larger difference to be that Yeats was a better literary theorist than he was an occultist. *A Vision* can be translated into aesthetic metaphors, as Mrs. Vendler shows, but a good deal of it obdurately resists such translation, or translates only by severe reduction. *Per Amica Silentia Lunae,* even in its more spectral second book, is closer to an aesthetic treatise, with poetic influence a more major concern in it than the vagaries of ghosts. Or rather, its ghosts are poetic ghosts, imprisoned imaginations and influences, like Shelley's, that linger and haunt and will not permit themselves to be lost.

Near the close of Section XII of "Anima Hominis," Yeats says of his "vision" that "it compels us to cover all it cannot incorporate," [by which] he means, to cover all of his life that seems merely accidental, and so irrelevant to meditation upon the Mask. Whether overtly or not, he is remembering the Shadow of Milton or Covering Cherub he had encountered in Blake. [Elsewhere] I sketched a theory of poetic influence (partly derived by me from Blake and Yeats) in which influence is seen both as blessing and as curse. The first comes about through the later poet's swerve away from his Great Original, by a revisionary act of misinterpretation, and such a process is illustrated by "Anima Hominis," as I have tried to show. The second process, that of accepting the curse of the Original's (and tradition's) too-great achievement, is handled differently by Yeats than by any other poet I know, for perhaps no other major poet is so much of a Gnostic in his mature vision. In "Anima Mundi," Yeats takes on the curse of poetic influence as a Gnostic adept would; he enters the Shadow of the Cherub not to redeem it (as Blake's Milton did) nor even to redeem himself, but to attain what he will come to call justice, a passionate fullness, not of experience or of being, but of an instantaneous knowing. There are triumphs of this momentary knowing throughout the later lyrics, and a prolonged defence of it in those books of *A Vision* that deal with history and the dead. The lyric triumphs and the defence (and the application of the attained Gnosis in some of the later plays) are more disputable than they would be if Yeats had been able to keep to the mood of "Anima Mundi," but bitterness kept breaking in, and the eloquence of reverie was abandoned. In May 1917, Yeats had much cause for embitterment, yet a beautiful kind of slow wonder dominates "Anima Mundi," and induces even the contrary reader to set aside his wariness. In temperament, Yeats has little in common with the Cambridge Platonist Henry More, who is so evident here, but he finds the art (as Pater did) to assume a mood he rarely sustained elsewhere. It is the mood of the beautiful sentence of Browne that Yeats quotes in his 1914 treatise, "Swedenborg, Mediums, and the Desolate Places," a prelude to "Anima Mundi":

I do think that many mysteries ascribed to our own invention
have been the courteous revelations of spirits; for those noble
essences in heaven bear a friendly regard unto their fellow creatures on earth.

In this spirit, "Anima Mundi" begins, with Yeats genially immersing
his mind in "the general mind" of Eastern poets, Connaught old women,
and mediums in Soho. From this, it is an easy step to the suspension of will
and intellect, that images may pass before him. But these images, throughout
the treatise, are not particularly random, and generally turn themselves into
the central images of Romantic poetry. So, this first evocation attains its
climax in the "immortal sea" of Wordsworth's "Intimations" Ode, and
subsequent sections will end with references to Coleridge, Blake, Spenser,
and Shelley. The *anima mundi,* though Yeats quotes from "More and the
Platonists," not surprisingly turns out to be the general mind of Romantic
poetic tradition, as Yeats has fused it together. The explorers who perhaps
knew all the shores where Wordsworth's children sport appear to be the
poets who found their first seminary in Spenser's Garden of Adonis, from
which Yeats quotes two instructive passages. The women of Connaught and
Soho are more than an amiable fiction, but something less than Yeats's
Muses. And though we hear the vocabulary of the spiritual Alchemists in
Section III, the table of elements given is Blake's, down to the bird born
out of the simplifying, reductive fire, from which Mystery rises again at the
close of "Night VIII" of *The Four Zoas.* Yeats goes on, in Section IV, to
desire contact with "those minds that I could divine," but chooses to quote
Coleridge's fine lyric, "Phantom," so as to give coherence to those minds.

In so occultizing Romantic tradition Yeats merely gave birth to the
bad line of pseudo-scholars who have been reducing Blake, Shelley, Keats,
Spenser, and of course Yeats himself to esoteric doctrine in recent times.
But his motive was more honorable than what animates these literary Ros-
icrucians. His *anima mundi* as a poet is not in itself at all original, and
something in his creativity feared the Covering Cherub, the negative strength
of Romantic tradition. Thus, in Section VI, he goes to Henry More and
anonymous mediums for speculation upon the after-life, yet his pragmatic
finding is the staple of Romantic poetry. Beauty, he tells us, is "but bodily
life in some ideal condition," and he ends the section by quoting *The Marriage
of Heaven and Hell:* "God only acts or is in existing beings or men." In
between, he gives us the kernel of the after life as the soul's "plastic power"
which can mould whatever "to any shape it will by an act of imagination."
When, in his next section, he needs to image forth the *anima mundi* he

resorts to the opinions of Shelley and to the central image of all English Romanticism, Spenser's Garden of Adonis:

> There is the first seminary
> Of all things that are born to live and die
> According to their kynds.

Though he holds that coherence is provided by the occult image, he can show us only a coherence made by the poets themselves. The dead, like the spiritists who study them, become metaphors for Romantic art, rather than principles who inform that art. So the freedom of the dead, or Condition of Fire, itself is able to illustrate nothing, but is clarified for us when Yeats quotes his own lyric, "The Moods," from *The Wind among the Reeds,* immensely more coherent than Section X, and enabling us to see what these "fire-born moods" are.

Yeats was rarely a self-deceiver, and I think plainly attempts to deceive us here, presenting us with rhetoric, by his own definition. He tells us that the dead are the source of everything we call instinct, and so of our passions, but what he means is that our passions imitate art, and that tradition has taken the place of instinct. Similarly, he wishes us to believe that we communicate with *anima mundi* through the famous and passionate dead, but what he means is precisely what the fiercely skeptical Shelley meant by the survival of Keats in *Adonais,* and he not only needs Shelley to explain his thought, but he must both distort the context and misquote when he cites *Adonais.* Shelley writes of the crisis of young poets:

> The splendours of the firmament of time
> May be eclipsed, but are extinguished not;
> Like stars to their appointed height they climb,
> And death is a low mist which cannot blot
> The brightness it may veil. When lofty thought
> Lifts a young heart above its mortal lair,
> And love and life contend in it, for what
> Shall be its earthly doom, the dead live there
> And move like winds of light on dark and stormy air.

This intricate stanza firmly holds to the Shelleyan attitude that is best described as a visionary skepticism, longing for imaginative survival yet remembering always: "All that we have a right to infer from our ignorance of the cause of any event is that we do not know it. . . ." Yeats, despite his own temperamental skepticism, adopted always the contrary attitude, inferring from his ignorance a range of occult causes. In Section XIII of

"Anima Mundi" he deals with "the most wise dead," who "certainly" return from the grave, and he remembers a doctrine of Henry More, on the music of the shades, that he had quoted in "Swedenborg, Mediums, and the Desolate Places." He applies it here, saying that men have affirmed always "that when the soul is troubled, those that are a shade and a song: 'live there,/And live like winds of light on dark or stormy air.' " Shelley's context, the "there" of what Yeats quotes, is the uplifted heart of the young poet, and not the haunted state Yeats makes of it, while the misquotation of "live" for "move," whether deliberate or not, is immensely illuminating, as another instance of the happily perverse workings of poetic influence. One remembers Shelley's brief, pungent essay, "On a Future State," where he remarks of the assertions made by those of "the secret persuasion" of an occult survival: "They persuade, indeed, only those who desire to be persuaded."

Shelley, as elsewhere in "Anima Mundi," provides the key to Yeats's discourse: the "passionate dead" live only in our imagination, and their dream is only of our life. Alas that they do wear our colors there, though Yeats exultantly cries of them that they are rammed with life (itself a tag from another poet, Jonson). Though in *A Vision* Yeats will depart from his uneasiness, and will postulate a world of the dead quite unlike the world of the living, here in *Per Amica Silentia Lunae* he is more of a poet and less of a necromancer, and he profits by his uneasiness, as do we. The Condition of Fire, with its purifying simplification through intensity, is precisely the Romantic Imagination, the burning fountain of *Adonais,* and the apparently mysterious Sections XV through XXI of "Anima Mundi" are an extended commentary upon *Adonais,* its stanza LIV in particular. The climax to this commentary, in Section XXI, is also the height of Yeats's visionary argument in *Per Amica Silentia Lunae.* Remembering that Shelley calls our minds "mirrors of the fire for which all thirst" Yeats asks the inevitable question, for Gnostic or naturalist alike, "What or who has cracked the mirror?" And, for answer, he turns to study his own self again, finding in the Paterian privileged moment his only true access to the *anima mundi,* and so presenting his genuine defence of poetry. What he describes is the basis of the poem "Demon and Beast," but his description here is more in the Romantic tradition. If, in the pulsation of an artery or displaced epiphany, he finds himself "in the place where the daemon is," this is still no victory, until the *daemon* "is with me," a work the poet must perform for himself.

HAROLD BLOOM

A Vision: *The Dead and History*

Emerson identified the Sphinx with nature, and his curious poem "The Sphinx" is another precursor to aspects of *A Vision*. Emerson thought the poet could unriddle the Sphinx by a perception of identities among the diverse particulars nature presented. If Yeats read Emerson on history, and he is likely to have done so, he would have encountered a very Yeatsian defiance of natural mystery: "This human mind wrote history, and this must read it. The Sphinx must solve her own riddle. If the whole of history is in one man, it is all to be explained from individual experience." Emerson and Yeats both believed "there is one mind common to all individual men," a mind sovereign and solitary, whose laws were immutable and could be discovered by men. Yet to read Emerson's essay on history and *A Vision* together is to see how rapidly the affinity between these poetic theorists of history is dissolved. Where Emerson kept away from system, and turned to poetry for his history, Yeats enters the labyrinth of system, and turns for knowledge to the dead. A fit epigraph for the aspects of *A Vision* this chapter discusses, perhaps for all of the book, can be found in Emerson's *Journals:*

> Miss Bridge, a mantua maker in Concord, became a "Medium," and gave up her old trade for this new one; and is to charge a pistareen a spasm, and nine dollars for a fit. This is the Rat-revelation, the gospel that comes by taps in the wall, and thumps in the table-drawer. The spirits make themselves of no reputation. They are rats and mice of society. And one of the demure disciples

From *Yeats.* © 1970 by Oxford University Press, Inc.

of the rat-tat-too, the other day, remarked that "this, like every
other communication from the spiritual world, began very low."
It was not ill said; for Christianity began in a manger, and the
knuckle dispensation in a rat-hole.

"The spirits make themselves of no reputation"; Book II of *A Vision*,
"The Completed Symbol," begins by apologizing for having delayed un-
wittingly in giving us the Four Principles, the innate ground of the Four
Faculties that we have studied already. Either the spirits were frustrated, or
the poet was careless. The Principles are Husk, Passionate Body, Spirit, and
Celestial Body, corresponding in *daimonic* existence to Will, Mask, Creative
Mind, and Body of Fate in human existence, as Yeats conceives it. Having
learned one barbaric terminology, the reader is reluctant to learn another,
but Yeats has his justification, even as Blake did when he created both an
eternal and a temporal mythology. Blake's Faculties are Orc, Satan-Jehovah
(in a brilliant compounding of the opposites of the orthodox), Los, and the
Covering Cherub, the fallen forms of the Zoas or primal beings; Blake's
Principles are the eternal forms of the same beings; Luvah, Urizen, Urthona,
and Tharmas. The double mythology in each poet is necessary because vision,
in their sense, is always at least double, of the experiential world and the
world of Giant Forms (to use Blake's phrase) from which experience has
fallen away. The Faculties or fallen Zoas are "man's voluntary and acquired
powers and their objects;" the Principles or unfallen Zoas are "the innate
ground" of our powers, centered in our consciousness even as the powers
are centered in our wills. Yeats's most direct passage of explanation is dense,
and demands explication:

> The *Principles* are the *Faculties* transferred, as it were, from a
> concave to a convex mirror, or vice versa. They are *Husk, Passionate
> Body, Spirit* and *Celestial Body. Spirit* and *Celestial Body* are mind
> and its object (the Divine Ideas in their unity), while *Husk* and
> *Passionate Body,* which correspond to *Will* and *Mask,* are sense
> (impulse, images; hearing, seeing, etc., images that we associate
> with ourselves—the ear, the eye, etc.) and the objects of sense.
> *Husk* is symbolically the human body. The *Principles* through
> their conflict reveal reality but create nothing. They find their
> unity in the *Celestial Body.* The *Faculties* find theirs in the *Mask.*

We must recall that the Faculties are voluntary, in the sense that we
accumulate them in the course of our experience. Not that we are free to
will them, but they reside in what Yeats calls Will, which is more of an

accumulated superego. The Husk, being an intrinsic Principle, always existent, is a kind of transcendental superego; if we can think of what a god's own censor might be, we have something close to Yeats's Husk. When Yeats says, darkly, that *"Husk* is symbolically the human body," he is recalling what I judge to be the Blakean origin of the term, in the great line from the apocalyptic *Night the Ninth* of *The Four Zoas:* "and all Nations were threshed out and the stars threshed from their husks." Yeats re-wrote the line as the epigraph to his *Crossways* group of early lyrics ("The stars are threshed, and the souls are threshed from their husks," a strong line but written by Yeats and not, as he says, by Blake), and since the revision of Blake presumably was an unconscious misremembering, the implied interpretation of Blake's "husk" would make the Husk the human body, as it is in *A Vision.* "My body is that part of the world which my thoughts can change," Lichtenberg remarks, in making much the same point that Yeats makes about the Husk. Husk is sense in sense's aspects of impulses and images, which shape the body and make it the manifestation of the unconscious, as a phenomenological psychiatrist might say, or of a transcendental superego, as the occultist Yeats in effect would say. The objects of sense come together in Passionate Body, the transcendental form of the Mask or questing libido. But, whereas the Faculties find their union in the Mask, the Principles cannot find theirs in the Passionate Body, for the conflict of the Principles is revelatory but not creative, and the Passionate Body remains always a manifold of sensations, subject to natural entropy.

Though a touch strained as symbolism, these first two Principles are not difficult to apprehend. But Spirit and Celestial Body, eternal mind and its object, are much more opaque to the understanding than eternal sense and its object. Partly this is because they dominate the world of the dead or, as Yeats terms it, "the period between lives." Spirit or unfallen mind is what Blake calles Urthona, or Coleridge (following the Kantians) "reason." This is not so much the conciousness of any particular visionary—be he poet or philosopher—but visionary consciousness itself, and perhaps Yeats should have called it The Spirit, if he had to use the misleading word "spirit" at all. Celestial Body, the object of the Spirit, is not as badly named since it means "the Divine Ideas in their Unity," and these Ideas for Yeats are Neoplatonic. Blake called his equivalent symbol Tharmas, the original unity of all the Zoas or warring beings in his pantheon. Like the unfallen Tharmas, the Celestial Body is a collective entity in the form of energy, rather than anything corporeal, and can best be thought of as a kind of transcendental id, even as the Spirit is a transcendental ego. "Trancendental," because we are now in the world of *daimons* and of the dead, and not of natural men, and also because we are now in the world that Yeats wants to call reality. When we die, consciousness passes from Husk to Spirit, and so only the imagination survives the ruin of sense. The Spirit turns from the objects of sense, or Passionate Body, "and clings to *Celestial Body* until they are one and there is only *Spirit;* pure mind, containing within itself pure truth." Or, very simply, Yeats is saying that after death we become all Imagination.

But for Yeats, the Imagination is *daimonic,* and this makes it impossible to understand Books II and III of *A Vision* without struggling with the meaning of Yeats's *daimons.* Husk is not human sense, but "the *Daimon's* hunger to make apparent to itself certain Daimons, and the organs of sense are that hunger made visible. The *Passionate Body* is the sum of those *Daimons.*" This kills the deepest interest we can feel in Yeats's mythology at this point, for there are no psychological correlatives to this part of the mythology, as there abundantly are when we read of the Faculties in Book I. The distance from human analogues is still greater when Yeats speaks of Spirit as "the *Daimon's* knowledge, for in the *Spirit* it knows all other *Daimons* as the Divine Ideas in their unity. They are one in the *Celestial Body.*" This then is not human knowledge, except insofar as our knowledge is revelation or *daimonic* thought, the thought of the poet of Phase 17 when he approaches most closely to Unity of Being. One mark of Yeats's vivifying power is that suddenly he is able to raise his own abstractions into an intensity of imaginative concern, mostly by invoking the central tropes of Blake's great ballad, *The Mental Traveller:*

> The *Spirit* cannot know the *Daimons* in their unity until it has first perceived them as the objects of sense, the *Passionate Body* exists that it may "save the *Celestial Body* from solitude." In the symbolism the *Celestial Body* is said to age as the *Passionate Body* grows young, sometimes the *Celestial Body* is a prisoner in a tower rescued by the *Spirit.* Sometimes, grown old, it becomes the personification of evil. It pursues, persecutes, and imprisons the *Daimons.*

As a note to this passage, Yeats refers us to "The Mental Traveller," but the reference is redundant. Though Blake presents a more inclusive dialectic in the poem, covering the relations of man to every confining context, Yeats is not mistaken in following out one strand only, the wars of love and jealousy fought between poetic consciousness and the Muse. The Female of "The Mental Traveller," Yeats takes as the composite form of his *daimons,* and the passage just quoted relies for its coherence on this identification. Because poet and Muse are fated to meet only in opposition, the

human and the *daimonic* alternately persecute one another. Yeats characteristically sides with the female figure in Blake's poem, a point obscured by
some earlier critics of *A Vision.* Thus, in the passage above, the male of the
poem momentarily is the Celestial Body, and the female the Passionate
Body. Translated, Yeats's passage reads: the poetic mind cannot know the
ultimate forms of poetic thought until it perceives these first as sensuous
forms, which exist so as to provide a bridge or ladder between poet and
archetypes. But there is an opposition between the forms of thought and of
sense, and if either expands, it must be at the other's expense. As a poet's
mind comes closer to the ultimate forms, the sensuous ones recede, as at
the opening of "Byzantium." "The unpurged images of day" belong to the
Passionate Body; the image, "more shade than man, more image than a
shade," belongs to the Celestial Body, which dominates in the night, or the
death that for Yeats is only an interval between lives. In "A Dialogue of
Self and Soul," when the Soul summons the Self to climb the ancient winding
stair of Yeats's tower, the purpose of the steep ascent is to rescue the Celestial
Body, held prisoner through the long day of the poet's life that is drawing
to its end. Yet those same archetypes, grown old in their unity, can so
reduce the Passionate Body as to tyrannize over the *daimons,* for even the
Muse cannot bear altogether to be cut off from the sensuous realm or, as
Yeats phrases it, "the *Daimon* seeks through the *Husk* that in *Passionate Body*
which it needs."

Yeats cares about only the two Principles that govern the dead, because
Husk and Passionate Body not only disappear when life is over, but are past
and present respectively during life, while Spirit and Celestial Body are
always to be realized, are the future. Yeats knows two futures, the dead and
history, and most of *A Vision* after Book I is a sustained meditation on one
of these or the other. Though the Yeatsian vision of history begins to be
expounded in Book II, after the definition of the Principles, this exposition
belongs mostly to Books IV and V, while the world of the dead is examined
in Book III. For convenience of discussion, I turn now to Book III and the
dead, after which I will return to Book II before describing the major aspects
of Yeats's theory of history.

Book III, "The Soul in Judgment," is uniquely the book of the *daimon*
and so belongs to the Muse, and it would be a comfort if this meant the
book concerned aesthetic process, as Helen Vendler tried to demonstrate.
Unfortunately, Yeats is perfectly categorical in making this his Book of the
Dead, and a dismal book it is. I am haunted, each time I read it, by memories
of Wallace Stevens's fine insistence that poetry is a satisfying of the desire
for resemblance:

What a ghastly situation it would be if the world of the dead was actually different from the world of the living and, if as life ends, instead of passing to a former Victorian sphere, we passed into a land in which none of our problems had been solved, after all, and nothing resembled anything we have ever known and nothing resembled anything else in shape, in color, in sound, in look or otherwise. To say farewell to our generation and to look forward to a continuation in a Jerusalem of pure surrealism would account for the taste for oblivion.

These are the remarks of a poet who believed that "the brilliance of earth is the brilliance of every paradise." "The Soul in Judgment" portrays not a paradise, but a purgatory, though it is surely the oddest purgatory ever imagined by a poet. The spirit of Book III was best conveyed by Yeats himself, in conversation with Dorothy Wellesley:

He had been talking rather wildly about the after life. Finally I asked him: "What do you believe happens to us immediately after death?" He replied: "after a person dies he does not realize that he is dead." I: "In what state is he?" W.B.Y.: "In some half-conscious state." I said: "Like the period between waking and sleeping?" W.B.Y.: "Yes." I: "How long does this state last?" W.B.Y.: "Perhaps some twenty years." "And after that" I asked, "what happens next?" He replied: "again a period which is Purgatory. The length of that phase depends upon the sins of the man when upon this earth." And then again I asked: "And after that?" I do not remember his actual words, but he spoke of the return of the soul to God.

This is simpler than Book III's account of the dead, and considerably more conventional in its moral implications. Yeats, in Book III, divides "the period between death and birth" into six states:

1. The Vision of the Blood Kindred
2. Meditation
3. Shiftings
4. Beatitude
5. Purification
6. Foreknowledge

The Vision of the Blood Kindred is a farewell to the world of sense, of unpurged images, to the Passionate Body and those bound to us through it. The Meditation is a state in which Husk and Passionate Body vanish, their place taken by Spirit and Celestial Body. There are three phases in the state of Meditation: the Dreaming Back, the Return, and the Phantasmagoria. The dead, in The Vision of the Blood Kindred, say farewell to things as they are, to the whole universe of impulses and images. What follows, in the Meditation, is a vision of the completed life under the aspect of coherence, the bundle of impulses and images, appetites and moods, now gathered together as an achieved form. Certainly Yeats's hidden analogue for the Meditation is the act of making a poem as "Byzantium" shows, but the Meditation itself is not a creative state. Rather, it is a troubled and imperfect process, in which creativity rids itself of organic sense only through long and painful dreams of the past, the Dreaming Back. For the unpurged images of day remain stubborn; they may recede, but they do not vanish, and so long as they are present the Spirit clings to them and cannot find the Celestial Body, as it must. When the Dreaming Back is over, the Spirit enters the Return phase of the Meditation, which:

> has for its object the *Spirit's* separation from the *Passionate Body,* considered as nature, and from the *Husk* considered as pleasure and pain. In the *Dreaming Back,* the *Spirit* is compelled to live over and over again the events that had most moved it; there can be nothing new, but the old events stand forth in a light which is dim or bright according to the intensity of the passion that accompanied them. They occur in the order of their intensity or luminosity, the more intense first, and the painful are commonly the more intense, and repeat themselves again and again. In the *Return,* upon the other hand, the *Spirit* must live through past events in the order of their occurrence, because it is compelled by the *Celestial Body* to trace every passionate event to its cause until all are related and understood, turned into knowledge, made a part of itself.

The resemblance at the close of this passage to the Self's culminating stanza in "A Dialogue of Self and Soul" is palpable. What should be noted is that the Dreaming Back is closer to the poetic process than the more spiritually advanced Return is. We are compelled to recognize again, in pondering a passage like this, that *A Vision* is not primarily a study of poetic consciousness, but a Gnostic scripture or apocalypse. Why should the Celestial Body, or Divine Ideas in their Unity, compel the Spirit to such a measuring and tracing of causes? Yeats's answer would be that this is a condition if freedom is to be attained. But is it a poetic condition? The

purgatorial notion of intense memory as a painful necessity is to be followed
by a pernicious casuistry, and the result is to be freedom. Yeats falls down
imaginatively in finding the process of liberation, yet his aim is imaginative
in the highest degree, for he sees that the Spirit's freedom is entirely in its
own gift. Movingly, he cites William Morris, to him "the happiest of the
poets," as he thinks of "the Homeric contrast between Heracles passing
through the night, bow in hand, and Heracles, the freed spirit, a happy
god among the gods." The passage he quotes, in Morris's translation, is
much more Morris than Homer:

> And Heracles the mighty I saw when these went by;
> His image indeed: for himself mid the gods that never die
> Sits glad at the feast, and Hebe fair-ankled there doth hold,
> The daughter of Zeus the mighty and Hera shod with gold.

Heracles as image walks in Hades, but his true imaginative form is
among the blessed. It is a sharp descent from this to Yeats's subsequent
observation that "after its imprisonment by some event in the *Dreaming
Back,* the *Spirit* relives that event in the *Return* and turns it into knowledge,
and then falls into the *Dreaming Back* once more." The cycles of "The Mental
Traveller," which Yeats does not want to escape, are hardly presented by
Blake as being the true form of imagination, but precisely as the image of
fallen man rotating in the hell of nature. For Yeats, the freedom of the
complete Meditation is a "more happy or fortunate . . . next incarnation,"
hence the necessity of the third phase, of "what is called the *Phantasmagoria,*
which exists to exhaust, not nature, not pain and pleasure, but emotion,
and is the work of *Teaching Spirits.*" The Phantasmagoria is a parody of
poetry, even as the Return is an antithesis of poetic imagination. For the
Phantasmagoria is simply our capacity for nightmare, the Spirit's hideous
ability to see itself tortured by flames and persecuted by demons, the very
real Boschian hell of failed vision. Yeats speaks of the Phantasmagoria as
completing "not only life but imagination," a use of "completing" which
does not reveal the poet in the fullness of his freedom.

The Gnostic coloring of Yeats's Book of the Dead darkens further after
this, for the Spirit is still unsatisfied after the Phantasmagoria, and requires
the third state, the Shiftings, before it casts off moral good and moral evil
as being irrelevant to its own freedom. What is "shifted" here is simply the
whole morality of a man—"In so far as the man did good without knowing
evil, or evil without knowing good, his nature is reversed until that knowledge is obtained." This, for Yeats, is the start of "true life" or freedom,
lived in the presence of the Celestial Body. The model here is certainly the

Blake of *The Marriage of Heaven and Hell,* but the result is parody of Blake, whose rhetoric may look like this simplistic Yeatsian antinomianism, but whose dialectic in the *Marriage* exposes the inadequacy of all mere moral inversions. But Yeats sees himself as having married good and evil together, and his alternate name for the next stage, the Beatitude, is the Marriage. The Beatitude is described both as a state of unconsciousness, and as a privileged moment of consciousness, a time of complete equilibrium or wholeness, clearly akin again to the aesthetic analogue which Yeats has been picking up and dropping almost at will.

The Spirit is now prepared for its perfection, before the movement toward rebirth begins. Yeats calls this fifth and perfect stage the Purification, but his term must be understood very narrowly, for the perfection is rather narrow itself. One thinks of the line revised out of the manuscript of "Byzantium": "all my intricacies grown sweet and clear," for what the Spirit has been freed of, in this Purification, is all complexity, and not just the sensuous complexities of blood and mire. "All memory has vanished, the *Spirit* no longer knows what its name has been, it is at last free and in relation to *Spirits* free like itself." I think it important to recognize here that the aesthetic analogue has dropped out again, for while the Celestial Body now dominates, a new Husk and Passionate Body have been born. Translated, that means we are both in a supersensuous and a sensuous realm, which means that the state is now occult, opaque to the resources of Yeats's language anyway. We are being told about somehow existent beings, and not about fictive ones. As might be predicted, Yeats is forced into obscurantism, and his description of the Purification is less coherent than it seems. But it is also the only description in *A Vision* that matters nearly as much as the earlier description of Phase 15, and a commentator on *A Vision* is obliged to enter into its difficulties.

What is the Spirit's purpose, for Yeats, which is only another form of the question, what can be achieved in the world of the dead, or the space between lives? Yeats insists upon purpose here; "the *Spirit* must substitute for the *Celestial Body,* seen as a Whole, its own particular aim." The Protestant element in Yeats, which is mostly the residual Protestantism preserved in the poetic tradition of English Romanticism, is dominant here, and not his esoteric Neoplatonism, for which the seeing as a Whole of the Celestial Body would more than suffice. When the purified Spirit has substituted its own particular aim for the Celestial Body, "it becomes self-shaping, self-moving, plastic to itself, as that self has been shaped by past lives." Yeats necessarily is interested only in unique natures (like those of lyrical poets of the seventeenth phase) and a Spirit possessing such a nature cannot be reborn until the appropriately unique circumstances exist to make rebirth possible. An extraordinary notion begins to be shaped; the unique Spirit may linger in the Purification for centuries, while it attempts to complete various syntheses abandoned, perforce incomplete, in its past life. Yeats is sensible enough to insist that "only the living create," which means that the Spirit must seek out a living man to assist it in completing such syntheses, as for instance Yeats's Instructors sought him out to teach him the system "not for my sake, but their own." This casts a fine illumination upon "All Souls' Night," the celebratory verse epilogue of *A Vision,* for presumably it implicitly salutes Yeats's own Instructors, who are made free by the poet's completion of his book to leave the Purification and reach the Foreknowledge, the stage of being directly before rebirth.

Yeats has been approaching his own center of vision again, and suddenly he takes us to it. "The *Spirit's* aim, however, appears before it as a form of perfection, for during the *Purification* those forms copied in the Arts and Sciences are present as the *Celestial Body*." In one sense, this is again Yeats's recognition that only the living create, though here the recognition is disguised by its backward presentation, as we are told that the Celestial Body provides the archetype that human creativity copies. But we, and even Yeats, know these forms only through the arts and sciences, which is closer to the point of Yeats's source here, Blake's "the bright sculptures of Los's Hall." Yeats's deep concern here is with his own lifetime desires as a poet, for which he now seeks (but scarcely achieves) a definitive rationalization. The Spirits' aim is perfection, but they can find such perfection only by acting in unison with one another, an ironic reversal of Yeats's distinction between living men, where the *primary* are condemned to communal desire, and the *antithetical* to a proud solitude (the distinction defined for Yeats by the "Preface" to Shelley's "Alastor"). The form of perfection for the dead "is a shared purpose or idea." Musing on this community of Spirits, Yeats suddenly clarifies more than he might have known, or been comfortable in knowing:

> I connect them in my imagination with an early conviction of mine, that the creative power of the lyric poet depends upon his accepting some one of a few traditional attitudes, lover, sage, hero, scorner of life. They bring us back to the spiritual norm.

Shelley haunts this passage, which indeed recalls not only *The Philosophy of Shelley's Poetry,* but also the account of Shelley's self-discovery as a poet in the description of Phase 17. Yeat's vision of perfection in his death-between-lives is a transcendental version of his lifelong vision of a possible poet, of the Shelley-free-of-limitations that he himself aspired to become. The condition of freedom (as much freedom as Yeats's system could allow) is the gift of the Romantic imagination, of simplification through intensity, here and in Eternity. Necessarily Yeats invokes the Thirteenth Cone, which he expounded in Book II, but which we have refrained from examining until now, at this climax of *A Vision.* Speaking of the Spirits, in their Purification, Yeats binds together his immanent and transcendental realms, the worlds of the Faculties and of the Principles:

> They may, however, if permitted by the *Thirteenth Cone,* so act upon the events of our lives as to compel us to attend to that perfection which, though it seems theirs, is the work of our own *Daimon.*

A Vision sees its God or "the ultimate reality . . . symbolised as a phaseless sphere." This sphere is called the Thirteenth Cone, a happily Urizenic name for God. Behind this name is Yeats's complicated myth of history, a fuller account of which is best postponed to a discussion of Books IV and V. Only a few rudiments are necessary for understanding the Thirteenth Cone. Each Great Wheel of twenty-eight incarnations is also conceived as a historical cycle or gyre of some twenty-two hundred years. Twelve such gyres form a single Great Year of twenty-six thousand years, on the model of the Platonic Year (which was, however, thirty-six thousand years, as Yeats knew). But the historical geometry of *A Vision* still awaits us in later books; the immediate meaning of the thirteenth Cone, for Books II and III, is man's freedom, or all of freedom that Yeats desires, anyway. Insofar as a gyre is an individual human life, it always intersects its own double, and the point of intersection determines a corresponding and opposite point on the other gyre. This corresponding point on the other cone "is always called by my instructors the Thirteenth Cycle or *Thirteenth Cone.*" Yeats is always difficult when he speaks of deliverance, and we need to attend him closely:

> It is that cycle which may deliver us from the twelve cycles of time and space. The cone which intersects ours is a cone in so far as we think of it as the antithesis to our thesis, but if the time has come for our deliverance it is the phaseless sphere, sometimes called the Thirteenth Sphere, for every lesser cycle contains within itself a sphere that is, as it were, the reflection or messenger of the final deliverance. Within it live all souls that have been set free and every *Daimon* and *Ghostly Self;* our expanding cone seems to cut through its gyre; spiritual influx is from its circumference, animate life from its centre.

The Ghostly Self Yeats had defined earlier as the *daimon* "when it inhabits the sphere," that is, the *daimon* withdrawn by the Thirteenth Sphere to itself. Critics have described the Thirteenth Cone as the re-entry of God into Yeats's system, but that hardly helps in defining it. Yeats ends the passage above with an illuminating reference to Shelley, while the use he makes of circumference and center is very close to Blake's in *Jerusalem*. For Blake and Shelley freedom lay not in the will, but in the imagination which struggled with the will. In Blake, the Yeatsian will is the Spectre of Urthona, who struggles with Los the creative mind; in Shelley, the will is Prometheus still trapped by hatred for Jupiter, who is will incarnate, and in Shelley we are doomed to become whatever we are unwise enough to hate. For Yeats, freedom is neither in the will nor in the imagination, but only in the inexplicable intervention of miracle, the Thirteenth Cone. Though there is genuine incoherence in this intervention, Yeats saves himself from the full consequences of that incoherence by his customarily subtle vacillation, which is his form of the Byronic "mobility," or his own version of a kind of *sprezzatura*. Only the Thirteenth Cone delivers us from the cycles of time and space, but Yeats is a half-hearted Gnostic, and rather wary of such deliverance. He triumphs over his own system by not always wanting to be one of those "souls that have been set free." Like his own Spenser, he loves the journey, and not the destination.

We left the death-between-lives at the close of the fifth stage, or Purification, where Yeats tell us that the Thirteenth Cone, our freedom, may permit the purified Spirits to so act upon us that we are compelled to become poets, "to attend to that perfection which, though it seems theirs, is the work of our own Daimon." Here the Spirits become, not quite a composite Muse, but a complete Mnemosyne, or mother of the Muses. But we are not to assume their benevolence, which is part of the point of the sixth stage or poise before rebirth, called the Foreknowledge. The Spirit (presumably most, or almost all Spirits) must be reborn, but not until the state of Foreknowledge substitutes for the perfection of the community of Spirits the next incarnation, which must be completely known as a vision, and be accepted by the individual Spirit. The next incarnation, for Yeats, is very arbitrary, and has nothing to do with our previous performances, being merely decreed by fate. And the Spirits, here also, are liable to make themselves of no reputation, but are "frustrators," like the beings who keep scrambling the airwaves between Yeats and his Instructors. Indeed, they operate as a kind of group superego; they play a part, Yeats says, "resembling that of the 'censor' in modern psychology." In the Foreknowledge, the only power the Spirit has is to delay indefinitely its own rebirth. Yet, if the

Thirteenth Cone chooses to help (we are not told why it should), the Spirit "can so shape circumstances as to make possible the rebirth of a unique nature," like presumably another lyrical poet of the seventeenth phase. That completes the technical account of the death-between-lives in Yeats, and if he had left it there, it would be rather too much less than would suffice. Fortunately, he makes something of an imaginative recovery in the remaining sections (X through XII) of Book III.

The last sentence describing the Foreknowledge reminds us that the Book is called "The Soul in Judgment": "During its sleep in the womb the Spirit accepts its future life, declares it just." "Just" in what sense? And how does Yeats mean us to interpret his use of "expiation"?

> The more complete the expiation, or the less the need for it, the
> more fortunate the succeeding life. The more fully a life is lived,
> the less the need for—or the more complete is—the expiation.

This is very Emersonian, and very effective, and clearly Yeats is persuasively re-defining "expiation," which appears to mean something like "using up the entire human potential, including all the capacity for significant emotion." If this is so, then the Spirit, declaring its future life to be "just," declares it to be more aesthetically complete, fuller, than the lives it lived before. Similarly Yeats himself, introducing *A Vision,* when he says of his gyres that "they have helped me to hold in a single thought reality and justice," means an aesthetically gratifying wholeness by "justice." Yeats found something of this "justice" in Lawrence's *The Rainbow* and *Women in Love,* novels he pioneered in admiring greatly. "Justice" is a grim quality in "The Mental Traveller" also, and I suspect Yeats admired that poem so intensely because, like Lawrence in his best novels, it seems to bring its persons together again and again until all possible passionate relations are exhausted. In Yeats the supernaturalist (the Lawrence of the tales is a supernaturalist also) the possibility of passionate relations is expanded to include the *daimon,* and Romantic love is even explained as "expiation for the *Daimon,* for passionate love is from the *Daimon* which seeks by union with some other *Daimon* to reconstruct above the antinomies its own true nature." On this account, all love must fail, and Yeats's own frustration in loving Maud Gonne is ascribed to a supernatural necessity. Little wonder that Yeats adds, with a finely savage urbanity: "We get happiness, my instructors say, from those we have served, ecstasy from those we have wronged."

In this dubious ecstasy, founded upon victimage, the obscure final section of "The Soul in Judgment" finds its subject. Section XII expounds two relationships, called Victimage for the Dead and Victimage for the

Ghostly Self or for the *daimon* absorbed into the purified Spirits. *"Victimage for the Dead* arises through such act as prevents the union of two incarnate *daimons* and is therefore the prevention or refusal of a particular experience, but *Victimage* for a *Spirit of the Thirteenth Cone* results from the prevention or refusal of experience itself." "Victimage" here means the opposite of the "justice" that is completion; to be victimized is to be denied the fullness of possible experience. Most simply, Victimage for the Dead is what Blake attacked in the "Proverbs of Hell" in his *The Marriage of Heaven and Hell.* To nurse an unacted desire is to murder an infant joy in its cradle, and victimizes the dead, in the ironic sense of the self-victimization of the dead-in-life. But the deeper Victimage, for the Spirit of the Thirteenth Cone, or the Divine Freedom, is a greater perversity of the spirit, and comes from Yeats's vision of death-in-life as the ultimate enemy of the imagination. Yeats comes closest to Blake and Shelley here, but is prevented from identifying with them by his perfectly sincere Gnosticism.

When the Spirit of the Thirteenth Cone is starved, it revenges itself upon refused experience, and tortures the unwilling dross of nature by inflicting upon nature a frustrate spiritually, which in turn produces only a greater asceticism or refusal of experience. This hideous cycle Yeats calls Victimage for the Ghostly Self, and says of it that it is "the sole means for acquiring a supernatural guide," which illuminates a dark aspect of "Byzantium," and perhaps several other major lyrics as well. Yeats's particular interest is reserved for a harsher state: "Sometimes, however, *Victimage for the Ghostly Self* and *Victimage for the Dead* coincide and produce lives tortured throughout by spirituality and passion." A life so tortured, never to break into fulfillment, is a life of cruelty and ignorance (cruelty to the self, ignorance toward others), and though Yeats says that such a life is evil, it is for him a kind of necessary evil, for it alone "makes possible the conscious union of the *Daimons* of Man and Woman or that of the *Daimon* of the Living and a *Spirit of the Thirteenth Cone*, which is the deliverance from birth and death."

It is not without considerable revulsion, or at least skepticism, that most readers (I trust, perhaps naively) could entertain such doctrine, for Yeats is not persuasively redefining cruelty and ignorance. He means cruelty and ignorance, in the contexts of spirituality and passion. As to passion, it is difficult to argue with any strong poet's dialectic of Romantic love, however savagely presented, and Yeats meets any protest in the matter of spirituality by coldly remarking: "All imaginable relations may arise between a man and his God." With that warning, Yeats is ready to pass from the dead to history, for his vision of history is his central relation to his God, a Gnostic "composite God" of process and entropy, whose cruelty answers our ignorance.

"The Great Year of the Ancients," Book IV of *A Vision*, has no admirers, while Book V, "Dove or Swan," rightly does. "Dove or Swan" is the only part of *A Vision* that can be judged an aesthetic achievement in its own right, though it is not as beautiful as *Per Amica Silentia Lunae.* "The Great Year of the Ancients" is a ramble but a ramble around two ideas Yeats could neither clarify nor discard, though their value to him in organizing poems and plays was always partly vitiated by their essential incoherence. The Great Year is, for Yeats, the promise of Eternal Recurrence, and the dialectic between *antithetical* and *primary* (Caesar and Christ, in Book IV, as derived from Mommsen) the promise of return to a world-order closer to his heart's desires. Blake made his myth of the Seven Eyes of God (characteristically drawing upon Scripture, and not an occult source) for reasons Yeats insisted upon misunderstanding. "The Mental Traveller," and other cyclic poems down to (but not including) *The Four Zoas* were intended by Blake not as promise or comfort but as moral prophecy in the Hebraic tradition, as terrible depictions of what was and what would be unless men awoke to their own humanity. For Blake the Great Year of the Ancients, like every other vision of mere recurrence, was a dehumanizing idea, and a reading of Book IV of *A Vision* necessarily shows Blake to have been correct. Nietzsche is a formidable antagonist for Blake when he insists upon the heroism necessary to endure the idea of Eternal Recurrence, but Yeats is manifestly less formidable when he adopts the Nietzschean principle that there is no redemption from recurrence. Section XVII of Book IV is the paradigm of the whole, and will stand for it here. Yeats awaits the *antithetical* intellectual influx:

> At the birth of Christ religious life becomes *primary,* secular life *antithetical*—man gives to Caesar the things that are Caesar's. A *primary* dispensation looking beyond itself toward a transcendant power is dogmatic, levelling, unifying, feminine, humane, peace its means and end; an *antithetical* dispensation obeys imminent power, is expressive, hierarchical, multiple, masculine, harsh, surgical.

This is a contrast, despite its masking terms, between death-in-life and vitality, a Romantic dialectic irrelevantly transferred to an alien context. The contrast, as Yvor Winters insisted, is of no value in itself; one can go further, and ask if the contrast, so applied, is not a barrier even to aesthetic values? To Yeats, it was a value because it became a condition for his creative freedom; thus, the passage just quoted precedes a citation of the Sphinx, the "gaze blank and pitiless as the sun," of "The Second Coming," here called by Yeats the actual intervention of the *"Thirteenth Cone*, the sphere, the unique." Whenever Yeats anticipated the approaching influx, he anticipated also his own creative maturation. The only importance Book IV of *A Vision* has for the student of Yeats is just this; we must see that our horror is his ecstasy, his as poet even if not as man.

When the student of Yeats passes on to Book V of *A Vision*, "Dove or Swan," he can be grateful that the poet has taken over completely from his astral Instructors. The defences of *A Vision* by such Yeats scholars as Whitaker and Vendler are convincing when "Dove or Swan" is in question. Like *Per Amica Silentia Lunae*, "Dove or Swan" is a superb and controlled marmoreal reverie, worthy of Sir Thomas Browne or of Pater (who suggested to Yeats more than its mood). The central belief of "Dove or Swan" is well summarized by Whitaker: "the acceptance of history is at one with freedom and creativity." Though Whitaker denies that "Dove or Swan" is deterministic, since it leaves to the contemplative poet the inner freedom of his reverie, a more objective reading of the book makes clear that Yeats is involved in self-contradiction. This is certainly no more damaging than self-contradiction is to many prose-poems. We have to judge "Dove or Swan" not by its coherence and insight as serious philosophy of history (as such, it is merely maddening) but as a reverie upon such a philosophy, a reverie beautifully proportioned and eloquently adjusted to many of our deepest imaginative needs. Where the first four books of *A Vision* fail such judgment, "Dove or Swan" triumphs, and provides the entire work with as much of a purely aesthetic justification as it can be said to have.

"Dove or Swan" is flanked by two lyrics, "Leda and the Swan" and "All Souls' Night," which define between them the extraordinary range of the book, from the rape of Leda to the poet Yeats drinking wine at midnight, at Oxford in the autumn of 1920. The Christian Era is approaching its end, sinking into rigid age and the final loss of control over its own thought:

> A civilisation is a struggle to keep self-control, and in this it is like some great tragic person, some Niobe who must display an almost superhuman will or the cry will not touch our sympathy. The loss of control over thought comes towards the end; first a sinking in upon the moral being, then the last surrender, the irrational cry, revelation—the scream of Juno's peacock.

Yeats grants Christian civilization the opportunity to expire in tragic dignity, but has no doubt that it must soon expire. He proceeds to trace three great wheels of time—2000 B.C. to A.D. 1, A.D. 1 to A.D. 1050, and

A.D. 1050 to the present day, or 1925. The first, or cycle of classical, *antithetical* civilization, reaches Phase 12 of the Great Wheel in the sixth century B.C., attaining personality but as yet no intellectual solitude, which for Yeats is the prime condition if lyric poetry is to be possible. Still a good Pre-Raphaelite, Yeats locates a Pre-Phidian stage (Phidias = Raphael) of art, a first discovery of solitude (Phases 13 and 14) "with a natural unsystematised beauty like that before Raphael." This art Yeats compares with Greek philosophy before Anaxagoras, and with the lost dramatists who wrote before Aeschylus and Sophocles, "both Phidian men." The age after Phidias is the art of Phases 16, 17 and 18, the art clustered round Unity of Being. Yeats recognizes three historical manifestations of Phase 15—Phidias, the artists of the reign of Justinian, Raphael. The phases just after, in each case, are those of the poets who meant most to Yeats, himself included. Partly, Yeats is exalting the Romantic art to which he adheres, but partly he is engaged in a much more valid and interesting activity, which is explaining Romanticism's conception of itself as renaissance not only of the Renaissance, but also of the two great periods earlier of which the Italian Renaissance was itself a renaissance, Periclean Athens, and Byzantium under Justinian.

It is in this explanation that "Dove or Swan" joins a vital tradition, and perhaps serves as its culmination. Yeats follows Pater in his Romantic versions of the Renaissance and of Athens, and derives his Byzantium from the French and English revival of interest, in the 1880's and later. Yeats's Byzantium, as Gordon and Fletcher have shown, is very close to Oscar Wilde's remarks on Byzantine art in "The Decay of Lying." Wilde read the essay aloud to Yeats on Christmas Day 1888, with lasting effect upon Yeats, subtly analyzed by Ellmann in his *Eminent Domain.* Wilde, rather than Pater (from whom, however, in this as in every other respect, Wilde derived) is the immediate source for the distinction between Caesar and Christ, upon which much of *A Vision* is founded. Condemning "our own imitative spirit," Wilde praised "Orientalism, with its frank rejection of imitation, its love of artistic convention, its dislike to the actual representation of any object in nature." This is of course Romantic Orientalism, and the Byzantium of Wilde and Yeats is in some ways closer to the moonlit world of the *Arabian Nights* than to mere history.

There are, for Yeats, as for Pater and Wilde, three full moons in the history of the arts. Yeats has the confidence to fix their dates, and the dialectical cunning to remind us that these eras of Phase 15 are also times of Phase 8 or 22 in larger cycles, and so times of trouble as well as of achievement. Or rather, to come closer to Yeats, the achievement is a resolution of the struggle of opposites that makes for the trouble:

Each age unwinds the thread another age had wound, and it
amuses one to remember that before Phidias, and his westward-
moving art, Persia fell, and that when full moon came round
again, amid eastward-moving thought, and brought Byzantine
glory, Rome fell; and that at the outset of our westward-moving
Renaissance Byzantium fell; all things dying each other's life,
living each other's death.

The age of Phidias is for Yeats a relatively cold splendor. With the
Incarnation, an extraordinary intensity enters into "Dove or Swan," particularly in one Paterian passage ambiguous and eloquent enough to have
achieved an independent fame, justly due its high purple:

We say of Him because His sacrifice was voluntary that He was
love itself, and yet that part of Him which made Christendom
was not love but pity, and not pity for intellectual despair, though
the man in Him, being *antithetical* like His age, knew it in the
Garden, but *primary* pity, that for the common lot, man's death,
seeing that He raised Lazarus, sickness, seeing that He healed
many, sin, seeing that He died.

The tone of this passage is perhaps too complex for mere analysis, the
complexity being due to Yeats's vacillation, which here approaches oscillation, between belief and unbelief. There is a similar puzzle in Pater's
attitude toward Christianity as a supreme example of "the religious sentiment," in the concluding pages of *Marius the Eipcurean,* a book Yeats had
absorbed with rare completeness. Read closely, the passage is in the tradition
of Blake's rejection of "pity" and Shelley's of "remorse," and appears to
question the spiritual value of the Incarnation for the imaginative or *antithetical* man. Like Blake and Shelley, Yeats finds more in Christ than "that
part of Him which made Christendom." As a polytheist, Yeats does find in
Christ "love itself," but also a human *antithetical* imagination, the poetic
mind of Phase 22, the phase evidently of the man Jesus, and of Flaubert,
of Herbert Spencer and of Marx, of Swedenborg and of Dostoevsky (and of
Darwin!), an astonishing company, selected with fine willfulness, and erratic
but genuine insight. The man of Phase 22, whose Will is balanced between
ambition and contemplation, may

become a destroyer and persecutor, a figure of tumult and of
violence; or as is more probable—for the violence of such a man
must be checked by moments of resignation or despair, premo-

nitions of balance—his system will become an instrument of destruction and of persecution in the hands of others.

Like Blake and Shelley, Yeats sets himself against the "system" of Christendom, while positing a Jesus more imaginative than Christendom worships. And he sets himself also against Christian love, too near allied to pity and too dangerously akin to remorse, for pity and remorse deaden the visionary imagination. This is perhaps the deepest lesson Yeats had learned from Blake and from Shelley, that creativity and love for a poet of the phases just past the full moon, poets who quested for apocalyptic Unity of Being, could come only through a difficult process of self-remaking, in which some of the prime apparent virtues of Christian tradition had to be redefined or even repudiated. The dance of opposites, which Yeats took too literally, is a metaphor of that remaking, and not the process itself. In one of his most remarkable self-revelations, Yeats converts his literalism of the imagination into another valuable insight, defining the difference between Christian love and his own:

> Love is created and preserved by intellectual analysis, for we love only that which is unique, and it belongs to contemplation, not to action, for we would not change that which we love. A lover will admit a greater beauty than that of his mistress but not its like, and surrenders his days to a delighted laborious study of all her ways and looks, and he pities only if something threatens that which has never been before and can never be again. Fragment delights in fragment and seeks possession, not service; whereas the Good Samaritan discovers himself in the likeness of another, covered with sores and abandoned by thieves upon the roadside, and in that other serves himself. The opposites are gone; he does not need his Lazarus; they do not each die the other's life, live the other's death.

Though this is marred by its formulaic ending (which must weary in time, surely, even the most devoted Yeatsians) it has in abundance the beauty of surprise. For Yeats's love is a cold passion, fostered by analysis. We love, he speculates, because our intellect tells us we have come upon uniqueness. This is hardly Romantic love, which knows that all things need to be made new before the imagination can marry what it has made. In Yeats's terms, Romantic love belongs to action, for Yeatsian love desires a stasis of the object of desire. Yeats is being true to his pervasive vision, for his love is Gnostic, fragment possessing fragment in desperate pursuit of the whole. The true center of Yeats's view is that this love is involuntary, though made by analysis, for analysis converts the lover's sense of the uniqueness of the mistress into love, but cannot make that sense. By the dialectics of *A Vision* the sacrifice of the seventeenth phase is involuntary, but that of the twenty-second voluntary. Yeats is fated not to be a Christian.

Once past his account of the beginnings of Christendom, Yeats is not stirred again, all through the decline of Rome, until the rise of Byzantium. By postulating a historically idealized version of his City of Art, Yeats follows the lead of Shelley in *Hellas* rather than Blake in *Jerusalem*. Blake's Golgonooza, like Spenser's Cleopolis, is a vision of what might be, not of what was. Shelley, in singing of an idealized Greece, was still skeptical enough not to commit himself to historical detail:

> Temples and towers,
> Citadels and marts, and they
> Who live and die there, have been ours,
> And may be thine, and must decay;
> But Greece and her foundations are
> Built below the tide of war,
> Based on the crystalline sea
> Of thought and its eternity;
> Her citizens, imperial spirits,
> Rule the present from the past,
> On all this world of men inherits
> Their seal is set.

Yeats's Byzantium is both built below, and yet swept by, the tide of war. The city begins to interest Yeats "the moment when Byzantium became Byzantine and substituted for formal Roman magnificence, with its glorification of physical power, an architecture that suggests the Sacred City in the Apocalypse of St. John." In the vision Yeats now allows himself, a historical city existed where belief flowered supernaturally into art, the art of "some philosophical worker in mosaic" showing forth divinity "as a lovely flexible presence like that of a perfect human body." Whitaker finds a qualification here and throughout Yeats's description of Byzantium, but such qualification is not evident to me. Certainly Yeats is not simple in his historical mythicizings, but if ever he wrote without ironical intent, it was certainly here:

> I think that in early Byzantium, maybe never before or since in
> recorded history, religious, aesthetic and practical life were one,

that architect and artificers—though not, it may be, poets, for language had been the instrument of controversy and must have grown abstract—spoke to the multitude and the few alike. The painter, the mosaic worker, the worker in gold and silver, the illuminator of sacred books, were almost impersonal, almost perhaps without the consciousness of individual design, absorbed in their subject-matter and that the vision of a whole people.

The admission as to poets is not so much an ironic qualification as it is an anxiety-reaction, since the historical evidence baffles Yeats. The Renaissance was hardly free of theological controversy, yet its languages did not grow abstract to inhibit its poets. Unable to find the great poetic period at this full moon, Yeats contents himself with the fulfillment of his communal ideal through the visual arts. If the entire passage be transposed into a description of an idealized poetry, we can see what Yeats hoped for in his own work. The poet speaks to multitude and esoteric group alike, and with an almost impersonal voice. It is difficult to see this fulfilled in any actual poet, Dante for instance is hardly without consciousness of individual design, but Yeats's dream is a moving one nevertheless.

As waking dream or Paterian reverie Yeats's description of Byzantium is most effective, but that it is conscious reverie need not render it ironical. Not Byzantium itself is being described, but the vison of a City of Art that runs through English Romantic tradition, from Blake and Shelley through the late phase of which Yeats is the culmination, the movement of Ruskin, Morris, and the Pre-Raphaelites. Because of the fame of the two "Byzantium" poems, Yeats critics have made more of Byzantium than Yeats himself did. The later Yeats tended to find only two full moons in the history of civilization, Greece and the Renaissance, and placed more stress upon Greece.

From Byzantium to the Renaissance is, for Yeats, a story of cultural decline, one that is a little surprising for the heir of the Pre-Raphaelites and their medieval Romanticism. But Yeats's Romanticism is not of the Gothicizing variety; he is the involuntary heir of Wordsworth in his longing for creative solitude, and he associates poetic solitude with the breaking-up of religious syntheses. The longing "for a solitary human body" as an erotic ideal becomes fused, for Yeats, with "something we may call intellectual beauty or compare perhaps to that kind of bodily beauty which Castiglione called 'the spoil or monument of the victory of the soul.' " This is hardly Shelley's "intellectual beauty," which was to be apprehended just beyond the range of the senses, but is a direct sensuous ideal: "Intellect and emotion, primary curiosity and the *antithetical* dream, are for the moment one." This might be Pater on the Renaissance, the difference being not in any Yeatsian irony of apprehension, since an *antithetical* dream is a self-conscious one, but in the more direct assertion of Unity of Being that Yeats allows himself.

When the perfection of Phase 15 is past, Renaissance art loses its disinterestedness in "a sudden rush and storm." Power is purchased at the cost of knowledge, and "the Soul's unity has been found and lost." With this dispersal, Yeats begins an account of English poetic history that constitutes the last movement of "Dove or Swan." The history, from Shakespeare to the Generation of 1914, is one of decline, but of a dialectical kind, as befits Yeats's system. Where no negative criticism entered Yeats's remarks on Dante, the description of Shakespeare is refreshingly equivocal:

> I see in Shakespeare a man in whom human personality, hitherto restrained by its dependence upon Christendom or by its own need for self-control, burst like a shell. Perhaps secular intellect, setting itself free after five hundred years of struggle, has made him the greatest of dramatists, and yet because an *antithetical* age alone could confer upon an art like his the unity of a painting or of a temple pediment, we might, had the total works of Sophocles survived—they too born of a like struggle though with a different enemy—not think him greatest. Do we not feel an unrest like that of travel itself when we watch those personages, more living than ourselves, amid so much that is irrelevant and heterogeneous, amid so much *primary* curiosity, when we are carried from Rome to Venice, from Egypt to Saxon England, or in the one play from Roman to Christian mythology?

Shakespeare's age is Phase 16, but he lives out of phase, being a man of Phase 20. Because he was out of phase, according to Yeats, Shakespeare became a dramatist rather than a lyric poet or man of action "drunk with his own wine." The great tragedies show Yeats not Unity of Being, but rather "a crowd of men and women who are still shaken by thought that passes from man to man in psychological contagion." Yet these personages, Yeats quietly concedes, are "more living than ourselves." Shakespeare's art caused always a feeling of unrest in Yeats, as indeed it had to, the feeling helping to save Yeats from writing a kind of drama in which he must have failed. For Yeats was too genuinely apocalyptic to live easily with any conceptions of tragedy that the Renaissance had developed; a difficulty that needs to be met when discussing Yeats's later plays.

After Shakespeare, the major English poets do not baffle Yeats's categories so badly, the sad result being that his remarks on them in "Dove or Swan" are less interesting. Milton, for the Romantics the poetic father who had to be overcome, is for Yeats only an attempted return, made too late, to the outworn synthesis of the Sistine Chapel. Milton's fault, we are told, is in his negative attitude toward classical mythology, and he is dismissed for "his unreality and his cold rhetoric." The mystery of Poetic Influence remains, for Yeats is to Blake and Shelley what they are to Milton, a son who makes himself strong by creatively misinterpreting the father. In Milton, Yeats acknowledges "the music and magnificence of the still violent gyre," which is more than J. B. Yeats would recognize. Like his corporeal father, the poet Yeats felt that Milton had entertained too many opinions, a curious prejudice on the part of two of the most opinionated of men.

The world of Cowley and Dryden is, for Yeats, one in which "belief dies out." A weary world "begins to long for the arbitrary and accidental, for the grotesque, the repulsive and the terrible, that it may be cured of desire." The accent is that of Pater describing Rome in its Decadence; for Yeats this later decadence goes from 1650 to 1875, Phases 19, 20, and 21 of an ebbing gyre. In this Yeats sees three epicycles—Augustan and the Age of Sensibility, Romantic, post-Romantic. For the first, at this point in his life, Yeats has little regard: "It is external, sentimental and logical—the poetry of Pope and Gray, the philosophy of Johnson and of Rousseau— equally simple in emotion or in thought, the old oscillation in a new form." The oscillation between *The Dunciad* and *The Bard,* and between the wisdom of Johnson and of Rousseau, has rarely been so undervalued or so misunderstood. A wonderful critical recovery is made when Yeats describes the onset of Romanticism (without using that term). In Yeats's theory, Romanticism is only a foreshadowing of the revelation that is soon to come, but only through reading this shadow can knowledge be found:

> In frail women's faces the soul awakes—all its prepossessions,
> the accumulated learning of centuries swept away—and looks out
> upon us wise and foolish like the dawn. Then it is every-
> where. . . . In poetry alone it finds its full expression, for it is
> a quality of the emotional nature (*Celestial Body* acting through
> *Mask*); and creates all that is most beautiful in modern English
> poetry from Blake to Arnold, all that is not a fading echo.

Yeats sees his own role as carrying expression of "the new emotion" over into an overt *antithetical* wisdom, of which Blake, "Coventry Patmore at moments," and above all the Nietzsche of Eternal Recurrence were the forerunners. This role is uniquely reserved for him in the period from 1875 to 1927, for reasons that the later version of *A Vision* cannot explain, because it excludes the last few pages of "Dove or Swan." In the first published *Vision* of 1925, Yeats examines his literary contemporaries in those pages. In 1925 we are at Phase 23, "the first where there is hatred of the abstract, where the intellect turns upon itself." Brooding on the art of Pound, Eliot, Joyce, Pirandello, Yeats does not find any mastery of *antithetical* wisdom but only a "technical inspiration" that wholly separates "myth—the *Mask*"— from fact. That was never his way, he implicitly insists, and he shows more sympathy for the mystical communalism of Peguy and Claudel, little as he resembles them in aspiration. Looking ahead to the waning phases of our gyre, Yeats utters the only one of his prophecies that chills me, for its insights are convincing and ominous:

> I foresee a time when the majority of men will so accept an historical tradition that they will quarrel, not as to who can impose his personality upon others but as to who can best embody the common aim, when all personality will seem an impurity— "sentimentality," "sullenness," "egotism,"—something that revolts not morals alone but good taste. There will be no longer great intellect for a ceaseless activity will be required of all; and where rights are swallowed up in duties, and solitude is difficult, creation except among avowedly archaistic and unpopular groups will grow impossible.

This is a Romantic vision of the death of desire, an extension of the implicit darker prophecies of Shelley's "The Defence of Poetry." Mankind moves toward a democratic and *primary* Decadence, unfavorably contrasted to the Decadence of the ancient world and his own day traced by Pater. The new influx of irrational force will awake into life not the apocalyptic forms dreamed by the prophets—Milton's and Blake's Human Form Divine, Nietzsche's superman, Patmore's New Catholic—"but organic groups, *covens* of physical or intellectual kin melted out of the frozen mass." In this coming horror Yeats looks for salvation to a small band of imaginative men, like himself, who will develop "a form of philosophy" like that roughed out in *A Vision*. This philosophy "will call that good which a man can contemplate himself as doing always and no other doing at all." This is too curious an ethic to bear commentary, and as always there are two rival strands in Yeats's apocalyptic anyway, one which would best suit a kind of amalgam of Carlyle and a Rosicrucian, or the later Lawrence, and a rather different one that is pure Blake and Shelley. The latter one is allowed a luminous but momentary expression when Yeats says: "Men will no longer separate the idea of God from that of human genius, human productivity in all its forms," but the

Fascist-Gnostic amalgam dominates the conclusion of the original "Dove or Swan." Thus we are told that men of learning, wealth, and rank "will be given power, less because of that they promise than of that they seem and are." But even these Elect "once formed must obey irrational force," yield themselves to "fanaticism and a terror" and, best of all, "oppress the ignorant—even the innocent—as Christianity oppressed the wise."

It is a relief then to return to the revised *Vision* to read the mellower conclusion that Yeats composed during 1934–36, where we find the aged poet sitting in his chair turning a symbol and not a civilization over in his mind. "Dove or Swan" is a majestic reverie, but more than a disconcerting one, for the *daimons* sometimes show greater exuberance in it than Yeats does. But in "The End of the Cycle" we hear a personality meditating, as we did in *Per Amica Silentia Lunae,* and this personality is rich and somber enough to doubt all speculation, its own included. The Thirteenth Cone or God is in every man and is his freedom, and it keeps the secret of futurity, as its ancestor Demogorgon did: "The deep truth is imageless." So self-admonished, the Blakean and Shelleyan imagination asserts itself in Yeats and ends *A Vision* with the greatest and most humanistic of his insights, more definitively expressed for being an open question addressed to the poet's own vacillation:

> Shall we follow the image of Heracles that walks through the darkness bow in hand, or mount to that other Heracles, man, not image, he that has for his bride Hebe, "the daughter of Zeus, the mighty, and Hera, shod with gold"?

"Man, not image" is a Blakean and Shelleyan motto, but hardly an inscription on the gate into Byzantium.

DENIS DONOGHUE

Yeats's Theater

Yeats registered the tension between history and symbol in theatrical terms, mainly because he conceived of action as resolving the antinomies of consciousness and experience. He was fond of quoting Goethe's saying that we never learn to know ourselves by thought, but by action. Thought is inclined to dispose its findings in some form of dualism, but action is unitary. In 1904 Yeats wrote:

> There are two kinds of poetry, and they are commingled in all the greatest works. When the tide of life sinks low there are pictures, as in the 'Ode on a Grecian Urn' and in Virgil at the plucking of the Golden Bough. The pictures make us sorrowful. We share the poet's separation from what he describes. It is life in the mirror, and our desire for it is as the desire of the lost souls for God; but when Lucifer stands among his friends, when Villon sings his dead ladies to so gallant a rhythm, when Timon makes his epitaph, we feel no sorrow, for life herself has made one of her eternal gestures, has called up into our hearts her energy that is eternal delight.
>
> (*Explorations*)

The quotation from Blake is typical of Yeats at this period: in these essays, later collected as *The Irish Dramatic Movement*, he calls upon Ireland to live and act as if under Blake's sign. "In Ireland," he goes on, "where the tide of life is rising, we turn, not to picture-making, but to the imagination of

---

From *William Butler Yeats*. © 1971 by Denis Donoghue. The Viking Press, 1971. Originally entitled "His Theatre."

personality—to drama, gesture." The tone is hectic. Yeats is determined
that the political vacuum caused by the fall of Parnell will be filled by
national feeling; literature and drama are the chosen means. He was excited
by the opening of the Abbey Theatre, which he helped to found as the focus
of an entire country, climax of a national drama. His early essays, and
especially those which he published in *Samhain* from 1901, were attempts
to provide Ireland with an artistic conscience; something to live up to, as
in the early years of the Abbey, and something to be rebuked by, when the
Abbey went its disappointing way. Even under Yeats's leadership the Abbey
showed many bad plays; nevertheless he thought that the theater would
bring national life to consciousness: he supposed that the Abbey would go
its own vulgar way eventually, and he was dispirited when it did.

In "William Blake and the Imagination" Yeats distinguished between
reason and imagination in much the same spirit as his distinction between
picture and drama:

> The reason, and by the reason he [Blake] meant deductions from
> the observations of the senses, binds us to mortality because it
> binds us to the senses, and divides us from each other by showing
> us our clashing interests; but imagination divides us from mor-
> tality by the immortality of beauty, and binds us to each other
> by opening the secret doors of all hearts. . . . Passions, because
> most living, are most holy . . . and man shall enter eternity
> borne upon their wings.
>
> *(Essays and Introductions)*

Yeats is paraphrasing Blake, and the language is not entirely convincing,
the wish is father to the style; but its bearing is clear. He is calling Ireland
to order, that is, to energy. She is to play a role comparable to the poet's.
"Somebody has said that all sound philosophy is but biography," he wrote,
"and what I myself did, getting into an original relation to Irish life, creating
in myself a new character, a new pose—in the French sense of the word—
the literary mind of Ireland must do as a whole, always understanding that
the result must be no bundle of formulas, not faggots but a fire." Marshall
McLuhan has pointed out, following Yeats, that passionate life does not
produce subtle characters: Heathcliff is less complex than Edgar Linton.
Passion obliterates difference. Yeats's relation to passion is a variant of his
relation to simplicity and power, hence to the simplicity of fire. The unpopular theater that he sought, when the Abbey had made itself falsely
popular, was to be a place of passion and imagination. It would have an
audience, fit though few, "like a secret society," admission "by favour." It

might be in London rather than in Dublin; it might be anywhere. Lady
Cunard's drawing room in Cavendish Square would suit, and might be turned
to the secret purpose of ritual for an evening or two. Drama might be an
extension of the séance. It is hard to imagine a Blake among the audience,
incidentally; Yeats's later theater resuscitates the idiom of Mallarmé, with
qualifying intonations from Nietzsche and from the Noh drama. Mallarmé
had already provided an aesthetic for the unpopular theater:

> I believe that Literature, recovered from its source, which is Art
> and Science, will provide us with a Theater whose performances
> will be the true modern form of worship: a Book, an explanation
> of man, sufficient for our finest dreams. I believe that all of this
> is written in nature in such a way that only those are permitted
> to close their eyes to it who are interested in seeing nothing.
> This work exists: everyone has attempted it, unwittingly. There
> is no one, genius or clown, who has not unwittingly come upon
> a trace of it. To reveal it, to raise a corner of the veil of what
> such a poem can be, is in my isolation at once pleasure and
> torture.

It is often said that the Noh drama was a revelation to Yeats and that
it changed his theater into something rich, strange, and Oriental. But the
sense of life and the sense of drama which those plays stimulated were already
active in him, waiting to find an appropriate form. He always despised the
bourgeois theater as he despised everything from that source; he spoke of
"the succession of nervous tremors which the plays of commerce, like the
novels of commerce, have substituted for the purification that comes with
pity and terror to the imagination and intellect." He quotes "solider Aristotle" here rather than, say, William Archer, but Mallarmé is closer to
his interests than either. When he came upon the few Noh plays he was
ever to meet, issuing from the diverse hands of Ernest Fenollosa, Tokuboku
Hirata, and Ezra Pound, he received them in Mallarmé's spirit. "I have
invented a form of drama," he wrote in "Certain Noble Plays of Japan,"
"distinguished, indirect, and symbolic, and having no need of mob or Press
to pay its way—an aristocratic form." The mask and headdress to be worn
"by the player who will speak the part of Cuchulain" in At the Hawk's Well
"will appear perhaps like an image seen in reverie by some Orphic wor-
shipper." "I hope to have attained," he says, "the distance from life which
can make credible strange events, elaborate words." Masks would guard the
play against theater business, nervous tremors, vulgarity of movement. Michio Ito, the Japanese dancer who inspired Yeats to this exaltation, held life

beautifully at a distance, receding "into some more powerful life" than the pushing world. "The arts which interest me," Yeats wrote, "while seeming to separate from the world and us a group of figures, images, symbols, enable us to pass for a few moments into a deep of the mind that had hitherto been too subtle for our habitation." The imaginative power of the Japanese plays made each play an image, a concentration of dramatic energy: the play in performance became a symbol, and was revered for doing so. As for the first Japanese audiences, "I know that some among them would have understood the prose of Pater, the painting of Puvis de Chavannes, the poetry of Mallarmé and Verlaine."

The Symbolist theory of drama, such as it was, would have served Yeats's purpose admirably, save that he had already become an equivocal Symbolist, if not a lapsed member of the faith, and that he had to accommodate the theory to his "tragic sense of life." Implicit in his commitment to subjectivity and the antithetical life was the need to present the modern predicament as tragic: "We begin to live when we have conceived life as tragedy." His idiom of drama, gesture, intensity, tragedy, and so forth could not well be fulfilled in Mallarmé's *culte* or even, strictly speaking, in the Noh plays, since the tragic situation is transcended rather than resolved there. Nietzsche provided the most powerful aesthetic of tragedy, consistent with the burden of Romantic experience. So in "Estrangement" and elsewhere Yeats associates tragedy with passion rather than with character; with self-creation—"A poet creates tragedy from his own soul, that soul which is alike in all men"; with ecstasy, "which is from the contemplation of things vaster than the individual and imperfectly seen, perhaps, by all those that still live." Passion "looks beyond mankind and asks no pity, not even of God." In "The Tragic Theatre" he writes that "tragic art, passionate art, the drowner of dykes, the confounder of understanding, moves us by setting us to reverie, by alluring us almost to the intensity of trance." What he calls tragic ecstasy is "the best that art—perhaps that life—can give." As in "Lapis Lazuli":

> They know that Hamlet and Lear are gay;
> Gaiety transfiguring all that dread.

Comedy has a low place; it is linked to character, to clashes on the surface of life, therapeutically useful at best, as when Yeats rid himself of intractable feelings in *The Player Queen* by turning them into farce.

The theory is clear, but the practice is difficult. The plays to study most closely are those in which a common aim is subject to stresses of feeling and form over a period of many years. I refer to the theatrical celebration of the Cuchulain saga, which began several years before Yeats had encountered the Noh plays and persisted long after he had received and to some extent discarded the Noh form. The Cuchulain plays are crucial in his theater because like the poems they are primarily concerned to dramatize the Hero: "Nietzsche is born, / Because the hero's crescent is the twelfth," as Yeats wrote in "The Phases of the Moon," a poem to keep in mind beside this passage from *A Vision:* ". . . of the hero, of the man who overcomes himself, and so no longer needs . . . the submission of others, or . . . conviction of others to prove his victory. The sanity of the being is no longer from its relation to facts, but from its approximation to its own unity." This is virtually transcribed from Nietzsche's "Of Self-Overcoming"—"*Der Selbst-Überwindung*"—in the second book of *Zarathustra*. Cuchulain is an Irish hero, but he is also a Dionysian Superman. Nietzsche says in *The Will to Power* that man's faith in himself is sustained by the few, those of inexhaustible fertility and power. Yeats wanted his Cuchulain to play a similar role in Irish life. Lady Gregory's *Cuchulain of Muirthemne* was for that reason "the best book that has ever come out of Ireland," meaning the most inspiring.

On Baile's Strand is the earliest of the Cuchulain plays, the product of Yeats's association with Lady Gregory in search of Ireland's soul. He started working on the play in 1901, finished the first version in 1903, and stayed tinkering with it for a second version in 1906. Regardless of the official endorsement of personality, the play is based upon contrasts of character, particularly Cuchulain and Conchubar. Yeats found that the presentation of the material in dramatic form brought a commitment to time and therefore to body and character. Writing to Frank Fay, who was to play Cuchulain, he referred to the source of the play, the chapter called "The Only Son of Aoife" in *Cuchulain of Muirthemne,* but he told Fay to remember "that epic and folk literature can ignore time as drama cannot—Helen never ages, Cuchulain never ages":

> I have to recognise that he does, for he has a son who is old
> enough to fight him. I have also to make the refusal of the son's
> affection tragic by suggesting in Cuchulain's character a shadow
> of something a little proud, barren and restless, as if out of sheer
> strength of heart or from accident he had put affection away.
> . . . Probably his very strength of character made him put off
> illusions and dreams (that make young men a woman's servant)
> and made him become quite early in life a deliberate lover, a
> man of pleasure who can never really surrender himself. . . . The

touch of something hard, repellent yet alluring, self assertive yet self immolating, is not all but it must be there. He is the fool—wandering passive, houseless and almost loveless. Conchubar is reason that is blind because it can only reason because it is cold. Are they not the cold moon and the hot sun?

(Letters)

The structure depends on the contrast between the two principals: Cuchulain the tragic hero, Conchubar the pragmatic man, more an antique Roman than a Celt. Cuchulain's passion for Aoife is careless, "A brief forgiveness between opposites / That have been hatreds for three times the age / Of this long-'stablished ground." As Emer says in *The Green Helmet:*

> For I am moon to that sun,
> I am steel to that fire.

Cuchulain is associated with the hawk, "one of the natural symbols of subjectivity," as Yeats later wrote in *Plays and Controversies.* To give the play greater density and reverberation, Yeats added to the two principals their counter-truths, the Fool and the Blind Man, and set them quarreling in a lower key, parody figures in relation to the main plot. The aim was to gain "emotion of multitude": in an essay of that title from the same period, Yeats says that Shakespearean drama "gets the emotion of multitude out of the sub-plot which copies the main plot, much as a shadow upon the wall copies one's body in the firelight":

> We think of *King Lear* less as the history of one man and his
> sorrows than as the history of a whole evil time. Lear's shadow
> is in Gloucester, who also has ungrateful children, and the mind
> goes on imagining other shadows, shadow beyond shadow, till
> it has pictured the world.
>
> (Essays and Introductions)

The theory is "that there cannot be great art without the little limited life of the fable, which is always the better the simpler it is, and the rich, far-wandering, many-imaged life of the half-seen world beyond it." I read this as Yeats's version of history and symbol, fact and paradigm; the little limited life of history enlarged and sent wandering through the mind by the symbolic forces it has touched. The Fool and the Blind Man wear masks, lest our minds see nothing but character.

The play is understandable in fairly conventional terms. Conchubar stands for reason's click-clack; he is a solid bourgeois citizen, timid, prudent, with a shrewd perception of the main chance; the Blind Man is his shadow. Cuchulain is the hero of action, with lidless eyes that face the sun. The themes are those of *In the Seven Woods;* much of the feeling of the play is common to that book and the love poems in *The Green Helmet and Other Poems.* This gives the play a certain radiance and it leaves a much more vivid impression than its pedantic scheme of contrasts would imply. Yeats is using the resources of the theater, so far as he commands them, to thwart the play of commerce and its attendant vulgarity. His scheme is too deliberate to be convincing, and it is saved by what he could not prevent, the personal feeling arising from his doomed love for Maud Gonne. The same feeling is felt again in *The Green Helmet,* but it is turned to hauteur as in such poems as "No Second Troy" and "Pardon, Old Fathers." The play is called "an heroic farce," and this is accurate, but the effect of the Red Man is to restore it to the serious heroic theme at the end:

> And I choose the laughing lip
> That shall not turn from laughing, whatever rise
>   or fall;
> The heart that grows no bitterer although betrayed
>   by all;
> The hand that loves to scatter; the life like a
>   gambler's throw.
>
> *(Collected Plays)*

This second Cuchulain play does not call for much comment, however; it is not injured if we think of it as left over from *On Baile's Strand.*

At the Hawk's Well (1916) is the first Cuchulain play written directly from Yeats's experience of the Noh. The movements of the actors "suggest a marionette," with masks by Edmund Dulac, dance by Ito, music of drum, gong, and zither. The substance of the play is still the pain of subjectivity, but the conflict is not merely the clash of prudence and passion. Imaginative energy has to reckon with the claims of domestic life and also with the enmity of the Absolute, "unfaltering, unmoistened eyes." So the play cannot be construed in terms of character; one of its achievements is to bring personality, in Yeats's usage, to the stage. There is an immediate gain in power of concentration: formally, the play proceeds not by adding one event to another but by releasing a cadence of energy, so that the fall of the cadence coincides with the end of the play. In that respect the play is a unified image. The Guardian of the Well deceives Cuchulain as she has deceived the Old Man; the deceit is embodied in the hawk dance. But the play is bluntly described by reference to dramatic event; it calls for description by way of rhythm, cadence, climax. The subjective Hero confronts his own vision as valiantly as he confronts the Guardian; the form of the drama is the form of self-definition. The most important discovery that Yeats made in the Noh was a form capable of gathering energy within its own movement: conflict is internal and external; no feeling is allowed to escape from the form. We are made to feel that Cuchulain contains all relevant energy within himself, and that the hawk dance merely brings out what is already implicit in the hero. The play gives a powerful impression of internal force; it is the threatrical form of self-conquest. In *A Vision* Yeats speaks of "a noble extravagance, an overflowing fountain of personal life," again of "a mind alone with the object of his desire." The great achievement of *At the Hawk's Well* is a theatrical form in which multiplicity is brought to unity, scattered emotions to the unity of passion. If soliloquy could be conceived as dynamic, it would take such a form. Conflict is continuous, but it is derived from within as much as from without, from the creative joy with which the hero overcomes himself. The energy in question is free, gratuitous.

In *The Only Jealousy of Emer* this motive is directed toward Fand. Cuchulain is a phantom, a shade, dreaming back in solitude, but fixed, for the moment, at a point of age, burdened by "old memories" and "intricacies of blind remorse." Fand calls him to that condition, described in "Vacillation," in which, remorse cast out, the soul is blessed. The play enables Yeats to bring into drama all those feelings which are sustained by symbols—the spirits of the dead, the world of essence, dreams, archetypes. But it turns, too, upon finite values: Emer's self-sacrifice, conflict between the motives which drive Cuchulain to Fand—"a statue of solitude"—and those which drive him to Eithne—"I have been in some strange place and am afraid." But the particular feeling turns upon freedom: the sense in which it is indeed free, subjective, antithetical, and the sense in which, ostensibly free, it receives the form of fatality.

The Death of Cuchulain (1938) is the last play in the cycle. By now, the Noh drama has ceased to answer every need; Yeats was no longer willing to hand over every relevant feeling to its determination within the chosen form. His relation to his own feeling is turbulent, often self-destructive. Cuchulain's story is given as a play within a play, and the external drama is enacted in the larger setting of Yeats's last poems. The play may still be understood in itself, but barely, and the last moments would bewilder an audience not attuned to the poet's late rhetoric.

It begins with a stage manager, the Old Man, speaking for Yeats, denouncing middle-class preoccupations "in this vile age." There is to be music, "the music of the beggar-man, Homer's music"; a dance, too, "Emer must dance, there must be severed heads—I am old, I belong to mythology— severed heads for her to dance before." But the dancer must be "the tragicomedian dancer, the tragic dancer, upon the same neck love and loathing, life and death": not "the dancers painted by Degas," with their chambermaid faces. (I see no evidence, incidentally, that a Symbolist dancer would be right for the occasion—Mallarmé's Loie Fuller, for instance; the dancer must respond to the impurity of Yeats's tone.) Then the play begins. Eithne Inguba has come with a message from Emer: Cuchulain must fight Maeve's "Connacht ruffians." Cuchulain thinks that Eithne is sending him to his death, her eye upon a younger man, but it does not matter. Eithne denounces him as an old, forgiving man, lacking "the passion necessary to life"; but she has not betrayed him. It hardly matters. Cuchulain is still the Red Man's hero, and when a question of truth arises, he says like a good Nietzschean, "I make the truth!" He goes out to fight, returns mortally wounded. Aoife enters to finish him off, her hatred fulfilled. They talk of old fidelities. So that he may die upon his feet, Cuchulain fastens himself to a pillar stone with a belt, and Aoife helps him, winding her veil about him. "But do not spoil your veil," Cuchulain says. "Your veils are beautiful, some with threads of gold." The Blind Man comes in, Cuchulain's shadow from *On Baile's Strand*. Maeve has paid him to kill Cuchulain. Aoife leaves. Cuchulain does not resist; he is merely fulfilling his destiny.

There is a passage in *A Vision* where Yeats, speaking of the period between death and rebirth, says of one of its phases, the Return, that in it the spirit "must live through past events in the order of their occurrence, because it is compelled by the Celestial Body to trace every passionate event to its cause until all are related and understood, turned into knowledge, made a part of itself." Nothing that happens to Cuchulain matters now, for that reason. His feeling has concentrated itself upon one limit, the vision of his next incarnation in the form of a bird:

> There floats out there
> The shape that I shall take when I am dead,
> My soul's first shape, a soft feathery shape,
> And is not that a strange shape for the soul
> Of a great fighting-man?

Strange or not, it is the sole object of Cuchulain's vision. "I say it is about to sing," he declares, when the Old Man kills him. The stage darkens. The Morrigu, goddess of war, arranges a dance of the severed head. Emer dances, and "a few faint bird notes" are heard. When the stage brightens, Emer has gone, the scene is modern; three musicians appear in ragged clothes, and one of them sings a harlot's song to the beggar man.

The song is difficult. There are signs that the play was not entirely complete when Yeats put it aside. "The flesh my flesh has gripped / I both adore and loathe," the harlot sings, and we recall the Old Man's dancer, "upon the same neck love and loathing." The harlot then says:

> Are those things that men adore and loathe
> Their sole reality?

and I suppose we take the question in the general setting of opposites, death-in-life and life-in-death; though it obviously comes from perturbation, as if the strategy of self and mask, long maintained, were now at a point of collapse. The questions which follow are only barely related to Heraclitean aphorisms:

> What stood in the Post Office
> With Pearse and Connolly?
> What comes out of the mountain
> Where men first shed their blood?
> Who thought Cuchulain till it seemed
> He stood where they had stood?
> No body like his body
> Has modern woman borne,
> But an old man looking on life
> Imagines it in scorn.
> A statue's there to mark the place,
> By Oliver Sheppard done.
> So ends the tale that the harlot
> Sang to the beggar-man.

It is sometimes maintained, partly on the evidence of these lines, that Yeats is repudiating, once for all, the whole heroic ideal, imagining it in scorn. The evidence can be read in another way. True, Cuchulain is no longer the man of action, though he goes willingly to the fight. He is no longer interested in the external marks of heroism, because his existence is purely internal; he lives now in the dream, concentrating whatever will he has upon the next turn of his gyre. In the poem "Cuchulain Comforted" the hero, a shade among shades, is in the phase which Yeats in *A Vision* calls the Shiftings, when the spirit is purified of good and evil. "In so far as the man did good without knowing evil, or evil without knowing good, his nature

is reversed until that knowledge is obtained." Cuchulain obtains the knowledge by meeting his opposites, the "convicted cowards," and his comfort is
in assent to the process. In the play he is heroic in the degree of that assent.
Still available to the Irish as paradigm, he stands beside Pearse and Connolly
in the General Post Office in 1916; they act their heroism through his. This
is what comes out of the mountain, though "thought" is a poor word for
the feelings which brought him forth. Pearse and Connolly are not shamed
in Cuchulain's eyes, nor is the heroic ideal lost in him. The Old Man's scorn
is visited not upon Cuchulain, Pearse, or Connolly, but upon a world which
has let them down. Sheppard's statue of Cuchulain is there "to mark the
spot" in the G.P.O., and without it we should have forgotten the passion
that produced the Rebellion. In "The Statues," a companion poem to *The
Death of Cuchulain,* Yeats asks:

> When Pearse summoned Cuchulain to his side,
> What stalked through the Post Office?

The verbs show that what stalked was heroic, superhuman. The poem is
more coherent than the harlot's song because it turns upon the idea of the
completed symbol and finds sanction in the Grecian statues. In the play,
Yeats finds an appropriate "end" for Cuchulain, in conspiring with his fate,
but not for his modern audience: in the poem, a mutual end is given in the
statue. In "The Mandukya Upanishad" he writes of "the dreamer creating
his dream, the sculptor toiling to set free the imprisoned image": Michel-
angelo's labor, especially. Partly, this is what Yeats tried to do in *The Death
of Cuchulain;* he sets his hero free but would not give us the same freedom.
This may account for the acrid tone in the Old Man's gloss; though it is
clear that Yeats wanted his note to be "wild" in the special sense indicated
in a late poem, "Those Images":

> Seek those images
> That constitute the wild,
> The lion and the virgin,
> The harlot and the child.

These "make the Muses sing" because they are the ageless forms of energy,
lyric figures active in the human play: they are what psychology, "that
modish curiosity," tries to pervert.

It is clear, when one thinks of the Cuchulain plays as a cycle, that *At
the Hawk's Well* and *The Only Jealousy of Emer* are the most successful; feeling
and form are indistinguishable. Everything comes together—theme, gesture,
rhythm, dance. If form means achieved content, as modern critics say, these

plays are formal satisfactions. *On Baile's Strand,* beautiful as it is and drawn from the same sources of feeling, has an air of existing at one remove from Yeats's deepest concerns, and the reason must be a defect of form. The play gives an impression of being a made thing, if well-made; it does not move to its own tune. In *The Death of Cuchulain* the dance form has not survived at all: like nearly everything else at this late stage—Symbolism, mask, role-playing—the form exists so that it may be abused, and most of the feeling is in the abuse. The play is remarkably powerful, as many of Yeats's last poems are, but its feeling spills out on all sides: we love it for the recklessness with which it turns against itself. A theater in which the Noh, Nietzsche, Mallarmé, and Yeats would find themselves simultaneously acknowledged would be a monster. Yeats did not devise such a thing; it may always have been a chimera. One or another personality must predominate. In that respect the most fortunate dominance was the Noh, because it enabled Yeats to "climb to his proper dark" out of the conventional theater. Mallarmé qualifies Yeats's theater, gives it a nuance of feeling not otherwise possible; Nietzsche brought turbulence, inciting Yeats to release his own.

We began with conflict, a natural point of departure for a commentary on Yeats as dramatic poet. Then we noted Yeats's dramatic sense in relation to tragedy and ritual, his sluggish access to comedy, thinking of that form in sullen association with character, surface, mimicry, and intrigue. We should now look somewhat beyond conflict, if that is possible, to see the form of its resolution, but bearing in mind that the process is more important than the end. One of the peculiar aspects of Yeats's imagination, however, is that it readily consorts with stillness: recall how often he refers to trance when another dramatist would sound the noise of battle. Sometimes he describes trance in lively fashion—he speaks of the intensity of trance, taking the harm out of it—but the association is odd. Stillness is the end that Yeats's drama proposes; trance and silence are its forms. He writes of "that stilling and slowing which turns the imagination in upon itself," and the direction is approved: he deplored stage trappings, coming and going across the boards, because they kept the mind vainly busy. Drama should release its audience from the chains of mortality; it should speak only to make silence deeper.

This is one kind of resolution. Another is the recognition, beyond conflict, that a miracle has taken place, the divine spirits have descended to earth, and the name of the event is beauty. The First Musician's song at the beginning of *The Only Jealousy of Emer* resumes the theme in notes first heard in "Adam's Curse":

> What death? what discipline?
> What bonds no man could unbind,
> Being imagined within
> The labyrinth of the mind,
> What pursuing or fleeing,
> What wounds, what bloody press,
> Dragged into being
> This loveliness?
>
> (*Collected Plays*)

and in "The Phases of the Moon" Aherne tells Robartes what he does not need to be told, that "all dreams of the soul / End in a beautiful man's or woman's body." A corresponding miracle is growth, as in the flowering of a tree. In these instances the miracle is pure grace, a gift, marriage of heaven and earth: our part is to receive it. A corresponding grace may come from within, its sign the dance, "body swayed to music," an act of the imagination for which body provides the visible means. Finally, there is flame, a consummation of being which destroys being, but grand for that reason. Flame transmutes substance, changing it into a higher form, so its imagery is equally available to alchemist and lover; the flame is sexual and magical. I mention these ends not to exhaust them but to say that they are never transcendental. Yeats is determined to press the human imagination to its limit; he delights to live, imaginatively, at the end of the line. But he is never willing to release himself, once for all, from the human cycle. When he speaks of God, mostly he means that form of death which the imagination proposes as its highest limit. By symbol, he means what the imagination has taken to itself as a permanent possession. In this setting, what the theater offered him, and especially the Noh drama, was a means of registering the double conflict of life: external, the hero's war against circumstance; internal, when the hero's imagination lives by challenging itself, one image provokes another, and energy acts within its own circle. The external conflict might have been enacted in conventional ways; the theater is rich in these. Internal conflict, on the other hand, needed something like the Noh, if not solely the Noh, and the dance is its exemplary gesture.

Of the drama in its bearing upon his life and work, Yeats has written in "The Circus Animals' Desertion," an authoritative poem on the loss of inspiration. Lacking a theme, the poet must be "satisfied with my heart," heart meaning self and the values endorsed in the "Dialogue of Self and Soul" and "Vacillation," the values for which Homer is Yeats's example.

The circus animals, images and symbols which obeyed his call, are departed, and he views them in that light. Rehearsing old themes in the absence of new ones, he recalls "The Wanderings of Oisin," *The Countess Cathleen,* and *On Baile's Strand,* not in themselves but in their personal source, his desolate love for Maud Gonne. In the third stanza he refers to "a dream" brought forth from this pain, "and soon enough / This dream itself had all my thought and love." In the dialectic of Yeats's poems generally, heart or self is set off against soul or spirit; in this poem, heart is associated with old age and soul with symbol, magic, inspiration. Poetry is featured as compensation for the failure of love, and though it is called "dream" we should try thinking of it as vision, too, as in "Dream of the noble and the beggar-man"; otherwise it appears mere wish-fulfillment. By this reading, dream is related to fact as shade to person; shade, engendered by illimitable desire. Feeling, thwarted, compensates for lack by setting up a dream, a vision, a poem. And soon the dream takes all his thought and love:

> And when the Fool and Blind Man stole the bread
> Cuchulain fought the ungovernable sea;
> Heart-mysteries there, and yet when all is said
> It was the dream itself enchanted me:
> Character isolated by a deed
> To engross the present and dominate memory.
> Players and painted stage took all my love,
> And not those things that they were emblems of.

The lines are not so forthcoming as they seem. The heart-mysteries in *On Baile's Strand* are presumably contained in Cuchulain's heroic but crazed fight with the waves; the personal application to Yeats's love may be assumed. The dream is again the vision of art, at whatever cost, and the enchantment is compensation for the lost magic of love. But then the dream is described: character isolated by a deed, Cuchulain's character isolated and turned into personality, assimilated to Yeats's general idiom of lonely, antithetical heroes. It is not clear whether the dream is the art itself, the achievement of the play, or the image, Cuchulain dominating memory with his great gesture. It makes a difference. If the dream is art, then the personal suffering is consigned to the form, the impersonality of art, and passion is well spent in the work. If it is Cuchulain, then Yeats the defeated lover is still present and has merely translated his passion into mythic frenzy. The last lines of the stanza move toward art and away from Cuchulain, but the assertion seems excessive, Yeats is protesting his "pure poetry" too much. "Those masterful images because complete / Grew in pure mind," he begins the last stanza, as if he were referring to heuristic fictions; "masterful" is repeated from "masterful Heaven" in the third stanza, so I assume it means that the images have the same power to save their poet's soul. Emblems, pure mind, players and painted stage; but they began from the rag bag of experience, odds and ends, casual appurtenances of "heart":

> Now that my ladder's gone,
> I must lie down where all the ladders start,
> In the foul rag-and-bone shop of the heart.

These lines have been interpreted as denoting a willing commitment to "life," even without the glow of inspiration, but I am not sure this is right, especially when I recall "the mill of the mind, / Consuming its rag and bone" from "An Acre of Grass." It is true that "foul" is often a word of praise in Yeats's poems (especially in the Crazy Jane sequence, though not in the later "Bronze Head") when the values of self or heart are dominant. The ladder is the winding stair of the tower, the climb to symbol, Platonic frenzy, inspiration. But the lines seem to me a rueful acknowledgement of the facts, not a Wordsworthian assertion that what is left will be a more substantial joy than the original.

As always, it is worth while consulting the poems before and after this one in the *Collected Poems*. Before, Crazy Jane is meditating on this vile age: last night she dreamed of Cuchulain and his Emer:

> Thereupon,
> Propped upon my two knees,
> I kissed a stone;
> I lay stretched out in the dirt
> And I cried tears down.

It is clearly relevant, one loss calling to another. In the poem immediately following, a poet, wearied of politics and noise, looks at a girl:

> But O that I were young again
> And held her in my arms!

And in the next poem, "The Man and the Echo," Yeats tries to cheer himself up, justifying his life's work while fearing that it may all be a dream. In this larger context the last lines of "The Circus Animals' Desertion" ask to be read as moral accountancy, balancing profit and loss. Yeats was always concerned with the enforced choice between perfection of the life and perfection of the work, with the relation between "the day's vanity" and "the night's remorse." Now, feeling loss which he interprets as remorse, he looks for vanity. Hence the dream, which at this stage seems precariously balanced between two meanings, illusion and vision, though leaning somewhat toward the first. In "The Gyres" Yeats leans the other way: "For painted forms or boxes of make-up / In ancient tombs I sighed, but not again."

It is perhaps surprising that Yeats's plays figure so largely in "The Circus Animals' Desertion"; he cannot have thought them as important as his poems. I think he felt that, important or not in their own right, they played a crucial part in his life. A poet who commits himself to action rather than knowledge, conflict rather than peace, is bound to seek appropriate forms in the theater. Plays are the natural culmination of Yeats's idiom: mask, role, opposites, conflict, discipline, body and soul. The theater also allowed Yeats to express his heart-mysteries while seeming to present a tale of Cuchulain, Forgael, Dectora. But the largest consideration is that the theater allowed him to devise "masterful images," starting from the bundle of accident and incoherence. The plays are therefore part of the grand intention, to make himself over again: that the images live in the realm of action means that they are unquestionable.

HERBERT J. LEVINE

"But Now I Add Another Thought": Yeats's Daimonic Tradition

In middle age, surrounded by evidence of his failures in public life, in love, and in his occult search for visionary revelation, Yeats desperately needed to articulate a myth to account for the adversities of his fate. "There is a hand not ours in the events of life," he wrote in *Per Amica Silentia Lunae.* Yeats had spent his entire life piecing together a personal religion and could not simply announce that he now believed in a providential God. He preferred to claim that the controlling hand belonged to the supernatural Daimon, a figure with a long mythographic tradition stretching from Hesiod to Pater, to which he felt he was adding his unique contribution: "But now I add another thought." Most recent scholarship has stressed the occult rather than the literary tradition behind Yeats's conception of the Daimon. The present essay changes that emphasis. After briefly laying out Yeats's theory of the Daimon as articulated in *Per Amica,* I will attempt to show what Yeats borrowed from the literary daimonic traditions known to him and to suggest the impact of his daimonic theory of creativity on the great poetry of his maturity.

Always the dramatist, Yeats shapes his daimonic speculations into a scenario: The Daimon, in all ways opposite to the individual he singles out, is bound to him with the intensity of a lover, and in fact conspires with the man's sweetheart against him. He will not loosen his controlling grip until he has led his chosen one to perform "the hardest work among those not impossible." The chosen man must internalize the power and wear the mask of his spirit guide, though these will bring him only disappointment and

From *Studies in the Literary Imagination* 14, no. 1 (Spring 1981). © 1981 by the Department of English, Georgia State University.

defeat in the world. He reacts stubbornly to the Daimon's mastery, wishing for the return of his individuality. Meanwhile, the Daimon bears his man's stubbornness as he would a lover's fickleness, and forces him "again and again to the place of choice," where he must become hero, saint, or holy fool in his own poetic world, or else remain just another figure in the casual comedy.

The climax of this scenario of loving struggle between man and Daimon comes at a moment of innocence that precedes creation:

> I am in the place where the Daimon is, but I do not think he is with me until I begin to make a new personality, selecting among those images, seeking always to satisfy a hunger grown out of conceit with daily diet; and yet as I write the words 'I select,' I am full of uncertainty, not knowing when I am the finger, when the clay.

In fashioning a poetic self, Yeats enters into a creative partnership with his God-surrogate, the Daimon, that at its best breaks down the boundaries of the ego, allowing the poet to wonder like a Biblical prophet whether he is the agent or simply the vessel of divine revelation. In Yeats's daimonic aesthetic, visionary and spiritual fulfillment follow from radical self-limitation: "I shall find the dark grow luminous, the void fruitful when I understand I have nothing, that the ringers in the tower have appointed for the hymen of the soul a passing bell." The central lesson of *Per Amica* and its dominating Daimon is that the poetic image does not belong to "Anima Hominis" but to "Anima Mundi." It is therefore the poet's responsibility to shake off the merely personal as he creates and to subordinate self-expression to the claims that the world soul makes upon him: "Surely some revelation is at hand" [*The Collected Poems of W. B. Yeats;* all further references to this text will be abbreviated as *CP*].

Before we can comment on Yeats's claims that his theory of the daimonic anti-self was a unique addition to the literature of the Daimon, we must briefly survey that literature. Yeats was no classicist; he knew the ancient literature primarily at second-hand, in syncretist compilations by the seventeeth-century Cambridge neo-Platonists More, Cudworth, and Glanvil, or in similar summary works by Plutarch. Elsewhere . . ., James Olney surveys the similarities between Yeatsian and Jungian Daimons and those of the pre-Socratics and Plato, so we need only touch on the ancient traditions before turning to their re-discovery and adaptation by the Romantic poets and critics, whom Yeats knew firsthand.

The Greek word daimon may come from one of two words: *daiomai* or *daemonas*—meaning "to divide" and "skilled," thus a skillful being who divides up the fates of humans. To the ancients, the *daimon* was a subsidiary god, the tutelary genius of a place or a person. The *daimon* itself was morally neutral, but could be used by the higher gods malevolently or beneficently. Some *daimones* viciously drove people toward negative, irrational behavior (in our idiom, such were "possessed by a demon"); other *daimones* brought people divine messages. It is in this latter light that we see the *daimon* Eros in Plato's *Symposium*, who attempts to draw men up toward divinity, or similarly, the soul in the *Timaeus*, conceived as an inner *daimon* whose dictates we must obey in order to realize the immortal potential in each of us. Most importantly for Yeats, men as different as Socrates and Empedocles used the figure of an inner *daimon* in defining their identities. Know thyself, know thy *daimon*, or destiny.

The Romantic writers rediscovered the mythological *daimon*, lost during the intervening Christian centuries, and restored it to literature. For some of the Romantics, as for Yeats, it was an article of faith that individuals of genius (itself a Greek synonym) were driven by an inner *daimon;* Goethe cited Napoleon as a daimonic character and Coleridge called opium "the avenging Daemon" of his life. Blake did not refer explicitly to the *daimon*, but the identification between man and an inner *daimon* is clear in his Aristophanic myth of Spectre and Emanation. In a prelapsarian state, the two were united, but in the world of generation they are divided and endlessly pursue one another to reattain wholeness. Yeats similarly envisions the momentary creative union of poet and Daimon as a Blakean apocalypse that prefigures the ultimate beatitude of the soul at the end of its temporal journey.

Yeats also appropriates more conventional mythological uses of the *daimon* found in such Romantic poems as *The Rime of the Ancient Mariner*, "Alastor," and *Manfred*. In these works, vengeful or tutelary spirits function as allegorical aspects of the hero: "Death-in-Life" wins the sinful mariner; an "Alastor," a beautiful female *daimon* who represents the poet's own Spirit of Solitude, lures him to his death. The heroes of such poems themselves attain daimonic consciousness as they become aware that the normal boundaries of their egos have expanded through symbolic communication with supernatural agents. They understand that their freedom is limited, yet their energy is focused and expanded, sometimes, as in the case of Manfred, even gaining them power over the daimonic realm itself. In coming to terms with their destinies, they are willing to bear a curse as a mark of their specialness. From his youth onwards, Yeats was attracted to such characters in Romantic poems, and in his cycle of Cuchulain plays, he borrows from them both the daimonic machinery of spirits and the figure of the daimonic hero, who willingly embraces the daimonic Muse who governs his accursed destiny.

Per Amica represents Yeats's belated attempt to court and embrace both Iseult Gonne and the daimonic destiny that ruled his unhappy life and poetic enterprise. As such, it bears a remarkable similarity to DeQuincey's autobiographical reverie of self-justification, "Levana and Our Ladies of Sorrow," a work that summarizes a whole complex of Romantic ideas about daimonic powers. Like Yeats, DeQuincey felt himself cursed as a lover, yet because of that curse, blessed as a visionary. His autobiographical myth focuses on three *femmes fatales,* daimonic sisters who first plague his heart with Tears, Sighs, and Darkness, but in the end, raise him up, as the name "Levana" implies, to unfold "the capacities of his spirit." Like Yeats's daimonic partner in creation, they speak to their chosen one in the language of vision: "*They* wheeled in mazes; *I* spelled the steps. *They* telegraphed from afar; *I* read the signals. *They* conspired together, and on the mirrors of darkness *my* eye traced the plots. *Theirs* were the symbols; *mine* are the words." DeQuincey's ladies have power over his life for good or for evil; they communicate symbolically through dream and vision; they concentrate their power over him by demanding that he worship and serve them as his muses. In short, they are everything that Yeats claimed of his Daimon. Yeats never cited DeQuincey to my knowledge, though he probably knew the "Levana" essay, which was available in his own library, and he may well have echoed another passage from the *Suspiria.* Yeats was trying to overcome a pervasive melancholy in writing *Per Amica,* so he naturally preferred to distance himself from a figure as morbid as DeQuincey and rely instead on more integrated personalities like Dante and Goethe, Carlylean poet-heroes who could testify with unquestioned authority to the uncanny daimonic presence at work in their creative processes.

Yeats is constantly announcing in both prose and verse that he has found wisdom, yet he asks us to bear in mind that "Those men that in their writings are most wise / Own nothing but their blind, stupefied hearts" (*CP*). Yeats cannot possibly own the images that he sees in his mind's eye, for they bear the consciousness of other lives and destinies. Such images Yeats calls daimonic. For instance, the imagined seashell with which Yeats sets the scene in *The Only Jealousy of Emer* is itself a small vessel of collective consciousness, a miniature version of the "Anima Mundi":

> What death? What discipline?
> What bonds no man could unbind,

Being imagined within
The labyrinth of the mind,
What pursuing or fleeing,
What wounds, what bloody press,
Dragged into being
This loveliness?

Yeats learned from Walter Pater, another inheritor of daimonic tradition, how to project the psychic life behind the image. Pater's evocation of the Mona Lisa is the literary image which most closely resembles Yeats's conception of the "Anima Mundi" as a storehouse of collective experience. For Pater, the Mona Lisa summarizes in itself "the modern idea"; associations drawn from geography, history and legend attain the status of universal myth in the unique presence of the image. Yeats writes that she is the synthetic image of all "human experience no longer shut into brief lives." At the same time, behind her mask is a "private reality . . . always hidden" that "must be the sole source of pain, stupefaction, evil." In a poem like "Leda and the Swan," Yeats learned to maintain this dual focus on the individual's pain in its relation to the collective experience of Western culture.

In such doubleness lies the essence of Yeats's daimonic art. We sense the private reality that is the source of his pain, but we know that at his best, when he is "in the place where the Daimon is," it is never his intention to express merely that private reality. "When a vast image out of *Spiritus Mundi*" troubles Yeats's sight we know that he is looking at a visionary world that he can only see with the help of the Daimon's vision. Because Yeats secularized the daimonic in so many of his poems, through rituals of visitation and narrations of sudden, puzzling intercessions, his readers tend to take the daimonic double vision for granted. Yeats never did. For him, it represented the long-sought and infrequent reward of his "secret discipline / Wherein the gazing heart doubles her might."

The daimonic ideal to which Yeats continued to aspire is the "radical innocence" he celebrates in "A Prayer for My Daughter," in which the soul learns "that its own sweet will is Heaven's will." Realizing as he did that the common condition of our life is hatred, Yeats does not pretend to be immune to the passions that divide us from one another and from Heaven's will. In "Demon and Beast," for instance, he exalts a brief interlude when he is no longer a "demoniac" (*CP*), he says, but is momentarily freed from the pervasive demons of hatred and desire and can laugh in the sun, at one with man and beast. The poem takes pains to point out that the demonism of hatred and desire *is* the human norm and that it is best counteracted by those, like the saints of the final stanza, who are daimonically inspired by an ecstatic vision that is antithetical to the ways of the world.

Yeats knew that, unlike the saint, he could not withdraw from the world to pursue a private vision of beatitude. He had struck out on a prophetic path in "The Second Coming," taking it upon himself to chronicle the chaos and unrelieved violence that was to become the unfortunate hallmark of the twentieth century. The daimonic poet knows that evil exists in the mind's eye as well as in the world, and that it is his responsibility to shadow forth "How the daemonic rage / Imagined everything" (*CP*). Without succumbing either to hatred or to self-righteous withdrawal, Yeats had to respond to the universal "Vision of Evil," in which he and all humankind shared.

In "Meditations in Time of Civil War," the poet climbs to the top of the tower and is overwhelmed by "Monstrous familiar images" that "swim to the mind's eye" (*CP*). He envisions a rage-driven multitude, biting and tearing at one another, shouting for vengeance, vengeance upon the murderers of Jacques Molay. "And I," writes Yeats, "my wits astray / Because of all that senseless tumult, all but cried / For vengeance on the murderers of Jacques Molay" (*CP*). It matters little that the man has been dead for six centuries; irrational violence persists and revisits its fury upon us in every generation. The raging troop is replaced in the mind's eye with a fairy-tale vision of magical unicorns bearing ladies on their backs. And this vision gives place in its turn to brazen hawks, immune to reverie, to hatred, or to softening pity: "Nothing but grip of claw, and the eye's complacency, The innumerable clanging wings that have put out the moon" (*CP*).

Yeats titles this poem "I See Phantoms of Hatred and of the Heart's Fullness and of the Coming Emptiness." It would be easy for a visionary poet to offer the "eye's complacency" as a response to the demons of vengeance, cloying loveliness, and indifference that haunt his world. Or like Milton's "Il Penseroso," invoked in Yeats's poem, the poet can indulge in the pleasures of melancholy reflection. Yeats knows how hard he must fight against his natural self and the tendency to seek the contentments of a normal life into which the Daimon will not bring his horrifying visions of the future. Bravely, Yeats shoulders the burden of being an unwanted prophet to his age, and, in the last stanza, comes to terms with his life as a daimonic poet:

> I turn away and shut the door, and on the stair
> Wonder how many times I could have proved my worth
> In something that all others understand or share;
> But O! ambitious heart, had such a proof drawn forth

> A company of friends, a conscience set at ease,
> It had but made us pine the more. The abstract joy,
> The half-read wisdom of daemonic images,
> Suffice the ageing man as once the growing boy.
>
> (*CP*)

Yeats is responsible for interpreting "the half-read wisdom" of the daimonic images he has envisioned, but only that half accessible to human understanding. Though he may have envisioned the impending destruction of his civilization, the poet remains radically innocent. The vision comes to him as Heaven's will, sent by its messenger, the immemorial Daimon.

Already amidst the visionary greatness of "Meditations in Time of Civil War," we begin to sense the lack of human sympathy that separates Yeats's late poems from us. If we look at Yeats's later conception of the Daimon in *A Vision*, we can easily see what he lost. The 1925 *Vision* is still close to *Per Amica* in preserving the passionate personal bond between man and Daimon, now envisioned as being of the opposite sex. The Daimons, however, operate only in a metaphysical realm, where they contrive to use men as instruments for their own inhuman fulfillment. This inhumanity increases in the 1937 *Vision*. Once as personal as a lover, the Daimon becomes an impersonal cosmic stage-manager handing out roles and pulling on the strings, as in the puppet-like Commedia Dell'Arte. No longer actively mediating between the poet's choice of masks and images and the "Anima Mundi," he becomes simply another category, in fact containing all other categories within him, but ultimately just another category as passionless and undramatized as the rest of *A Vision's* machinery. The individual is subsumed by the Daimon's memory in the inevitable cycles of mankind: "Now his wars on God begin; / At stroke of midnight God shall win" (*CP*).

Yeats's unique contribution to the several millenia of daimonic tradition is his sense of an absolute opposition and struggle between man and Daimon, a Blakean feature of his thought which grew more pronounced with time, though without Blake's apocalyptic hope for reconciliation. This concept removes Yeats entirely from the Platonic use of the *daimon,* which is based on a principle of likeness between man's soul and his *daimon.* Yeats rejected Shelley's Platonic epipsyche, an ideal image of soul drawn from the poet's own soul, because it was nothing more than an allegorical reflection of aspirations already well known to the poet. Yeats needed his Daimon to help him confront otherness, growing out of his conviction that in the resulting painful struggle, a man comes upon what lies buried deep inside him, whether it be the unconscious strivings of the soul exalted by Plato or Shelley or the unconscious Vision of Evil known by Dante. It behooves us to know both visions, Yeats felt, but expecially the Vision of Evil, since it so shapes the world of horror and violence in which we live. The Daimon drew Yeats deeper into "the desolation of reality" (*CP*). It is little wonder that we prefer the "radical innocence" of Yeats's first years courting his daimonic Muse, when the dark grew luminous and the void fruitful.

PAUL DE MAN

Imagery in Yeats

With striking critical insight, Yeats has described his own poetic development by opposing it to the concept of *Bildung,* as it appears in the German
romantic tradition. He knew this tradition only through Goethe, one of his
father's favorite authors, but the reference to *Wilhelm Meister* is singularly
apt: "I still think that in a species of man, wherein I count myself, nothing
so much matters as Unity of Being, but if I seek it as Goethe sought, who
was not of that species, I but combine in myself, and perhaps as it now
seems, looking backward, in others also, incompatibles. Goethe, in whom
objectivity and subjectivity were intermixed . . . could but seek it as Wilhelm Meister seeks it, intellectually, critically, and through a multitude of
deliberately chosen experiences; events and forms of skill gathered as if for
a collector's cabinet; whereas true Unity of Being, where all the nature
murmurs in response if but a single note be touched, is found emotionally,
instinctively, by the rejection of all experience not of the right quality, and
by the limitation of its quantity."

It is well to bear this in mind when trying to impress a framework of
order on Yeats's work. We cannot expect the gradual development of a
Mallarmé, a consciousness which comes to know itself by observing the
reflections of its own experiences, but rather an *a priori* commitment that
maintains itself in the face of all attacks and temptations. The movement
of *Bildung* is one of repeated defeats, never altogether wasteful because, no
matter how tragic the damage to individuals, they result in an enrichment
of the spirit. Blind hope rushes into action to meet disaster; Faust embarks

From *The Rhetoric of Romanticism.* © 1984 by Columbia University Press. Originally entitled
"Image and Emblem in Yeats."

forcefully on the impossible, causes ruin and destruction to others and to himself, with no gain but some increased wisdom of his limitations. The impossibility of the quest unveils gradually, and an awareness of the ultimate absurdity of the enterprise appears as the crowning achievement, at the end of the drama. The pattern of Yeats's poetic development, however, is Quixotic rather than Faustian. The irrevocable commitment seems to be made from the start, absurdity and all, and the subsequent test is merely one of loyalty and perseverance.

Such a pattern could be simple enough, much simpler, in fact, than the succession of assertions and denials that characterize a movement of becoming. But in Yeats's case, the original commitment is particularly elusive. There is bound to be a fundamental complication associated with an ideal which is persistently referred to as Unity of Being, but most frequently expressed, as in the above quotation, by such terms as "to reject" or "to limit"—terms that suggest plurality rather than unity. And there may well be true incoherence at the core of a system which, like *A Vision,* claims to be both cyclical, a mere repetition of a movement resulting from tensions between irreconcilable opposites, and dialectical, a progression of antinomies toward their ultimate reconciliation. A "Unity of Being" which has to be understood in opposition to another "Unity of Being" is certainly not of a kind which can easily be defined. Behind the term "Unity of Being" is hidden a long history of conflicts and contradictions; when Yeats uses it to describe his poetry, an interpretation of the entire work is needed to know why he chooses to state it in this manner.

Yeats's actual commitment, which determines the intricate verbal strategy of his poetry, cannot be deduced, as was the case for Mallarmé, from his own explicit statements. Mallarmé's obligation is to the *truth* of his language; therefore, the complication of his intention is always exactly equal to the complication of his statement: this makes him, in spite of so many opinions to the contrary, into the very opposite of an "obscure" poet— although it certainly does not make him into a simple one. Yeats is very articulate about his poetic theories and discourses eloquently and abundantly on the subject, but his statements, whether they appear in the poetry or in his dramatic or critical writing, always have to be considered in the light of an intent that reaches beyond their particular meaning. His langauge is not the language of truth; it is determined by an intent which uses language and in which language is deeply involved, but which nevertheless finds its ultimate justification in a meta-logical and, at times, anti-logical realm.

In the case of a poet of this type, when no works or passages can be singled out and given true exegetic value, the best way to gain access to their true meaning is often to observe local accidents and anomalies of language by means of which actual intentions or commitments, hidden behind the statement, are revealed. By far the most conspicuous of such accidents are the several stylistic changes and incessant revisions that mark Yeats's career. His avowed opinions and convictions, as well as his public conception of his role as a poet, remain remarkably stable, but his poetry keeps varying in texture and in tone until the very last poems. These changes are not primarily thematic, even though they sometimes seem to be: Yeats's themes are in fact much less varied than his styles, and it is not always possible to establish a correlation between thematic and stylistic shifts. A strong feeling exists among commentators that if it were possible to account for the changes in manner, true insight would be gained in Yeats's fundamental hopes and preoccupations. The stylistic experimentations are prompted by his deepest concern; themes, declarations of purpose, aesthetic or pseudo-philosophical theories are subsidiary to this concern, put to use in its service. The key to a real understanding of Yeats's poetic enterprise, as well as of his place in the tradition of nineteenth-century poetry, is to be found in his stylistic evolution. This is true of all poets, to some extent, but it is true in a special sense for Yeats. In some—and Mallarmé is a case in point—the distinction between theme and style is not apparent, and one is free to move from stylistic to thematic considerations without encountering discontinuities; Yeats, on the other hand, consciously uses and exploits this very distinction for strategic purposes. By ignoring the formal aspects of his language, one allows oneself to be deliberately misled by the author's own devices.

Critics have been well aware of the importance of the stylistic element in Yeats, and most attempts at a general interpretation have actually been interpretations of the stylistic changes. Although no systematic study of the problem is as yet available, the more or less fragmentary and intuitive descriptions of the changes stress similar elements: the contrast between the vocabulary of the early and the later poetry; the passage from a purely lyrical to a more dramatic medium; the difference between the esoteric, hieratic imagery of the early and the much more concrete and natural imagery of the later poetry; the change from repetitive and incantatory rhythms to intricately varied and abrupt metrical patterns; the increased use of irony and ambiguity; the passage from a neoromantic Victorian "poetic" diction to a hardened "modern" form of address often said to be close to actual speech. There is at least some measure of agreement as to the general trend of these changes, although the findings are based, in general, on quick impressions rather than on exhaustive analysis. Stylistic criticism of Yeats would complicate this relatively simple picture a great deal.

Beyond this point, agreement vanishes. When it comes to an interpretation of the changes, opinions vary widely, quantitatively, qualitatively, and historically. Some see a total contrast between the early and the late Yeats, others maintain that it ". . . is a development rather than a conversion, a technical change rather than a substantial one." Some, a majority, see it as a movement toward a more "realistic," socially responsible, publicly committed poetry, while others stress the increased esotericism and hermeticism of the later poetry, less conventionally "literary" and more avowedly occult and initiatory. Some consider Yeats as the culmination and fulfillment of the romantic tradition, others as moving definitely outside of this tradition.

Before any other consideration, it should be pointed out that the change cannot be so easily observed as its obvious existence may lead one to believe. There is not one single change but several, and it is not certain that they tend in the same direction. Neither is it certain that objective characteristics of style (assuming even—which is not the case—that they had been accurately defined and described) can be easily and immediately translated in terms of poetic intent; that the prevalence of a more or less colloquial vocabulary, for instance, necessarily indicates a poetry closer to earth than conventionally "poetic" word choice; or that the frequent presence of natural imagery necessarily implies a concretization of experience; or that a dramatic syntax and structure is necessarily more socially concerned than a lyrical one. All such outward characteristics of style have to be placed within a highly complex network of motives and intentions before their tentative significance can be stated with some chance of accuracy.

For instance, to take a simple and well-studied example, Yeats's style underwent a considerable transformation between 1889, the date when his first volume of verse was published, and 1895, when he revised his early poems for a new edition (*Poems,* London, 1895); the alterations offer excellent material for a study of the development at that point. The conclusions are clear; the changes are attempts to eliminate the remnants of conventional romantic diction: inflected verb forms, partially elided prepositions, inversions, etc. In a way, this makes the language more natural and brings it closer to ordinary speech; words such as "you," "the," "always," "no," "from" are certainly closer to ordinary speech than "ye," "thy," "ever," "nay," "o'er," etc. But it could hardly be argued that this shift from conventionally "poetic" language to normal usage was accompanied by a parallel thematic change from an otherworldly realm back to earth; whatever the difference between the 1889 and the 1901 versions of a poem like "The Indian to His Love," they hardly make it less ethereal, though they make it a great deal less ridiculous. As for the new poems which Yeats is writing

around 1895 and which will be printed in book form in 1899 under the
title of *The Wind among the Reeds,* they are certainly not to be called earth-
bound or realistic. This change, although it is doubtlessly oriented toward
"natural" diction, occurs at a moment when the "substantial" evolution, as
revealed by the imagery, moves more and more radically away from nature.
We understand, then, that this particular change in diction (not in imagery)
between the 1889 edition of *The Wanderings of Oisin and Other Poems* and the
1895 edition of *Poems,* marks a development in technical skill. Yeats has
come into contact in London with his English fellow poets and he is "learning
his trade" *with* (not *from*) them, following a trend which was generally
prevalent among his contemporaries; a similar difference exists between the
diction of Swinburne and that of Dowson and Symons (both great admirers
of Verlaine) or between that of Tennyson and Lionel Johnson. This is indeed
a "technical change rather than a substantial one," but it is complicated by
the fact that at the same time a "substantial" development has taken place
(between *The Wanderings of Oisin and Other Poems* of 1889 and *The Countess
Cathleen and Various Legends and Lyrics* of 1891) that tends in the direction
opposite from the evolution in technique.

Later, when the major change occurs which is generally mentioned in
speaking of the transition from Yeats's early to his mature period (between
The Shadowy Waters, 1900, and *In the Seven Woods,* 1903), the hardening of
texture, the introduction of contemporary, topical allusions, a new abundance of natural imagery all have prompted the prevalent interpretation of
a definitive return to a certain form of realism. The stylistic equivalence of
this return is found in a parallel return to a syntax and diction that imitate
natural speech. So oversimplified are our notions of style, and so strongly
influenced by loose historical categories, that we tend to call "realistic" any
diction which is no longer Victorian. One commentator, at least, has been
curious enough to take a closer look, and drawn attention to the fact that
Yeats's mature diction is anything but mimetic, that it introduces again
many of the more "literary" forms of style which the early revisions had
been eager to eliminate, especially archaisms and inversions. Of course, they
are not the same kind of archaisms or inversions and they fulfull a different
expressive function, but their fundamental characteristic remains: they ac-
centuate the distinction between spoken and written language and widen
the gap between mimetic and expressive diction. In the middle and the later
Yeats, one is very far removed indeed from the Preface to the *Lyrical Ballads.*
The vocabulary and syntax of the poetry after 1904 is certainly not sufficient
proof that the change ought to be interpreted as a return to reality.

Our point is merely that if the study of stylistic changes is indeed the best way of access to the interpretation of Yeats, it is a key that should be used with great caution and with a steady awareness of the intentional principle that determined stylistic peculiarities. It is this pattern of intentions (which, in Yeats, differs from the thematic structure) which we want to observe. And, as in all romantic poetry, the most revealing stylistic unit will be the image.

Yeats's early poetry is, in his own words, "covered with embroideries," and much of its imagery is purely decorative. It is often similar in texture to this passage from *The Wanderings of Oisin:*

> A citron colour gloomed in her hair,
> But down to her feet white vesture flowed,
> And with the glimmering crimson glowed
> Of many a figured embroidery;
> And it was bound with a pearl-pale shell
> That wavered like the summer streams,
> As her soft bosom rose and fell.

This is pictorial, Pre-Raphaelite writing, with a picture-book delight in colors that exist merely for the color's sake; citron, white, and crimson, all in the span of three lines. In this context, the "pearl-pale shell" seems hardly more than another picturesque detail—although it could be more than this. Niamh, who is being described, is something of a siren, a water creature who rides the waves, and the decorative shell could point to her elemental nature. Very early in the poem, we are perhaps already dealing with an image which belongs to a much more complicated species; it refers, by means of a traditional pictorial emblem to a complex experience (the sea, and its dark attraction on Oisin); it contains mythological elements (the siren); and it refers to a specific natural element (water). But it appears among so much descriptive detail, devoid of metaphorical or emblematic depth, that it escapes notice in the crowded picture.

A little further along in the poem, the image of the shell reappears, when Niamh and Oisin are about to land on the first of their three islands:

> we rode on,
> Where many a trumpet-twisted shell
> That in immortal silence sleeps
> Dreaming of her own melting hues,
> Her golds, her ambers, and her blues,
> Pierced with soft light the shallowing deeps.

This image starts from the perception of an actual thing, the eye catching sight of the shells as the water grows shallow. The late version (which dates from a 1933 edition) still strengthens this effect by means of the exact visual detail "trumpet-twisted," but it is clear from the unaltered line, "Pierced with soft light the shallowing deeps," that the encounter with the natural, outward world has always been an essential part of the image. It grows, however, into much more than a descriptive or decorative detail. The transfer of the material attributes of shape and color into consciousness, which makes up the perception, is accompanied by a symmetrical transfer of acts of consciousness into the object: the shell is said to be "dreaming" and the verb "pierced" changes the passive process of being perceived into an act of volition; by then, the shell has both imagination and will, the main faculties of a conscious mind, and it has received them from a mere figure of speech.

This kind of image is very frequent in the early Yeats. It differs from mere personification, which has primarily a descriptive purpose and is based on mimetic devices; to say that the wind howls or that the sun smiles is to say something about the wind and the sun, but to write of shells "dreaming of their own hues" is to say something about the act of dreaming, not to describe the shells. Or rather, it is to say something about the power of symbolic language, which is able to cross the gap between subject and object without apparent effort, and to unite them within the single unit of the natural image. Behind such imagery stands the conception of fundamental unity of mind and matter, expanding from the particular oneness of the single image into universal unity, the *"ténébreuse et profonde unité . . . Ayant l'expansion des choses infinies"* of Baudelaire's famous sonnet "Correspondances."

Baudelaire can be mentioned with relevance at this point, certainly not as a source (for whatever contact Yeats had with French symbolism occurred later and even then Baudelaire was not the major influence), but because the conception of imagery, at the beginning of Yeats's work, places him so clearly within the general European tradition of symbolism. None of Yeats's immediate predecessors or contemporaries in England, even those, like Symons or Dowson, who came into much closer contact with France, is as closely akin to the symbolic language of Baudelaire and his successors. This becomes more apparent still in the lines

> a trumpet-twisted shell . . .
> Dreaming of her own melting hues,
> Her gold, her ambers, and her blues,

The verb "dreaming" transfers attributes of consciousness into the natural object and establishes the unity of a correspondence, but the content of the

dream is itself of great importance for the structure of image: the shell is
dreaming, not only of itself, but of its own most striking formal, material
features: the very colors by which it was originally perceived. The movement
of the image, which started in perception, then fused the perceived object
and the perceiving consciousness into one by means of a verbal transfer, now
returns to the original perception, making the object itself into the perceiver.
From purely perceptual, then metaphorical (or symbolic), the image has
become one of self-reflection, using the material properties of the object (the
colors) as a means to allow a self-reflective consciousness to originate. In the
process, the center of interest, which first resided in the colors as the qualities
by which the object was perceived, has shifted: the idea of a shell endowed
with the highest form of human consciousness (self-reflection) is in itself so
striking that the colors have lost most of their prominence; what arrests the
mind, no doubt, are no longer the "melting hues" but the shell dreaming
of its own beauty. The structure of the image has become that of self-
reflection. The poet is no longer contemplating a thing in nature, but the
workings of his own mind; the outside world is used as a pretext and a
mirror, and it loses all its substance. Imagery by "correspondences" ends
up in self-reflection, and the dominant mood of Yeats's earliest poetry is
one of narcissistic self-contemplation:

> they are always listening,
> The dewdrops, for the sound of their own dropping.
> ("The Sad Shepherd")

> A parrot sways upon a tree,
> Raging at his own image in the enamelled sea.
> ("The Indian to His Love")

One could speculate at length how a young poet, living in the peripheral, eccentric atmosphere of Dublin and the J. B. Yeats family, came
to write as by instinct in a style which has no immediate antecedent in the
English poetry of his day. It was natural enough for Mallarmé to think of
himself as one who had to begin where Baudelaire left off, but much more
difficult to explain how Yeats found himself unknowingly in the same predicament. His early poetic manner bears the obvious marks of the English
romantic and post-romantic tradition, of Tennyson and Swinburne, of the
romantic conception of Spenserian sensual imagery as it appears in Keats
and in the Pre-Raphaelites, of Shelley's near-emblematic symbolism. None
of these influences, however, can account for the combination of imagery
founded on correspondences between mind and matter, with conscious self-

contemplation, a combination which characterizes French rather than English poetry of the second half of the nineteenth century. Later, Yeats will discover his affinities with the *symbolistes,* but his poetry is never closer to theirs than before 1885, when he had little or no knowledge of their work.

J. HILLIS MILLER

Yeats: The Linguistic Moment

How can we include in a discourse, any *discourse, that which, being the very condition of discourse, would by its very essence escape discourse? If non-presence, the core and ultimate reason behind all discourse, becomes speech, can it—or should it—make itself heard in and through self-presence?*
—NICOLAS ABRAHAM,
"The Rind and the Core"

. . . . it is quite hopeless to try to penetrate directly to the nucleus of the pathogenic organization.
—SIGMUND FREUD,
Studies on Hysteria

My topic here is the topography of Yeats's "Nineteen Hundred and Nineteen." This topography is a certain structure of places, in both the spatial and rhetorical senses of that word. The structure incorporates also a non-place, not so much utopian as atopical, a place that is both there and not there. It is a certain crossroads to which all roads lead and yet which can be reached by no road. What can this mean?

Topography—the word indicates both an arrangement of places that is already there and the activity of graphing them, mapping them, transposing them from the real to its represention. This activity Yeats's poem already performs. It puts a multitude of elements within the space of the poem, laid out on the page as a map. The critic repeats that activity in his turn. He makes a new map of his own. These topographies are also topologies.

From *The Linguistic Moment: From Wordsworth to Stevens.* © 1985 by Princeton University Press. Originally entitled "Yeats."

They are a mapping that is a search for meaning, a search for the central *logos* that gives significance to the whole place and to the separate places within the place. This chapter makes its search in part through the implicit superimposition on Yeats's poem of several other "similar" spatial structures—a painting by Paul Klee, *Danceplay of the Red Skirts;* a poem by Wallace Stevens, "A Primitive Like an Orb"; an essay by Friedrich Nietzsche, "On Truth and Lies in a Nonmoral Sense"; and two passages by Sigmund Freud, one in *Studies on Hysteria,* the other in *The Interpretation of Dreams.* These might be thought of as transparent maps laid over the ground plan of "Nineteen Hundred and Nineteen," or perhaps projected there in an imaginary version of the Hinman collating machine. Their shadowy presence will allow me to raise in another way the question of what is meant by calling the poet's mapping a "transposition." They also raise the question of what is meant by saying two texts have "similar" spatial structures. The goal of this chapter is to reach the center of the labyrinth of the Yeats poem, but since reaching this goal directly is impossible, I have tried to get there by way of detours through other corridors in a group of analogous labyrinths. When the way is blocked by one route, one seeks another way in.

The implicit superimposition of diverse examples will also allow the raising of several more general questions. A lyric poem, for example, "Nineteen Hundred and Nineteen," has a temporal structure. Word follows word when we read it silently or aloud. Why do such poems so often use spatial figures to describe their own activity, just as the critic, in his turn, is so often drawn to spatial images in his mapping? This spatialization may be especially easy to investigate in a lyric poem of moderate length, such as "Nineteen Hundred and Nineteen" or "A Primitive Like an Orb." Is such a poem a separate genre, with its own form, different from the brief lyric poem, for example, a sonnet, "Leda and the Swan," say, or different from the group sequence, like Yeats's "A Woman Young and Old," or different from the long lyric philosophical poem, like Stevens's "An Ordinary Evening in New Haven"? If so, what are those formal properties? Why is it, finally, that this spatialization, which seems so effective as a means of interpreting the poem, tends ultimately to break down? It fails to account for the poem unless the image or the concept (it is both and neither) of the atopical is introduced. This introduction ruins the reader's initial enterprise of topographical mapping as a way of accounting for the poem.

That "Nineteen Hundred and Nineteen" raises the most urgent metaphysical, moral, historical, aesthetic, and political questions, there can be no doubt. Written as a response to the Black and Tan violence in Ireland and more generally to the disillusionment in the West after the First World

War, it joins such works as Paul Valéry's *"La crise de l'esprit"* and *Regards sur le monde actuel,* Oswald Spengler's *The Decline of the West,* T. S. Eliot's *The Waste Land,* and Virginia Woolf's *Mrs. Dalloway,* in asking why it is "no work can stand, / Whether health, wealth or peace of mind were spent / On master-work of intellect or hand, / No honour leave its mighty monument" [lines 35–38, *The Variorum Edition of the Poems;* all further references to this text will be abbreviated as *VPY*]. Yeats's poem asks also the ethical question: In the light of such knowledge, what should we now do? Knowing no work can stand, how should we then spend our time, from moment to moment, before we die?

The reader of a lyric poem raises certain questions, instinctively or by training in one version or another of the long Western tradition of rhetoric, of which Anglo-American New Criticism is only one of the latest. Who is speaking, from what place, and to whom? What form of order or unity does the poem have, allowing the reader to organize every detail around a beginning, middle, end, and generative center? What, finally, is the poem "about"? What is the literal, nonlinguistic thing, situation, event, state of mind, or supernatural reality to which it refers as to its center? This center is assumed to govern all the figurative language in the poem and to make the figures, figures of something or other nonfigurative.

In the case of Yeats, critics have tended to assume that it is Yeats himself speaking. He speaks directly from his real personal and historical situation, or he speaks by way of a persona, Crazy Jane or Ribh. The persona is a transposition of that real self of Yeats and may be translated back again. Critics have tended to assume that a poem by Yeats, like any good poem, will have an "organic unity"—leaf, blossom, and bole rooted in the particularities of Yeats's sense of his own life. Yeats's own early critical prose, in *Ideas of Good and Evil,* contains many powerful restatements of the Romantic doctrine of organic unity. For Yeats a poem must be a living whole, like a flower, or a tree, or the body of a beautiful woman dancing. Critics, finally, have tended to assume that the literal center which controls all those figures is either the objective historical world, or Yeats's subjectivity, his sense of that world, or the supernatural powers in which Yeats believed and of which all those figures are emblems. It is in this latter area that Yeats's critics have most disagreed, for example, Denis Donoghue or Richard Ellmann on the one hand and F. A. C. Wilson or Kathleen Raine on the other. It is here, also, that Yeats himself appears to be most vacillating and contradictory, to offer his critics most scope for disagreement.

It will be my position here, presented hypothetically in terms of a reading of one poem standing by synecdoche for them all, that Yeats, in

"Nineteen Hundred and Nineteen" at least, speaks as no one, from nowhere, at no time, to no identifiable listeners; that "Nineteen Hundred and Nineteen" can by no effort be shown to have an organic unity; and that there is no identifiable central, literal thing of which all else is figure. The poem, in short, is a "labyrinth of the wind" (line 121). This labyrinth has no center that can ever be named literally or be present, here and now, to perception or to experience. This absence redefines all the named elements in the poem and makes them neither literal nor figurative, neither emblems nor things. Such figures take place, in Joyce's phrase, "at no spatial time." The absence of an identifiable center disqualifies all the conceptual oppositions that the critic needs to interpret the poem but at the same time gives the poem its enigmatic power, as though it were that "stump on the Acropolis," the "ancient image made of olive wood" (lines 46, 6), both sign and thing, therefore neither unequivocally.

What are the elements that enter into the poem? What is their placing, and within a space of what shape? What the elements are, the basic alphabet of the poem's code, we know. Previous critics have identified them. Though the competent reader of Yeats will steer his way among them without difficulty, they appear, when the reader stands back a little and surveys the group, an amazingly heterogeneous lot. They represent by synecdoche the material that enters into Yeats's work generally. In fact each detail of the poem ("Phidias' famous ivories," "the circle of the moon" [lines 7, 3], and so on) tends to stand for an entire context—Greek civilization as a whole, Yeats's visionary phases of the moon, or whatever. The concentration and explosive intensity of the poem is achieved by this bringing together in abrupt juxtaposition detached parts that stand for large wholes. The parts have been cut by violence from these wholes and mutilated. Each stands for its context, across the gap of its incisive separation from it. This form of synecdoche is appropriate, since the emblems are uniformly of acts of violence by man against the cherished monuments of his own constructive power. An example is the burning, by incendiary or bigot, of "that stump upon the Acropolis," the "ancient image made of olive wood," already given an ironically diminishing epithet that suggests mutilation, as of a hand or leg cut off. What was already a stump is then burned, though it was the emblem, in its making, in its preservation, and in its destruction, of Athenian civilization. It was created by Athene to counter Erechtheus's spring of salt water, in their rivalry over who was to become deity of the city. Each image of Yeats's poem in complex ways records an act of violence and is put into the text by another act of sundering. The images are then placed side by side with more violence. They are heterogeneous materials yoked together by violence.

The poem contains events from 1919, "the present time" of the poem: "A drunken soldiery / Can leave the mother, murdered at her door, / To crawl in her own blood, and go scot-free" (line 26–28). This material is placed side by side with the Greek details from Sophocles, Thucydides, and Herodotus, the "ancient image made of olive wood," "Phidias' famous ivories / And all the golden grasshoppers and bees" (lines 6, 7–8). The latter images open the poem and precede the present-day material. To both of these are added elements from those "mummy truths" of *Per Amica Silentia Lunae* and *A Vision,* the latter at that moment still in progress: the circle of the moon, the "Platonic Year" that "Whirls out new right and wrong, / Whirls in the old instead" (lines 55–56), the notion that after death the soul sometimes cannot free itself from the habits of life. This idea also has a specific source in Blake's *Milton* and is as much literary as esoteric or Neoplatonic. Blake's "Mock on" is echoed in the fifth section of the poem: "Come let us mock at the great . . ." (line 93ff.). Then there are "Loie Fuller's Chinese dancers" (actually Japanese), with all their context of Art Nouveau decor and the Mallarméan symbolism of dancer and dance. Juxtaposed with all that is the image of the swan. This may come from Shelley's *Prometheus Unbound* or from Spenser, as well as from Yeats's experience of real swans in Ireland, those wild swans at Coole. He had also seen there weasels fighting in a hole, mentioned in line 32. The final stanza mixes Herodias's daughters, with their context of Oscar Wilde's *Salomé* and Arthur Symons's "The Dance of the Daughters of Herodias," Yeats's own plays for dancers on the theme of the severed head, and material from Irish history and folklore. The latter include the whirling wind of the hosting of the Sidhe, those apparitional riders on horses with flowers on their heads, and the story of the fourteenth-century witch, Dame Alice Kyteler, and her "insolent" incubus, Robert Artisson, "Robin son of Art."

Finally, there are elements that are in the poem, apparently, only as passing figures of speech: the sun ("as it were wax in the run's rays" [line 12]; "now but gape at the sun" [line 102]); the dragon ("It seemed that a dragon of air" [line 51]); the labyrinth ("A man in his own secret meditation / Is lost amid the labyrinth that he has made / In art or politics" [lines 69–71]; "the labyrinth of the wind" [line 121]). Or are they only passing figures of speech? If so, of what literal things are they the figures? What meaning do those weasels have? Are they merely a figure of the unbridled ferocity, now, of that *we* who speaks the poem, we "who are but weasels fighting in a hole"? This is just the question. What center, literal reference, or *logos,* in the sense of chief meaning, organizes all the heterogeneous material of the poem—esoteric, historical, Hellenic, Biblical, literary, traditional, and biographical—making it an integrated whole? What stands outside the dance and controls it, in the sense that all the emblems of the poem are emblems for that "what"? Is it Yeats himself, the mind of the poet, who names himself in the first person twice in the poem ("I am satisfied with that"; "What my laborious life imagined" [lines 61, 82])? Is it a collective consciousness, the *we* or Ireland or of Europe at this moment of history? Is it material, historical, objective "reality"? Is it some transcendent spiritual center or force? Could it be all four, or some vanishing point where they coincide?

The *now* of the poem seems firmly located in the year named in the title, and its *here* seems to be Ireland, the speaker the poet. "Now days are dragon-ridden, the nightmare / Rides upon sleep" (lines 25–26): "I am satisfied with that . . . ." That *I*, however, appears only briefly in the poem. It emerges as the separate subjectivity of the poet who thinks of destroying even "the half-imagined, the half-written page" (line 83), the page, it may be, we are at that moment reading in printed copy. The "image" (line 80) of the wild swan leaping into the desolate heaven brings a savage rage to destroy what he has half-imagined, even the image that has generated the wildness and rage, in a self-dismantling torsion whereby the image is the means of taking "the solitary soul" to a place where that image is an impediment to achieving the act or state of the soul of which it is an image. The soul cannot get there without the image, but cannot get there with the image either.

This drama of the solitary soul emerges only briefly in the third part of the poem from a speaking consciousness that is consistently collective, a *we*. That *we* at first seems to be *we Irish,* but even by the third stanza of the first part must include the English, too, by implication all Europeans who have endured the great war. Gradually, as the poem progresses, the consciousness becomes an absolutely all-inclusive *we,* a *we* any man or woman joins when he or she reads the poem and looks back over the panorama of world history. The poem is spoken by no one in particular. It is uttered by a vast, visionary, all-inclusive voice within which the personal *I* of the poet only momentarily identifies itself.

Passages from Yeats's prose, for example, from the position-taking summary essay of 1937, "A General Introduction for My Work," have often been cited to support the claim that Yeats's poems should be thought of as the intense speech of Yeats himself in a particular time, place, and situation. "I tried," says Yeats, "to make the language of poetry coincide with that of passionate, normal speech. I wanted to write in whatever language comes most naturally when we soliloquise, as I do all day long, upon the events of our own lives or of any life where we can see ourselves for the moment."

One need only read on to the next page, however, to discover that this "passionate, normal speech" in poetry is in fact not private and particular to the poet. It is not personal at all but another voice, universal, anonymous, depersonalizing, a voice speaking through the poet. It is the voice of human experience generally, of literary and philosophical tradition. It is the voice ultimately of "nothing," of that no one and no place from which the desolate winds blow in "Nineteen Hundred and Nineteen": "If I wrote of personal love or sorrow in free verse, or, in any rhythm that left it unchanged, amid all its accidence [sic], I would be full of self-contempt because of my egotism and indiscretion, and foresee the boredom of my reader. I must choose a traditional stanza, even what I alter must seem traditional. I commit my emotion to shepherds, herdsmen, camel-drivers, learned men, Milton's or Shelley's 'Platonist,' that tower Palmer drew. Talk to me of originality and I will turn on you with rage. I am a crowd, I am a lonely man, I am nothing."

The speaker of "Nineteen Hundred and Nineteen" is not the private person William Yeats, but Yeats as a part of that *we* who is a crowd, a lonely man, nothing. The time and the place of the poem undergo a similar expansion. As the poem progresses the now of the poem reveals itself to be not the historical now of 1919 but a perpetual now in which the dance of history has always already occurred and yet is always occuring again, as the "Platonic year / Whirls out new right and wrong, / Whirls in the old instead." In the last section of the poem "Herodias' daughters have returned again" and Robert Artisson "lurches past" (lines 118, 126), brought back from the fourteenth century into the perpetual present of the poem. Within that present all things, and the loss or "vanishing" of all things, are contemporary because all things are "image."

The place of the poem undergoes a similar expansion. At first it is Ireland at a certain moment in history, but the place rapidly becomes a vast all-inclusive space of visionary image large enough to contain Greece, Phidias's famous ivories and all the golden grasshoppers and bees, that swan, Loie Fuller's Chinese dancers, those weasels, Robert Artisson and Lady Kyteler. It is big enough also to contain the vanishing of all these, according to the universal law of the poem: "Man is in love and loves what vanishes, / What more is there to say?" (lines 42–43). It seems as if that hole in which the weasels fight must be a black hole.

The voice of the poem is the voice of the poem. The time of the poem is the time of the poem. The place of the poem is the place of the poem. What person, time, and place are these? What is the topography of this space? What are its loci, the *lieux* within its milieu?

The shape of the poem, it is easy to see, is a round. The poem is a circular labyrinth in which the various elements of each of the six sections rotate around a center that is never named (except in figure), in a constant double process of substitution. This spatial design of a whirlwind or maze is reinforced throughout the poem in overt images: in the "circle of the moon" at the opening, in the circular whirling of the dancers and of the great year, in the word *round,* with its rhyme, *enwound,* which echoes through the poem ("But wearied running round and round in their courses," etc., lines 43, 49, 52, 116), in the labyrinth that is twice named (lines 70, 121), in the circular movement, in the last section, first of the apparitional horsemen and then of the dance of Herodias's daughters. The latter are seen by countrymen in Ireland in those miniature cyclones of dust that blow across the fields and roads.

This overt naming of a certain topography is reinforced first by the structure of each separate section. Each section is circular. A small set of elements is set in relation in each: Greek ivories, grasshoppers, and bees are placed against details from contemporary history in the first, dancers are set against the Platonic year in the second, and so on. Each section is a circular round of displacements in which each element or category of elements gives way to another set to which it is figuratively compared. The swan is set against a solitary soul in the third poem; the *we* of the poem against weasels fighting in the third; the great, the wise, the good, and the mockers are juxtaposed in the formally symmetrical mocking stanzas of the fifth section; the ghostly riders, Herodias' daughters, Robert Artisson and Lady Kyteler are put side by side in the sixth. The actual form of figurative equivalence among the elements in each section is uncertain since it depends in each case on their common relationship to the absent center. All one can see is that each new element rapidly replaces the one before. Their relation is as much antagonistic as harmonious. They are opposites living one another's death, dying one another's life, old right and wrong against new, weasels fighting in a hole. As the images interact in their whirling, they almost immediately consume one another and vanish. This occurs most strikingly in the fourth section, which exhausts its elements in four brief lines:

> We, who seven years ago,
> Talked of honour and of truth,
> Shriek with pleasure if we show
> The weasel's twist, the weasel's tooth.
>
> (lines 89–92)

"Nineteen Hundred and Nineteen" is a discontinuous poem. It must constantly start again from nothing, the nothing of the blank space between each section, so rapidly do the elements in each section destroy one another and exhaust what can be said of them in their relationship. The reader feels in the poem a great urgency to say what can be said before that gong's "barbarous clangour" (line 58) announces the end of a given effort of artic- ulation. The speaking or writing constantly destroys itself, and this neces- sitates a constant new beginning.

The second form of substitution in the double circular form of the poem is that whereby each new section replaces the one before. All the sections are related to one another as the elements of each separate section are related. It seems as if the poet is forced to reach again and again the point, a point that is also a moment, a moment-point, "at no spatial time," in which he must say "Man is in love and loves what vanishes, / What more is there to say?" The space of the poem collapses in a moment and in a point that can be given no spatial location, can be mapped by no image placed in its rightful home in a visible topography.

Does the poem continuously self-destruct, or is its scattering caused by some force outside itself? The new elements in each section rapidly take on the whirlwind or labyrinth shape that dominates the whole. They then vanish in their turn in a new mutually destroying agon, to be replaced by a new whirlwind structure in symmetrical juxtaposition. Or are they sym- metrical? By what law or by what right, in the name of what common measure, may they be called "analogous"? Does the reader know that it is a "new whirlwind," or is it perhaps the same wind levelling whatever it encounters? This wind may be revealed only in its acts of destruction, since in itself it is invisible. It constantly needs new material, so hungry is it for annihilation, and so insatiable, it may be, to display its power. What is that wind? From what center or periphery, from what cave of the winds or "center on the horizon," to use Stevens's phrase, does it blow?

The interpreter, at this crucial point of the analysis, when he has encountered a crossroads or a blind alley in the labyrinth of the wind, may be helped by following the threads of other, analogous, versions of the "same" structure—in art, in poetry, in philosophy, and in psychoanalytic theory. The topology of a whirlwind or of a whirlpool, a swirling of elements around a missing or veiled center, is a common one in all these forms of expression, though of course it is not the only one. The abyssal structure of Stevens's "The Rock" is not the same as this whirlwind form, nor is the self-generating linear sequence of vision within vision of Shelley's "The Triumph of Life" the same, nor are the complex temporal reversals and substitutions of Hardy's lyrics the same. Each of my chapters here explores a different spatial representation of temporality. Just as the relation between the successive sections of Yeats's "Nineteen Hundred and Nineteen," across the blank spaces dividing each from each, stays problematic as long as the central ratio by which they may all be measured remains unidentified, so the sense in which topographical structures by different workers in different media may be said to be analogous is even more problematic. The notion of analogy, whether this is thought of as a logical or as a figurative relation, is precisely what is in question here. What is the *logos* in the name of which we may say that *A* is like *B,* or falls within the "same" conceptual category, or in the name of which we may create one of those ratios Aristotle finds at the base of one class of metaphors: *A* is to *B* as *C* is to *D,* "wild swan" is to "the solitary soul" as "we," these days, are to "weasels fighting in a hole," or as Lady Kyteler and Robert Artisson are to—to what? The dance of Herodias's daughters? The latter, however, is not quite the "same" relationship. Or is it? This is just the question. In any case, the whirlwind always turns on those little words *is* and *as.*

In the case of Stevens's "A Primitive Like an Orb," the invisible and unnamable power at the center of the labyrinth of words making up the poem is the rising or setting sun, "at the center on the horizon," (line 87) but the rule of the poem is that the word *sun* may not appear. As the sun may not be looked in the eye without blinding the looker, so the nonpresence, the core and ultimate reason behind all discourse, what Stevens here calls "the poem at the center of things," can only be named evasively, as something that "is and it / Is not and, therefore, is" (lines 13–14).

To give another example, one of the earliest great theoretical or metapsychological passages in Freud's work, in section 4 of *Studies on Hysteria,* presents a dazzling series of incompatible metaphorical models, each contradicting the one before, to express the fact that the "pathogenic nucleus" at the source of a given case of hysteria may not be reached or brought unchanged into the light of day, there to be seen and literally named. The work of the analyst is like that of the explorer of a labyrinth that has a center, but one that may by no procedures be reached as such. It has the nature of language or of signs and is the condition of the discourse of the hysteric, but it cannot be named directly, neither by the patient nor by the analyst. A more famous passage in *The Interpretation of Dreams* names this unreachable and unidentifiable "black hole" at the center of the maze of psychic life with the figure of the mushroom mycelium:

> Even in the best interpreted dreams, there is often a place that must be left in the dark because in the process of interpreting, one notices a tangle [*ein Knäuel*] of dream-thoughts arising, which

resists unravelling but has also made no further contributions [*keine weiteren Beiträge*] to the dream-content. This is the dream's navel, the place where it straddles the unknown [*dem Unerkannten aufsitzt*]. The dream-thoughts, to which interpretation leads one, are necessarily interminable [*ohne Abschluss*] and branch out on all sides into the netlike entanglement [*in die netzartige Verstrick-ung*] of our world of thought. Out of one of the denser places of this meshwork [*Geflechts*], the dreamwish rises like a mushroom out its mycelium.

This dark place, or a "similar" one at the center of his own thought, Friedrich Nietzsche, in "On Truth and Lies in a Nonmoral Sense," calls "the mysterious X [*das rätselhafte X*]." Perception is already a metaphor of this X. Language is therefore a metaphor of a metaphor, twice displaced. If language, in Nietzsche's celebrated formulation here, is "a movable host of metaphors, metonymies, and anthropomorphisms," these are not substitutes for literal names that could be given. All are, strictly speaking, catachreses, figures drawn from some other realm and transferred as the improper names for what has no proper name in any language. If lies are immoral because the truth should be given whenever possible, according to a categorical imperative, the "lies" of which Nietzsche speaks in this essay are "nonmoral" (*aussermoralischen*) because it would not be possible for anyone to give the true formulations of which they are the figurative deformations. How can it be immoral to tell a lie when there is no possibility of telling the truth?

The image of the labyrinth does not appear as such in Nietzsche's essay. Its place is taken by the figures of the beehive, the columbarium, the stratified pyramid, the spider web, the stately and apparently impregnable fortress, an astrological map of the heavens, and the design made in sand in response to musical vibrations. These reticulated patterns are figures for the edifices of thought philosophers and other conceptual thinkers make to "bar the foul storm out." At the same time they are figures for artistic constructions, motivated by feeling, in musical tones, in paint, or in poetic words. Art and philosophy at first seem rigorously opposed in Nietzsche's argument, but in the end they are seen as coming to the same thing, or to different versions of the same thing. However solid any one of these architectural constructions may appear, each is no more than a frail spider web over a rushing stream. Both artist and philosopher are, in Nietzsche's famous formulation, "as if hanging in dreams on the back of a tiger [*gleichsam auf dem Rücken eines Tigers in Träumen hängend*]."

In place of a full exploration of these analogous examples of the strange maze this chapter attempts to map, the maze whose center is "only . . . an X which remains inaccessible and indefinable for us [*nur ein für uns unzugängliches und undefinierbares* X]," I limit myself to a somewht more complete discussion of a single case. This is a graphic rather than verbal representation of the structure I claim is common to all these examples, the design of the labyrinth without attainable or representable center.

Paul Klee's *Tanzspiel der Rotröcke* [*Danceplay of the Red Skirts*] (1924) seems almost like a negative version of Stevens's "A Primitive Like an Orb." Klee's painting presents a spiral, whirlpool, or labyrinth design with a dark core rather than a bright one. What better representation in graphic form of the topographical structure that is my topic here than a dark orb where vision fails, as eyesight is blinded when it looks directly at the sun? Is that central region in the painting a hollow tunnel or is it a solid object, absorbing all the light, a kind of black hole? What can be seen, the red skirts, seems to have come from the dark sun or to be returning to it, so that the center is clearly hot enough and bright enough, dark with excessive bright. The dark orb at the center of the painting can be thought of as made of the superimposition of all the colors distributed across the surface of the painting: the browns, gray-greens, and yellows, as well as the reds.

The word *Tanzspiel* in the title suggests both dance and play, the latter in the sense of interplay or fluctuation (as one says, "there is play in this wheel"), as well as in the sense of game. Klee's painting is literally spatial, as no poem can be, except in the sense that the words are distributed spatially on the page. Nevertheless the topography of this painting is in its own way as enigmatic as that of "Nineteen Hundred and Nineteen." The figures in Klee's painting are clearly signs of some sort, not representations of some ballet that might be photographed. As enigmatic signs they must be interrogated. When they are interrogated they reveal themselves to create, in their play, there on the surface of the painting, a space that is as illogical, as disoriented, as unchartable, as the space of any poem.

One irreducible difference between any poem and any painting is that a painting is after all spatial. There it is, all at once, on the canvas, however complex the patterned echoes from one part of the painting to another may be. The basic resource of poetry, on the other hand, is repetition of the same structure with different materials along a temporal axis, as in "Nineteen Hundred and Nineteen." Klee presents only one version of his whirlpool pattern in this painting. He employs as elements only the repeated and fragmented doll-figure in the red skirt plus the architectural elements, perhaps real buildings, perhaps a stage set for a ballet: walls, roof, windows, and doors swirling with the skirts. What corresponds, in Klee's use of his medium, to the chainlike series of images in apposition in Stevens's "A Primitive Like an Orb," or to the sequence of sections, each developing its own set of figurative elements, in Yeats's poem, is of course the long sequence of Klee's paintings. Many, though not all, of these have the same topographical arrangement as *Tanzspiel der Rotröcke*. Each such painting develops with different elements the same enigma of the relation of visible and yet peripheral hieroglyphic figures, halfway between writing and representational mimesis, to an invisible center.

The puzzle, in Klee, lies also sometimes in the relation between the purely graphic elements in the painting and Klee's witty and poetic title for it. These titles often name the paintings only by figurative displacement. At any rate, since they are language, they are open to the kind of interpretation appropriate for language rather than for graphic figures. The title of *Tanzspiel der Rotröcke*, for example, not only contains the doubling play between dance and play in *Tanzspiel*. It also suggests that it is not the women who are dancing but the red skirts. It is either as though there were some compulsion in the skirts themselves that whirls them around without human intent, or as though some dragon of air had fallen among the skirts and whirled them and their wearers around on its own furious path, to put it in terms drawn from Yeats's "Nineteen Hundred and Nineteen."

The problems for interpretation in Klee's painting lie in this either/or and in related undecidable alternatives. Do the skirts impel themselves to dance or are they seized by the rotating force that spirals out from the center? Are the dancers, whole and fragmentary, along with the bits and pieces of buildings or scenery, coming out of the central obscurity, or are they going into it? Are they dispersing centrifugally and taking form as they get further from the formless center, or are they being sucked by centripetal force into the maelstrom? Are they being broken and dismembered more and more as they reach nearer to the center, until at last they vanish altogether in that dark core where all colors and shapes are combined? Are there in fact a multitude of red skirts, as the plural in the title suggests, or is there only one dancer shown simultaneously at different times and at different loci on the spiral leading toward and away from the center? Even if the skirts are plural, they are clearly representations of the same process at different stages. All the skirts are subject to the same forces. They are signs of that invisible energy from which they all come or to which they all return. This energy creates them or they create it, since the center draws its meaning from the peripheral signs for it. At the same time those signs, the identifiable shapes of dancers in red skirts, wholes or parts, draw their meaning from the central dark primitive core of which they are the signs. They create and reveal it

at once, make it and are made by it, in an oscillation of meaning like that
in Stevens's "A Primitive Like an Orb."

However the critic chooses to interpret the dynamic topology of Klee's
painting, it is clear that he must in one way or another recognize that its
meaning is generated by the alogical correspondence between the red-skirted
figures and the central orb around which they dance. Since that orb cannot
be represented visually except in figures that both falsify it and yet are the
only kind of representation it can have, it may be said that Klee's painting
is a visual representation of a catachresis. It presents signs that are neither
figurative nor literal. They refer by displacement to something that could
not be represented literally and so do not substitute for a literal picture that
just does not happen to have been given. . . .

These brief detours through maze-like displacements in Stevens, in
Klee, in Freud, and in Nietzsche have left still hanging unanswered the
questions I posed about Yeats's "Nineteen Hundred and Nineteen." The
detours were in search of answers to the questions: What is that destructive
wind that blows through Yeats's poem, levelling everything, even, repeatedly, the constructions of the poem itself? From what cave of the winds
does it blow? Is that cave at the center or at the periphery, at the center on
the horizon? Violence is the human and transhuman law. That law breaks
all political codes of law to fragments, as those ivories, golden grasshoppers
and bees, images of the gods, symbols of longevity and patiently constructed
work, are turned into objects for sale or broken into bits. If no work of
hand or intellect can stand, what then should man do?

The detours have identified a certain topographical pattern. This pattern
is duplicated, always with a difference, from poem to poem and within each
of the poems by Yeats and Stevens. It appears also in Klee, in Nietzsche,
and in Freud. The difference is that different materials, in each case, are
brought into proximity with an unnamable center. The various topologies
are also analogies for one another. To say that this topographical structure
is duplicated from text to text or from medium to medium must be taken
in a special sense, "anasemically," as Jacques Derrida or Nicholas Abraham
would say, that is, against the grain of the usual meaning of *analogy*. That
word traditionally suggests a circumferential similarity in wording between
diverse verbal elements. This similarity is justified by the common relation
of the elements to a presiding central word or *logos*—father, sun king, patron
of analogies. This center is the guarantee of the sibling kinship of what is
on the periphery. Do they not all have the same father? In the spatial design
mapped in various examples here there is no patronizing king, no sun, at
best a dark sun that is also an endless tunnel. The design is a topology

without any *logos* at the center. This means that the relation of analogy among peripheral elements or between superimposed versions of the "same" design must be redefined. The relation is an ana-analogy of elements that do not really belong together in the same space. The most heterogeneous elements can be brought together in the same place, as they conspicuously are in Yeats's poem. Their relation to one another is governed not by their reference to a common *logos* but by the fact that they are all catachreses for an unknown X around which they circle. The X is something that both makes them emblems and at the same time undermines their referential validity. It also separates them from one another across fissures that do not allow the resonances of analogy in the traditional metaphysical sense of that term. This means that the spatial model breaks down. This breaking down reveals the model to be the indispensable means of thinking about the structure in question, but indispensable only if it is carried to the point where it no longer functions and must be dispensed with. Why must we represent to ourselves in spatial terms what is not spatial but verbal and temporal? Why must this topographical structure always fail in the encounter with something that cannot be spatially located, that has no *topos* and no proper name?

This *it* is at a center that is no center but is missing there, and at the horizon but missing there, too. It is dispersed everywhere, not just outside, beyond the last wall, nor inside, at some inner core, like a hidden tomb or a corpse in a pyramid. Nor is this *it* in a transcendent realm. For Yeats as for Stevens, "the light / Of it is not a light apart, uphill." Yeats chooses firmly for the whirlpool, the gyre of immanent powers as against the waterfall of Platonic or Neoplatonic emanations dropping from the One in regular gradations. *It* is neither word, nor force, nor thing, nor subjective energy, nor spiritual entity, but all those "things" at once in a confusion that confounds the clear distinctions and binary oppositions between subject and object, between word and thing, between literal and figurative language, between this world and a supernal one, which are necessary to clear thought, whether in poetry, in philosophy, or in literary criticism. If the *it* is the cave of the wind that blows through the labyrinth of Yeats's poem, the thinking or the linguistic structures that lead to the intuition of this *it* must not be confused with any sort of trancendentalism, Platonic or otherwise, any thinking governed by the presence of presences, occult or otherwise, nor with a certain false Heideggerianism of the immanence of Being, nor with a nihilism of the abyss, the idea that nothing exists at the base but empty and factitious structures of signs. If the *it* is neither thought, nor thing, nor spirit, nor word, it is not nothing either. In the encounter with this *it,* the validity of the notion of the linguistic moment reaches its limit and dissolves before something that is not language, though it both motivates and disrupts language. This "something" nevertheless can only be approached through that language it disrupts when the final step across the threshold, the step that can never quite be taken, begins to be taken.

What I am calling the linguistic moment is the moment when a poem, or indeed any text, turns back on itself and puts its own medium in question, so that there is a momentum in the poem toward interrogating signs as such. This momentum may make a casual moment spread out to take up all the time of the poem, or to suspend time in a ceaseless hovering. This moment, when language is foregrounded, is indispensable to the putting in question of the presupposed structures of logocentric metaphysics: beginning, middle, end, organic unity, and underlying extra-linguistic ground—whether that ground in a given case is called being, consciousness, will, self, physical object, absolute spirit, presence, or whatever. In the end, however, having performed this deconstructive function, the linguistic moment reaches the term of its usefulness as a term or as an endpoint. Beyond this boundary, though encountered only through words, the linguistic moment dissolves before the *it.* The unknown X is beyond language, though it is what all language "names," in the gap which may not be closed between all words and any fixed identifiable referent, subjective, objective, natural, or supernatural. This *it* is what undermines all thinking, performing, and constructing, in art, poetry, science, politics, or philosophy, all the monuments made by the great, the wise, the good, and the mockers of all those in Yeats's poem. Because of the *it* all these monuments are inhabited from the beginning by the leveling wind. They are woven or molded of wind, for "A man in his own secret meditation / Is lost amid the labyrinth that he has made / In art or politics," and that labyrinth is "the labyrinth of the wind."

I have spoken of an intuition through language of what is beyond language but on which language rests, like a spider web on a roaring river or like a man asleep on the back of a tiger. In what way, exactly, is this "intuition" (this word too must be read here against the grain of its usual sense) expressed in the language of Yeats's "Nineteen Hundred and Nineteen"? The poem as a whole is not only written for the sake of its final section but rather leads up to its final section or reaches its climax in the final section. This section attains closest to the *it* from which the leveling wind blows. With a discussion of that section I shall conclude this chapter.

First a word should be said about the presence in Yeats's poem of the image of the sun that is the "central" figure in Stevens's "A Primitive Like an Orb." The sun is the basis of the "photological" tradition in Western thought from Plato on, for example, at the end of Book VI and the beginning of Book VII of the *Republic*. If the labyrinthine wind is the pervasive emblem in Yeats's poem, the sun is also twice mentioned, in ways that implicitly equate the levelling wind with the levelling sun. "Nineteen Hundred and Nineteen" is heliocentric too, as Yeats's work as a whole often is, as well as "centered" on that cavern from which the wind blows. It is as if the sun and the wind source were two foci of an ellipse, like one another and yet different. Around these foci the elements of the poem whirl like planets in their orbits.

If the wind levels all, there is something a little ominous, in spite of its benign action, about the way the sun works in the second stanza of the first section of the poem. "We too had many pretty toys when young," says the poet, among them "habits that made old wrong / Melt down as it were wax in the sun's rays." If the strong sun can so easily melt old wrong, might it not, almost by accident as it were, in its ubiquitous force, also melt old or new right, as the Platonic Year, a little later in the poem, with absolute indifference, "Whirls out new right and wrong, / Whirls in the old instead." The wax is implicit in that image of the golden bees, emblem in the opening stanza of the poem of the constructive power of Greek culture. What the bees in their architectural genius make, they make of wax, and Yeats has scarcely mentioned the bees before he reminds the reader in a seemingly casual simile of the vulnerability of wax to the sun's rays.

The second mention of the sun comes in the second stanza of the fifth section, the mocking poem. There the sun has its full function as the blinding center that cannot be looked at directly, or can be looked at directly only by blinded eyes. These eyes have been blinded, like those of Oedipus, by excess wisdom and gape open now like empty mouths, or like wounds. Though the sun cannot be looked at, all the calendars of seasonal and annual changes, all that can be known and studied, rotate around that dazzling invisible center:

> Come let us mock at the wise;
> With all those calendars whereon
> They fixed old aching eyes,
> They never saw how seasons run,
> And now but gape at the sun.
>
> (lines 98–102)

In the last section of the poem three images follow one another, each replacing the last when that last has hardly been presented, in the most rapid and most violent sequence of all. The sequence leads to the final violence of the last two lines: "To whom the love-lorn Lady Kyteler brought / Bronzed peacock feathers, red combs of her cocks" (lines 129–130), after which the poem, which has started and stopped and started again throughout, abruptly stops for good. The first image, of the apparitional horsemen, is replaced by that of the dance of Herodias's daughters, and that in turn by the insolent fiend, Robert Artisson, and the love-lorn Lady Kyteler. "I have assumed in this sixth poem," Yeats writes of the first image in his notes on the poem, "that these horsemen, now that the times worsen, give way to worse": "But wearied running round and round in their courses / All break and vanish, and evil gathers head" (lines 116–117). What this "evil" is, the reader knows, both from earlier passages in this poem and from Yeats's interpretation of our times elsewhere. Evil is the increase in violence and unreason threatening all orders of law and art, but preparing, it may be, a new annunciation, a reversal of the gyres whirling out new right and wrong, whirling in the old instead. As the poem moves from section to section and from image to image, the reader moves also closer and closer to the center of the labyrinth, whirlpool, or circling gyres. The final three images, in the last section, whirl the fastest and are closest to the absolute violence of the center, that unnamed crossroads where Lady Kyteler makes sacrifice to her incubus. That center is also at the periphery. According to Yeats's image of the turning, intersecting gyres, the approach toward the center on one gyre is accompanied by the furthest centrifugal receding out to the edge on the other, as "Things fall apart; the center cannot hold."

None of the three final images is interpreted within the poem. Each is only presented, "concretely described." Each is a vehicle with a missing tenor. The three images are figures, but there are no named or namable literals that they replace. In this they are what Yeats calls "emblems" and what traditional rhetoric calls "catachreses." They hang, hover, or turn in the void as signs of what cannot be signified directly. Their interpretation therefore cannot be, as with ordinary figurative images, by way of the relation of the figurative vehicle to the literal tenor it replaces. The interpretation must be lateral, around the chambers or corridors of the labyrinth. This displacement from figure to figure is allegorical in the sense in which Walter Benjamin or Paul de Man use the term. The meaning of a Yeatsian emblem can be identified not in relation to what the emblem signifies, in a sign-thing structure (that "thing" remains absent and without a literal name), but in relation to other emblems, whether in the same poem or in other texts in the tradition, in a sign-sign relation. This relation is characterized by the temporal gap between the two emblems and by their heterogeneity in relation to one another. They cannot be assimilated to some common essence or archetype. Distance and unlikeness separate emblem from emblem. Across that gulf the interpreter must leap. Moreover, the critic is also bound by the law that prohibits the poem from naming the *it* directly. His language can have at best the same status of perpetual displacement as the language of the poet. The critic can only move in his turn from emblem to emblem around the periphery, troping one in terms of the other. The critic's language may be defined as the continuous translation of what cannot be by any means ever given, by poet or critic, in the original language. The emblematic or allegorical method, for both poet and critic, is always the translation of what is already a translation rather than ever being the translation of an original. There is no original language for the *it*.

The final three images of "Nineteen Hundred and Nineteen" are a splendid example of Yeats's emblematic strategy and of the implicit invocation of an appropriate method for the interpretation of such emblems. The first image is that of the ghostly horsemen, "ancient inhabitants of the country," or "fallen angels" seen by Irish country people, according to Yeats's note. This image seems to make a reference back to the real horsemen and soldiers of the Black and Tan atrocities in section 1. The reader may at first mistakenly think the "violence upon the roads: violence of horses" is the same as that historical violence. In fact this image marks the transition to the overtly supernatural emblems of the final section. These are no earthly horsemen and riders. Such emblems are made of the transfiguration of natural objects, a certain way of seeing them as signs, as the countrymen see in those miniature whirling dust storms the dance of Herodias's daughters or the hosting of the Sidhe. "They [the Sidhe] journey in whirling winds," wrote Yeats in a note to "The Hosting of the Sidhe," "the winds that were called the dance of the daughters of Herodias in the Middle Ages, Herodias doubtless taking the place of some old goddess."

The ultimate key to unlock the farthest door before the final cryptic barrier of silence protecting the *it* within the labyrinth of the wind is the allegorical relation between the two final images. Both of these combine the erotic and the supernatural in a way characteristic of Yeats. The two images, however, are related in crisscross or chiasmus. From one image to the next the sexes or their relations change place, and there is also a displacement from center to periphery of the perpetrator of violence.

The *it* is given the allegorical name first of the absent and unattainable center of the dusty labyrinth of the wind made by the dance of Herodias' blind daughters:

> Herodias' daughters have returned again,
> A sudden blast of dusty wind and after

Thunder of feet, tumult of images,
Their purpose in the labyrinth of the wind;
And should some crazy hand dare touch a daughter
All turn with amorous cries, or angry cries,
According to the wind, for all are blind.

(lines 118–124)

Here the female comes from the center and the male is captivated by her, drawn fatally into the maelstrom. Herodias's daughters, of whom Salomé of course is one, are themselves mutilated, blinded as the old wise men who gape at the sun are blind. The context here is Yeats's own work in his late plays, *A Full Moon in March*, *The King of the Great Clock Tower*, and *The Death of Cuchulain*, and in addition his sources for the figure of this dance: the Bible, Heine, Oscar Wilde's *Salomé*, and Arthur Symons's poem, "The Dance of the Daughters of Herodias." Although these daughters are mutilated, they are for Yeats also emblems of a mutilating power in women, a power to unman and decapitate the men who love them as in the beheading of John the Baptist. Only a crazy hand would dare touch one. The daughters are emblems of the absence of any "head" meaning, underlying support for the meaning of all other signs. This meaning does not exist as something that can ever be named directly or confronted directly. It can only be named or confronted as an absence, like a missing head or a missing phallus. Herodias's daughters are, in Yeats's precise phrase, a "tumult of images," a storm of figures without ascertainable polar center.

This erotic relation is reversed in the final emblem. Now the male, Robert Artisson, comes from the center, and the enamored female, Lady Kyteler, is at the edge, drawn by infatuation toward that center. The mutilation or dismembering is now performed by the mortal woman in homage to her supernatural incubus, not by supernatural woman on mortal man. Lady Kyteler, though mortal, was a witch. She was as fatal to men as any of Herodias's daughters, having, it is supposed, killed by poison or enchantment four husbands, one after the other. Her own doom came in her submission to Robert Artisson, "an evil spirit," according to Yeats's note, "much run after in Kilkenny at the start of the fourteenth century." Lady Kyteler is supposed to have "had carnal knowledge" of Artisson. This demon, "named Son of Art, or Robin son of Art," was attracted into the natural world from his dwelling place in the supernatural by sacrifices made at crossroads, traditionally associated with ghosts, witches, and demons. Crossroads are in folklore at the borderland between the canny and the uncanny. Here, that crossroad, or those crossroads, since they are a multiple and ubiquitous focus, may be taken as the emblem of the absent center itself. It or they are never named in Yeats's poem, only in his sources. Dame Alice and her "band of heretical sorcerers," these sources say, "offered in sacrifice to demons living animals, which they dismembered, and then distributed at cross-roads to a certain evil spirit of low rank, named the Son of Art." In Yeats's poem Lady Kyteler dismembers peacocks, symbol for Yeats of annunciation ("the cry of Juno's peacock"), and cocks, offering to her insolent fiend bronzed peacock feathers starred or eyed, and red combs of her cock, images of unmanning once more, like the blindness of the gaping old men.

This act of dismembering causes Robert Artisson to manifest himself as the next emblem when Herodias's daughters vanish. Artisson is the version here of that "rough beast" in "The Second Coming" who "slouches towards Bethlehem to be born," or of that "brazen winged beast" of "laughing, ecstatic destruction" Yeats came to see "as always at my left side just out of the range of the sight":

> But now wind drops, dust settles; thereupon
> There lurches past, his great eyes without thought
> Under the shadow of stupid straw-pale locks,
> That insolent fiend Robert Artisson
> To whom the love-lorn Lady Kyteler brought
> Bronzed peacock feathers, red combs of her cocks.
>
> (lines 125–130)

The beheading, mutilation, or castration is performed first by supernatural women on mortal men, then by a mortal woman in homage to her supernatural lover. This reversible act of violence occurs across the barrier between the sexes. This is also the barrier between natural and supernatural, and between system, order, beauty, reason, on the one hand, and disorder, the foul storm, on the other. The reversal from Herodias's daughters to Lady Kyteler shows that the foul storm, which seems to blow from outside the human and natural world, is always already inside, intimate to man and to all his constructions, intrinsic to everything he has made.

"Nineteen Hundred and Nineteen" is a poem that systematically dismantles itself as system. It lacks the closed order of "organic unity." It keeps stopping and starting again and cannot be rationally integrated by interpretation. Also, it is about the ruination of system or order. It is about the way the "foul storm" cannot be barred out because it always gets incorporated into any system of art, of love, of politics, law, or philosophy and makes that system self-destruct, as "Nineteen Hundred and Nineteen" continually destroys itself.

This gives the answer to the questions I proposed at the beginning: "Why is it no work can last?" and "What should man do when he sees no monument of art or intellect can stand?" No work can last because any work is inhabited, undermined, by the *it* which destroys it. What one should do is some action like Yeats's in writing the poem. Destroying the half-imagined, the half-written page would accomplish nothing. To write a poem is a constructive act that at the same time participates in the destruction, as does Lady Kyteler in offering bronzed peacock feathers, red combs of her cocks. Such an act of mutilation as the poem performs does not end all things, but it approaches as close as possible to that cave of the winds by incorporating the wind's power into the labyrinth of the poem, in the words on the page. Things are preserved only in their destruction, by being turned into emblems, where they are in the closest proximity of signifying to the wind that destroys them. This means, for all the elements that enter into the poem—human, natural, and supernatural—being cut up and cut off from one another and from their natural contexts. Each is destroyed and renewed by being made into a sign that stands for that which there is no standing and no standing for.

Chronology

1865   William Butler Yeats born June 13, 1865 in Dublin. Yeats's family moves between Ireland and England several times.

1875–80   Yeats at Godolphin School, Hammersmith, England.

1882   First poems published.

1885   Yeats forms the Dublin Hermetic Society with a group of friends. He publishes a few poems in the *Dublin University Review*.

1886   Abandons art studies to write full-time.

1887   Yeats's family returns to London. His mother suffers a stroke which leaves her mentally impaired. Yeats joins the Blavatsky Lodge of the Theosophical Society in London and publishes his first poetry in English magazines.

1888   In London, Yeats meets Shaw, Wilde, William Morris, and W. E. Henley. Writes *Fairy and Folk Tales*.

1889   Publishes *The Wanderings of Oisin and Other Poems*. Is introduced to Maud Gonne by John O'Leary.

1890   Yeats is initiated into the Order of the Golden Dawn.

1892   Founds National Literary Society in Dublin. Publishes *The Countess Cathleen and Various Legends and Lyrics*.

1893   *The Celtic Twilight* and the three-volume *The Works of William Blake*.

1894   Meets Olivia Shakespear. *The Land of Heart's Desire* is performed in London.

1895   *Collected Poems* published. Edits *A Book of Irish Verse*.

1896   Has brief affair with Olivia Shakespear. Meets Lady Gregory in the West of Ireland. Meets John Synge.

1897   Spends the summer at Lady Gregory's home at Coole Park. *The Secret Rose* published.

1898   With Lady Gregory and Edward Martyn, forms Irish Literary Theatre.

1899   Rehearses for first performances of the Irish Literary Theatre. *The Wind among the Reeds* wins *Academy* prize for poetry.

1900   Yeats's mother dies. *The Shadowy Waters* appears.

1902   Yeats is made president of newly-founded Irish National Theatre Society. *Cathleen ni Hoolihan* produced.

1903   *In the Seven Woods* published. Yeats is devastated by Maud Gonne's marriage to John MacBride, and travels to America on a lecture tour.

1906   Named director of the Abbey Theatre with Lady Gregory and Synge. *Poems 1899–1905* published. Yeats's *Deirdre* performed at Abbey.

1907   Yeats defends Synge's *The Playboy of the Western World* after Abbey riots. Tours Italy with Lady Gregory and her son Robert.

1908   Eight-volume *Collected Edition* of his works finished, with complete revisions of early works. Yeats visits Maud Gonne in Paris, and studies French.

1909   Meets Ezra Pound. Synge dies.

1910   Receives Civil List pension of £150 per year. *The Green Helmet and Other Poems* published.

1911   Meets Georgie Hyde-Lees. In Paris with Lady Gregory. *Plays for Irish Theatre* published.

1912   Yeats lectures at Harvard on "The Theatre of Beauty." Ezra Pound reads aloud for Yeats and teaches him to fence.

1913   Yeats and Pound spend first of three successive winters at Stone Cottage, Sussex. *Poems Written in Discouragement* published.

1914   Lecture tour in America. *Responsibilities* appears.

1915   *At the Hawk's Well* produced in London, with masks by Edmund Dulac and dances by Michio Ito. Yeats declines offer of knighthood.

1916   Easter Rising in Dublin. Yeats writes "Easter 1916." John MacBride executed. Yeats visits Maud Gonne in Paris. Purchases Ballylee tower.

1917   Marriage to Georgie Hyde-Lees in London after refusals by Maud Gonne and her daughter Iseult.

1918   Restoration of Ballylee begins. Yeats writes *The Only Jealousy of Emer*.

1919   Anne Butler Yeats born February 26.

1920   Lecture tour in America.

1921   Michael Butler Yeats born August 22. *Michael Robartes and the Dancer* and *Four Plays for Dancers* published.

1922   Beginning of Irish civil war. Yeats's father dies. *The Trembling of the Veil* published. Yeats becomes member of the Irish Senate.

1923   Nobel Prize for Literature. Writes *The Bounty of Sweden*.

1925   First edition of *A Vision* published. O'Casey's *The Plough and the Stars* opens to riots at the Abbey.

1927   Serious influenza and lung congestion leads to collapse.

1928   Continued poor health. Yeats finishes his Senate term and travels to Rapallo. *The Tower* published.

1929   *Fighting the Waves* produced in Dublin. Yeats suffers relapse, diagnosed now as Malta fever.

1930   *The Words Upon the Window-Pane* performed at Abbey.

1931   At Coole Park with Lady Gregory.

1932   Death of Lady Gregory. Yeats goes on his last American lecture tour.

1933   *The King of the Great Clock Tower* written. *The Winding Stair* published.

1934   Sexual rejuvenation achieved through Steinach operation. *Wheels and Butterflies* published.

1935   *A Full Moon in March* published.

1936   Seriously ill again, Yeats travels to Majorca, London, and back to Ireland. Delivers BBC lecture on Modern Poetry.

1937   Second edition of *A Vision* and *Essays 1931–1936* published. Four more BBC broadcasts.

1938   *Purgatory* performed at the Abbey. Moves to south of France and writes *On the Boiler*. Begins *The Death of Cuchulain*.

1939   Yeats dies on January 28. Buried at Roquebrune, France.

1948   Yeats's body returned to Ireland aboard the Irish corvette *Macha*. Funeral procession from Galway to Sligo and then to Drumcliffe. Yeats's grave lies "under bare Ben Bulben's head" with a stone inscribed as Yeats directed in "Under Ben Bulben."

Contributors

HAROLD BLOOM, Sterling Professor of the Humanities at Yale University, is the author of *The Anxiety of Influence, Poetry and Repression,* and many other volumes of literary criticism. His forthcoming study, *Freud: Transference and Authority,* attempts a full-scale reading of all of Freud's major writings. A MacArthur Prize Fellow, he is general editor of five series of literary criticism published by Chelsea House.

HELEN VENDLER teaches at both Boston and Harvard Universities. Her books include studies of Yeats, Stevens, George Herbert, and Keats.

PRISCILLA WASHBURN SHAW is Professor of English and Comparative Literature at the University of California at Santa Cruz. She is the author of *Rilke, Valéry and Yeats: The Domain of the Self.*

THOMAS R. WHITAKER is Professor of English at Yale University. His books include *Swan and Shadow: Yeats's Dialogue with History* and *Fields of Play in Modern Drama.*

IAN FLETCHER, formerly of the University of Reading, is now Professor of English at the University of Arizona. He is the foremost authority on the English literature of the period 1880–1914, and is widely known for his writings on Yeats, Pater, Swinburne, and Lionel Johnson.

ALLEN R. GROSSMAN is Professor of English at Brandeis University, and is the author of *Poetic Knowledge* and *Of the Great House.*

RICHARD ELLMANN is Goldsmiths' Professor of English at New College, Oxford, and Research Professor of the Humanities at Emory University. He is the foremost scholar of Joyce and the author of *Yeats: The Man and the Masks* and *The Identity of Yeats.*

DENIS DONOGHUE is the Henry James Professor of Letters at New York University. His books include studies of Yeats, Swift, and Dickinson.

He is also the author of *Ferocious Alphabets* and *Sovereign Ghost: Studies in Imagination.*

HERBERT J. LEVINE is Assistant Professor of English at Franklin and Marshall College. He is the author of *Yeats's Daimonic Renewal.*

PAUL DE MAN was Sterling Professor of Comparative Literature at Yale University. His influential theoretical studies are gathered together in *Blindness and Insight, Allegories of Reading,* and *The Rhetoric of Romanticism.*

J. HILLIS MILLER is Frederick W. Hilles Professor of English and Comparative Literature at Yale University. Among his many books are *The Poetry of Reality* and *The Disappearance of God.*

Bibliography

Adams, Hazard. *Blake and Yeats: The Contrary Vision.* Ithaca, N.Y.: Cornell University Press, 1955.

————. "Some Yeatsian Versions of Comedy." In *In Excited Reverie: A Centenary Tribute to William Butler Yeats, 1865–1939,* edited by A. Norman Jeffares and K. G. W. Cross, 153–70. New York: St. Martin's Press, 1965.

Allen, James Lovic. "Yeats's Phase in the System of *A Vision.*" *Éire-Ireland* 8 (1973): 91–117.

Bloom, Harold. "The Internalization of Quest-Romance." In *Romanticism and Consciousness: Essays in Criticism,* edited by Harold Bloom, 3–24. New York: W. W. Norton, 1970.

Bornstein, George. *Yeats and Shelley.* Chicago: The University of Chicago Press, 1970.

Brooks, Cleanth. "Yeats: The Poet as Myth-Maker." *Modern Poetry and the Tradition.* Chapel Hill: University of North Carolina Press, 1939.

————. "Yeats's Great Rooted Blossomer." In *The Well-Wrought Urn: Studies in the Structure of Poetry.* New York: Harcourt, Brace & World, 1947.

Davie, Donald. "Yeats, Berkeley, and Romanticism." In *English Literature and British Philosophy,* edited by S. P. Rosenbaum. Chicago: The University of Chicago Press, 1971.

Donoghue, Denis. *William Butler Yeats.* New York: Viking, 1971.

Donoghue, Denis, and Mulryne, J. R., eds. *An Honoured Guest: New Essays on W. B. Yeats.* New York: St. Martin's Press, 1966.

Ellmann, Richard. *The Identity of Yeats.* 2d ed. New York: Oxford University Press, 1964.

————. *Yeats: The Man and the Masks.* New York: Macmillan, 1948.

Engelberg, Edward. *The Vast Design: Patterns in W. B. Yeats's Aesthetic.* Toronto: University of Toronto Press, 1964.

Finneran, Richard J. *The Prose Fiction of W. B. Yeats: The Search for "Those Simple Forms."* Dublin: Dolmen, 1973.

Flannery, Mary C. *Yeats and Magic: The Earlier Works.* New York: Harper & Row, 1978.

Frye, Northrop. *Anatomy of Criticism: Four Essays.* Princeton, N.J.: Princeton University Press, 1957.

———. "The Top of the Tower: A Study of the Imagery of Yeats." In *The Stubborn Structure: Essays on Criticism and Society,* 257–77. Ithaca, N.Y.: Cornell University Press, 1970.

———. "Yeats and the Language of Symbolism." In *Fables of Identity: Studies in Poetic Mythology,* 218–37. New York: Harcourt, Brace & World, 1963.

Gregory, Horace. "W. B. Yeats and the Mask of Jonathan Swift." *The Southern Review* 7 (1941–1942): 492–509.

Gwynn, Stephen, ed. *Scattering Branches: Tributes to the Memory of W. B. Yeats.* New York: Macmillan, 1940.

Harris, Daniel A. *Yeats: Coole Park & Ballylee.* Baltimore: The Johns Hopkins University Press, 1974.

Henn, T. R. *The Lonely Tower: Studies in the Poetry of W. B. Yeats.* 2d ed. London: Methuen, 1965.

Hirschberg, Stuart. "Why Yeats Saw Himself as a '*Daimonic* Man' of Phase 17: A Complementary View." *English Language Notes* 11 (1974): 202–6.

Hone, Joseph. *W. B. Yeats, 1865–1939.* 2d ed. London: Macmillan & Co., 1962.

Jeffares, A. Norman, ed. *Yeats, Sligo and Ireland.* Gerrards Cross, Buckinghamshire: Colin Smythe, Ltd., 1980.

———. *The Circus Animals: Essays on W. B. Yeats.* New York: Macmillan, 1970.

———. *A Commentary on the Collected Poems of W. B. Yeats.* Stanford, Ca.: Stanford University Press, 1968.

———. *W. B. Yeats: Man and Poet.* 2d ed. New York: Barnes & Noble, 1962.

Johnston, Dillon. "The Perpetual Self of Yeats's *Autobiographies.*" *Éire-Ireland* 9 (1974): 69–85.

Kermode, Frank. *Romantic Image.* London: Routledge & Kegan Paul, 1961.

Kline, Gloria C. *The Last Courtly Lover: Yeats and the Idea of Woman.* Ann Arbor: UMI Research Press, 1983.

Koch, Vivienne. *W. B. Yeats, The Tragic Phase: A Study of the Last Poems.* London: Routledge & Kegan Paul, 1951.

Laity, Cassandra. "Yeats and Florence Farr: The Influence of the 'New

Woman' Actress on Yeats's Changing Images of Women." *Modern Drama* 28 (1985): 620–37.

Langbaum, Robert. *The Mysteries of Identity: A Theme in Modern Literature.* New York: Oxford University Press, 1977.

Lentricchia, Frank. *The Gaiety of Language: An Essay on the Radical Poetics of W. B. Yeats and Wallace Stevens.* Berkeley: University of California Press, 1968.

Lester, John A., Jr. "Joyce, Yeats, and the Short Story." *English Literature in Transition* 15 (1972): 305–314.

Levin, Gerald. "The Yeats of the *Autobiographies:* A Man of Phase 17." *Texas Studies in Literature and Language* 6 (1964–1965): 398–405.

Levine, Bernard. *The Dissolving Image: The Spiritual-Esthetic Development of W. B. Yeats.* Detroit: Wayne State University Press, 1970.

Levine, Herbert J. *Yeats's Diamonic Renewal.* Ann Arbor: UMI Research Press, 1983.

Lynch, David. *Yeats: The Poetics of the Self.* Chicago: The University of Chicago Press, 1979.

Marcus, Phillip L. *Yeats and the Beginning of the Irish Renaissance.* Ithaca, N.Y.: Cornell University Press, 1970.

Miller, J. Hillis. *Poets of Reality: Six Twentieth-Century Writers.* Cambridge, Mass.: Belknap / Harvard University Press, 1965.

Moore, Virginia. *The Unicorn: William Butler Yeats's Search for Reality.* New York: Macmillan, 1954.

Murphy, Frank Hughes. *Yeats's Early Poetry: The Quest for Reconciliation.* Baton Rouge: Louisiana State University Press, 1975.

O'Driscoll, Robert. *Symbolism and Some Implications of the Symbolic Approach: W. B. Yeats during the Eighteen-Nineties.* Dublin: Dolmen, 1975.

Olney, James. *The Rhizome and the Flower: The Perennial Philosophy—Yeats and Jung.* Berkeley: University of California Press, 1980.

Parkinson, Thomas. *"W. B. Yeats, Self-Critic: A Study of His Early Verse" and "W. B. Yeats: The Later Poetry": Two Volumes in One.* Berkeley: University of California Press, 1971.

Perloff, Marjorie. "The Consolation Theme in Yeats's 'In Memory of Major Robert Gregory.' " *Modern Language Quarterly* 27 (1966): 306–322.

———. " 'The Tradition of Myself': The Autobiographical Mode of Yeats." *Journal of Modern Literature* 4 (1975): 529–73.

———. "Yeats and the Occasional Poem: 'Easter 1916.' " *Papers on Language and Literature* 4 (1968): 308–328.

Reugueiro, Helen. *The Limits of Imagination: Wordsworth, Yeats, and Stevens.* Ithaca, N.Y.: Cornell University Press, 1976.

Ronsley, Joseph. *Yeats's Autobiography: Life as Symbolic Pattern.* Cambridge, Mass.: Harvard University Press, 1968.

Rudd, Margaret. *Divided Image: A Study of William Blake and W. B. Yeats.* London: Routledge & Kegan Paul, 1953.

Saul, George Brandon. *Prolegomena to the Study of Yeats's Poems.* Philadelphia: University of Pennsylvania Press, 1957.

Schricker, Gale C. *A New Species of Man.* Lewisburg: Bucknell University Press, 1982.

Snukal, Robert. *High Talk: The Philosophical Poetry of W. B. Yeats.* Cambridge: Cambridge University Press, 1973.

Spivak, Gayatri Chakravorty. "Finding Feminist Readings: Dante–Yeats." *Social Text: Theory, Culture, and Ideology* 3 (1980): 73–87.

Stallworthy, Jon. *Between the Lines: Yeats's Poetry in the Making.* Oxford: Clarendon Press, 1963.

————. *Vision and Revision in Yeats's "Last Poems."* Oxford: Clarendon Press, 1969.

Wilson, F. A. C. *Yeats's Iconography.* New York: Macmillan, 1960.

Witt, Marion. "The Making of an Elegy: Yeats's 'In Memory of Major Robert Gregory.' " *Modern Philology* 48 (1950): 112–21.

Zabel, Morton Dauwen. "The Thinking of the Body: Yeats in the Autobiographies." *The Southern Review* 7 (1941–1942): 562–90.

Zwerdling, Alex. *Yeats and the Heroic Ideal.* New York: New York University Press, 1965.

Acknowledgments

"Introduction" (originally entitled "Yeats, Gnosticism, and the Sacred Void") by Harold Bloom from *Poetry and Repression: Revisionism from Blake to Stevens* © 1976 by Yale University. Reprinted by permission of Yale University Press.

"The Player Queen" by Helen Vendler from *Yeats's* Vision *and the Later Plays,* © 1963 by the President and Fellows of Harvard College. Reprinted by permission of Harvard University Press.

" 'Leda and the Swan' as Model" by Priscilla Washburn Shaw from *Rilke, Valéry and Yeats: The Domain of the Self,* © 1964 by Rutgers, The State University. Reprinted by permission of Rutgers University Press.

"Poet of Anglo-Ireland" by Thomas R. Whitaker from *Swan and Shadow: Yeats's Dialogue with History,* © 1964 by the University of North Carolina Press. Reprinted by permission.

"Rhythm and Pattern in *Autobiographies*" by Ian Fletcher from *An Honored Guest: New Essays on W. B. Yeats,* edited by Denis Donoghue and J. R. Mulryne, © 1965 by Edward Arnold (Publishers) Ltd. Reprinted by permission.

" 'The Moods': Tradition as Emotion" by Allen R. Grossmann from *Poetic Knowledge in the Early Years, A Study of* The Wind Among the Reeds, © 1969 by the Rectors and Visitors of the University of Virginia. Reprinted by permission of The University Press of Virginia.

"Oscar and Oisin" by Richard Ellmann from *Eminent Domain; Yeats Among Wilde, Joyce, Pound, Eliot, and Auden,* © 1965, 1966, 1967 by Richard Ellmann. Reprinted by permission of Oxford University Press.

"Toward *A Vision: Per Amica Silentia Lunae*" by Harold Bloom from *Yeats,* © 1970 by Oxford University Press, Inc. Reprinted by permission.

"*A Vision:* The Dead and History" by Harold Bloom from *Yeats,* © 1970 by Oxford University Press, Inc. Reprinted by permission.

"Yeats's Theatre" (originally entitled "His Theatre") by Denis Donoghue from *William Butler Yeats,* edited by Frank Kermode, © 1971 by Denis Donoghue. Reprinted by permission of Viking Penguin, Inc.

" 'But Now I Add Another Thought': Yeats's Daimonic Tradition" by Herbert J. Levine from *Studies In The Literary Imagination* 14, no. 1 (Spring 1981), © 1981 by the Department of English, Georgia State University. Reprinted by permission.

"Imagery in Yeats" (originally entitled "Image and Emblem in Yeats") by Paul de Man from *The Rhetoric of Romanticism,* © 1984 by Columbia University Press. Reprinted by permission.

"Yeats: The Linguistic Moment" (originally entitled "Yeats") by J. Hillis Miller from *The Linguistic Moment: from Wordsworth to Stevens,* © 1985 by Princeton University Press. Reprinted by permission.

Index

223